Confronting the Democratic Discourse of Librarianship

Confronting the Democratic Discourse of Librarianship

A Marxist Approach

Sam Popowich

Library Juice Press
Sacramento, CA

Published in 2019 by Library Juice Press.

Library Juice
PO Box 188784
Sacramento, CA 95818

http://litwinbooks.com/

This book is printed on acid-free paper.

Library of Congress Cataloging-in-Publication Data

Names: Popowich, Sam, author.
Title: Confronting the democratic discourse of librarianship : a Marxist
  approach / Sam Popowich.
Description: Sacramento, CA : Library Juice Press, 2019. | Includes
  bibliographical references and index.
Identifiers: LCCN 2019010997 | ISBN 9781634000871 (acid-free paper)
Subjects: LCSH: Libraries and society. | Libraries and society--United
  States. | Libraries--Political aspects. | Library science--Political
  aspects. | Libraries and state.
Classification: LCC Z716.4 .P67 2019 | DDC 021.2--dc23
LC record available at https://lccn.loc.gov/2019010997

Table of Contents

1   INTRODUCTION

15   CHAPTER ONE   The Democratic Discourse of Librarianship

53   CHAPTER TWO   Vectors of Oppression

87   CHAPTER THREE   Liberalism and the Enlightenment

121   CHAPTER FOUR   Ideology and Hegemony in the Marxist Tradition

171   CHAPTER FIVE   Three Hegemonies of Library History

207   CHAPTER SIX   The Library Myth

247   CHAPTER SEVEN   Truth Machines

269   CHAPTER EIGHT   Dual Power and Mathesis

293   CONCLUSION   Lives and Time

301   BIBLIOGRAPHY

319   INDEX

To the Dalhousie University School of Information Management
Class of 2007

This is why, from the viewpoint of dominant class interests, the less the dominated dream the *dream* of which I speak, in the confident way of which I speak, and the less they practice the political apprenticeship of committing themselves to a utopia, the more open they will become to "pragmatic" discourses, and the sounder the dominant classes will sleep.

Paolo Freire,
Pedagogy of Hope.

Utopian thinking demands a revision of Gramsci's famous slogan, which might now run: cynicism of the intellect, utopianism of the will.

Fredric Jameson,
An American Utopia: Dual Power and the Universal Army.

Introduction

"Cornerstones of liberty," "arsenals of a democratic culture," "essential to the functioning of a democratic society"—these ideas are widespread in librarianship. They form the basis of much of the discourse around service, ethics, law, rights, and responsibility, but they are rarely confronted in a radical way. Our professional discourse rarely challenges the fundamental idea that democracy is a characteristic of contemporary Western society. American, Canadian, or British society may be imperfect, corrupted, in decline, or under attack, but the presence of democracy itself is never seriously questioned. This book seeks to challenge that presumption and to see what consequences follow from that challenge.

The word "democracy" comes from the combination of two Greek words, δῆμος (*demos*, "people") and κράτος (*kratos*, power). Clearly, then, democracy implies a relationship between *people* and *power*—but what kind of relationship? This raises additional fundamental questions: who are the people? Who is included and excluded from the definition of "people"? What kind of power? where is power located, and what kind of power is it? Lenin once argued that the fundamental question of politics is "who for whom?", and it is this question that must be asked of any democratic discourse.

In the *Politics*, Aristotle includes democracy in his taxonomy of states, but categorized it as a "deviated" as opposed to a "correct" constitution. For Aristotle, governments could either have one ruler, a few rulers, or many rulers, and each of these regimes were either "correct" or "deviated."[1] There were six possible regimes in all:

	Correct	Deviation
One Ruler	Kingship	Tyranny
Few Rulers	Aristocracy	Oligarchy
Many Rulers	Polity	Democracy

Aristotle's classification of democracy as a "deviation" suggests that we need to be very careful when we use the term. For us, "democracy" is a positive expression of the power of a people in a particular kind of society, but we have to bear in mind that adopting the term uncritically or transhistorically makes us ignorant of changes in its meaning over time.

The insistence on libraries as institutions essential to democracy is longstanding and stems from the "missionary" origins of the profession at the end of the 19th century. Typically, what is meant by democracy in our discourse is unclear, accidentally or deliberately left vague enough to mean almost anything. Democracy, we might say, is in the eye of the beholder. It becomes an empty signifier which can take on a multitude of meanings, thereby becoming itself the site of political struggle. Alternatives to the democratic discourse of librarianship—the "social control" thesis, for example—arise occasionally, but the persistence and tenacity of the democratic discourse is significant, as its persistence holds not only within the profession, but in public perceptions of the library as well.

The professional and public view of libraries as essential to "democracy"—something the profession and the public believe characterizes Western society—is attractive, because on the one hand it provides a built-in and unassailable value to the work we do, one that is difficult to challenge or critique without challenging the democratic presumption of Western society itself. In a neoliberal world, libraries are constantly having to prove or communicate their

---

1   Aristotle, *The Politics* (London: Penguin Books, 1951), 189–90.

value, and an unquestionable connection to democracy—an unimpeachable good!—provides us with a solid foundation on which to argue our worth. But it also allows us to think well of the societies we live in, to give them a pass, to confuse "is" with "ought," as in "libraries *are* arsenals of a democratic culture" when what we mean is "libraries *ought to be* arsenals of a democratic culture." From a political perspective this allows us also to ignore the very real problems inherent in our social and political world: racism, sexism, intolerance, alienation, hatred, violence, and political manipulation. If we live in a truly democratic society then these things are aberrations, faults, mistakes, rather than structurally integral elements of a society based, not on democracy at all, but on oppression, exclusion, and domination. By claiming that our societies are indeed democratic we allow ourselves to believe that such problems are easily fixed without fundamentally changing the nature of our society. By extension, if libraries are essential to democratic societies, then they are fundamentally doing the right things, and any problems within the profession—lack of diversity, racism, sexism—can also be ignored in light of the "greater good" of the library's democratic mission. How one feels about the pace, amount, and kind of social change required depends on how you feel about the way the world is now, how it treats you and how it treats others—in other words, it varies according to privilege. A social reality mystified and obscured by privilege is difficult if not impossible to change.

This is no accident. A society based on economic exploitation, benefiting some and oppressing others, needs to maintain its hegemony by any means it can. When we think about the democratic discourse of librarianship in these terms—as political rhetoric and ideological narrative designed to uphold and protect the status quo—then the famous quote by Roosevelt, often used in such discussions, appears in a different light:

> Libraries are directly and immediately involved in the
> conflict which divides our world, and for two reasons;
> first, because they are essential to the functioning of a
> democratic society; second, because the contemporary
> conflict touches the integrity of scholarship, the freedom

of the mind, and even the survival of culture, and libraries are the great tools of scholarship, the great repositories of culture, and the great symbols of the freedom of the mind.

Roosevelt presumes that Western society must be democratic, because he is waging war against Nazi Germany, and it is easier to command the hearts and minds of citizens in a struggle between culture and barbarism, democracy and fascism, than it is to win them to the cause of American hegemony in an imperialist and colonialist world system. Upholding democracy means being on the ethical "right side" of history which makes it all the harder to challenge or criticize the policy and actions of the winners.

Demos

Who, then, are "the people" when we talk about democracy? Democracy has never included everyone. A well-known Canadian politics textbook argues that "democracy means that people share equally in political rule; it does not mean that they share equally (or even equitably) in wealth or social status" and claims that "the democrats of ancient Greece understood equality to mean that all citizens were equally capable of exercising political power."[2] Such claims, however, do two things: they limit politics to an analysis of the state and leaves "citizen" undefined. The limitation of the political to the state means that we can live in a democracy even if our social and economic relationships are undemocratic; as long as the government is "democratic" (whatever that means), what goes on in society is unimportant. On the other hand, how do we define citizenship? Aristotle claims that "there is no unanimity, no agreement as to what constitutes a citizen."[3] For the Athenians, every citizen

---

2   Patrick Malcolmson, Richard Myers, Gerald Baier, and Thomas M. J. Bateman, *The Canadian Regime: An Introduction to Parliamentary Government in Canada,* Sixth Edition (Toronto: University of Toronto Press, 2016), 6.

3   Aristotle, *Politics*, 168.

was expected to participate in political life, but not everyone was a citizen. Women and slaves were by definition not citizens, because they were not free and not male, and so were excluded from political life. As opposed to the abstract concept, democracy in the real world always rests on such exclusions.

Who, for example, constitutes the "all" in the "Free to All" of the Boston Public Library? Founded in 1848, Boston Public Library was a shining example of a period library historian Sidney Ditzion has described in glowing terms:

> The concepts of republicanism, risen from the enlightenment, advertised in the Revolution, strengthened in the philosophy of Jeffersonian and practiced in the era of Jacksonian democracy, were by mid-century deeply engraved in the popular mind. The doctrine of human rights, political equality, and residence of authority in the whole people, had become firmly fixed in the professed American credo.[4]

And yet, human rights, political equality, and "the whole people" excluded slaves not only in the south, but in the supposedly free states of the north as well. Only two years after the founding of the Boston Public Library ("free to all"), Congress passed the "Fugitive Slave Law," allowing escaped slaves in the north to be recaptured and returned to their owners. The democratic ideals Ditzion imagines to be "firmly fixed" in American society of the mid-19th century are ones which happily coexisted with legal slavery, not to mention the determined genocide of Indigenous populations across the entire continent.

Even after the Emancipation Proclamation and the Civil War, things weren't much better. In 1902 the newly opened Atlanta library (a Carnegie library) was closed to Black people. W. E. B.

---

4   Sidney Ditzion, *Arsenals of a Democratic Culture: A Social History of the American Public Library Movement in New England and the Middle States from 1850 to 1900*, (Chicago: American Library Association, 1947), 52.

Du Bois and other Black citizens of Atlanta argued that the library should be open to all those whose taxes paid for it. Du Bois wrote, "I am taxed for the Carnegie Public Library of Atlanta, where I cannot enter to draw my own books"[5]. Rather than desegregate the library, a separate library for Black people was opened in Atlanta, but not until 1921.

One counter-argument to such criticism is that democracy may not be perfect, but it is improving. And indeed, the history of the Global North since the Industrial Revolution does show a gradual rise in the standard of living (for some) and expansion of the franchise. Legal enfranchisement continued throughout the 20th century until we reached the state of full legal suffrage. But as we have seen in recent elections, technical disenfranchisement, in the form of property requirements, gerrymandering, restrictive ID laws, etc., have simply taken the place of legal disenfranchisement. Such measures are different than the kinds of physical exclusion we see either in legal disenfranchisement or in deportation (even Lincoln was in favour of deporting Black and Indigenous People from the "land of the free" after the Civil War). This is without even mentioning the potential for interference in elections themselves, as Russia may have done in the US and Britain, Canada has done in Honduras, and the US itself has a long history of doing in Central and South America (most recently in Venezuela). Essentially, however, all these measures are taken to restrict citizenship and the power of citizenship, to limit who "the people" are. More to the point, however, is that for those who have always been excluded from full citizenship—often, indeed, from humanity itself—such "improvements" mean very little. Injunctions to be patient, to subscribe to piecemeal reforms, to compromise and tolerance, are obscene in a world in which Black people, queer and trans people, the disabled and women are so dehumanized that their lives mean nothing in our "democracies." The fact that people are dying does not allow us the luxury of bourgeois deliberation and respect for propriety. We will return to the question of lives below.

---

5   Wiegand, *Part of Our Lives*, 84.

Kratos

There are many questions we can ask about power, but one of the most significant in terms of "democracy" is where power is located and what kind of power it is. Power is not decentralized and equal—we don't live in a communist or anarchist society—it resides somewhere. The amount of time, energy, and marketing that goes into an election cycle suggests that government is the site of power, but is this in fact the case? This may depend on another question about power: what *kind* is it? Does one kind of power—political power—reside in Parliament or the Presidency and another kind of power—social power, perhaps—reside somewhere else? Are these really different kinds of powers, or is one merely the institutionalized, legitimized form of the other? Do those who hold social power (men, the wealthy, and the white) also owe their political power to it? If, as democracy claims, there is no difference between the people "in power" and the people not in power, then there is no real difference between social power and political power, except that one is constitutionally entrenched. Political theorists such as Antonio Negri draw a distinction between the "constituted power" of the state and the "constituent power" of the multitude. Certain powers (plural) may be held by people within our political institutions—namely the power to decide on, enforce, and adjudicate laws—while other powers are decentralized and exist in civil society. But is the dividing line so neat, or are those who hold political power just as subject to civil power as the rest of us?

This distinction between political society and civil society, and the way power is structured within these two realms, raises questions about other ways in which our society and social life itself is segmented. For the Greeks, as we have seen, private power was the realm of the household—the realm of women and slaves, of *bios* or biological life and its needs. Public power, political power, on the other hand, was the realm of *zoe*, a higher kind of life only accessible to those whose biological needs were taken care of. Since women and slaves existed to care for the biological needs of men, men were "free" to participate in this higher life, the life of politics as opposed to the life of "economics," which just means "the laws or running of the household." So there are two realms of life: the economic, bio-logical life of necessity circumscribed by the household; and the po-litical, public life of freedom located in the *polis* (or, nowadays, po-litical institutions).

However, as society developed, a middle-ground opened up between the private world and the political world—we tend to think of this as the public sphere or civil society. The discourse of librarianship puts a lot of weight on the idea of the public sphere, drawn from the work of Habermas, because it is there that libraries operate. However, for Habermas, the public sphere was a sphere of liberal, bourgeois male property owners; it was a sphere where they could pursue their own public interests *precisely because they were denied access to political institutions reserved at the time to the monar-chy and the aristocracy.* Excluded from political life, the bourgeoi-sie set up its own social institutions as a means to consolidate social power until, in the first half of the 19th century, they took over po-litical power directly. The bourgeoisie itself called this new regime of bourgeois power not based on aristocratic privilege "democra-cy." As political life has been forced to include more people who are not white male property owners (which happens with the expan-sion of the franchise), the more the concept of democracy, civil life, and the public sphere has taken on new meanings, and from some perspectives has become eroded or debased. It is interesting to see how library theory falls in line with social and political changes. Li-brary writers like John Buschman and Ed D'Angelo decry the de-basement of liberal democratic society, arguing that various forces or processes (the "new public philosophy" for Buschman, postmod-ern consumerism for D'Angelo) have caused the decline of Amer-ican democracy and the ability of the library to play a role in sup-porting it. They see the past as a "golden age" of democracy and civil life—the period of classical liberalism for D'Angelo, the wel-fare state for Buschman—but this past was only a golden age to those who would have been considered citizens granted the right to political life. There was never a period of good capitalism when full democracy held sway.

Returning to the problem with limiting "politics" or pow-er to the state, we can conclude that "democracy"—including the extension of the franchise—only applies to the political sphere; the civil or social sphere is free to be as undemocratic as it likes. The American Library Association core principle of democracy refers only to the participation in the political sphere through voting. But while attention has been paid to democratizing our political institutions through enfranchisement and representation, we tend to ignore the question of democracy outside the political realm, in the public sphere or civil society. While we may think of the political realm as in some ways exercising a democratizing influence on civil society, through government programs and policies, for example, liberalism tends to think of the civil societies as private in the sense that they are autonomous from politics, outside or above politics. Because we tend to think of political power as properly restricted to our political institutions (decrying "political interference" in civil life), it makes no sense from a liberal perspective to think of the public sphere as democratic or not.

But what is this liberal perspective? Out of all the 17th and 18th century political philosophers, John Locke (1632–1704) has had the most direct influence on Anglo-American political thinking and the structure of the institutions of Britain, Canada, and the United States. Locke, along with others like Thomas Hobbes and Jean-Jacques Rousseau, believed in a primordial "state of nature" in which self-sufficient individuals existed in competition with each other (Hobbes called this condition the "war of all against all"). The state of nature was no guarantee of individual rights, as men (the sole concern of these theorists) competed to achieve their aims. Much of the political theory of this period was aimed at discerning the best form of state to guarantee social peace and individual rights. From Hobbes' experience of the English Civil War, he determined that the militarily-instituted state of monarchy was the most appropriate form of state to avoid the state of war, while for Locke, a state constituted by social contract and balanced by the power of the civil society was the most appropriate for the liberal bourgeois world that developed after the Civil War. We owe the division between legislative and executive (Cabinet and Parliament in the Westminster system, President and Congress in the American) to this theoretical structure of checks and balances.

Along with the structure of our political institutions, Locke's liberalism influenced much of the "common sense" way we think about the world. The view of society as fundamentally composed of individuals led to a hegemonic "methodological individualism" in the humanities and social sciences. The combined ideas of the social contract and the strict division of private and public interests have determined the view that the proper role of the political realm is to guarantee private rights and interests but not to interfere with or constrain them. This in turn is based on a concept of natural rights (rights inhering naturally in individuals), liberty (for those possessed of natural rights), and stable constitutionalism (to protect the liberty of those with natural rights). As we have seen, however, the bourgeois public sphere or civil realm only recognized white male property owners as individuals, therefore only they were possessed of natural rights and liberty and were entitled to the protection of the bourgeois state. The slow extension of the franchise has problematized this position, but has not resolved its contradictions.

Politics, in this view, becomes exclusively about deciding on, creating, and enforcing the minimum of laws to guarantee private interests and the maximum to penalize those who do not assimilate to the bourgeois norm. Making the country "good for business" is the aim of international relations, while lowering taxes and criminalizing the poor and the different the aim of domestic politics. Locke's vision of checks and balances take the form of lobby groups and political influence on the part of the wealthy, and occasional moments of resistance on the part of the marginalized and disenfranchised.

Lives and Time

The democratic discourse of librarianship positions public libraries as the perfect institutions of the public sphere or civil society—a catalyst for the forging of liberal communities by self-sufficient individuals that nevertheless does not impose its own values or ideologies on citizens. But this view only holds up if all is generally well in Western liberal democracies, if there is nothing fundamentally wrong with capitalism, or if there is, it is simply a question of

remedying it according to the values and principles of liberalism itself. This appears rhetorically as qualifiers to capitalism: the problem is with "crony" capitalism, "surveillance" capitalism, or "postmodern consumer" capitalism, but never with capitalism as such.
Generally speaking, this perspective survives only by ignoring two
concrete facts: that people—Black people, women, trans and queer
people, disabled people—are dying; and that we no longer have
all the time in the world to deliberate and come to a decision. This
perspective is only possible by denying—through the manipulation of history and ideology—the humanity of those who do not
fit the definition of citizenship or the *demos*, as well as denying the
ecological effects of capitalist accumulation on the planet. In the
current historical moment, we are faced with an acute and radical
challenge to both of these presumptions: Indigenous sovereignty
is tightly linked with environmental stewardship, #BlackLivesMat-
ter is connected to the police-industrial complex. Collective proposals like Alexandria Ocasio-Cortez' "Green New Deal" is faced
with an anti-environmentalist libertarian populism given ideological support by the White House itself. We can see the effects in the
incarceration and death toll among Black Americans, especially at
the hands of the police; in the current refugee/immigrant crises in
North America and Europe, sparked by the combined histories of
colonialism and economic expansion. The liberal model of the sanctity of (white, male, bourgeois) life and unlimited time for deliberation is challenged not only by radical social and demographic movements, but by the prospect of imminent climate apocalypse. The
International Panel on Climate Change gives us *at best* 12 years to
get our house in order, and in fact it may already be too late.

The requirement to take death and climate change seriously
has major implications on how we think about libraries and librarianship. The abstractions that suffuse our professional discourse—
neutrality, democracy, freedom, diversity, inclusion—are too easily recuperable by the racist and sexist structures of capitalist power
precisely because of their abstraction. Additionally, the political
economy of our institutions goes uninterrogated, so that even questions of labor, class, and precarity remain undertheorized. This is
admittedly changing—important work is currently being done on

unionization, collective action, race, gender, disability, and the political consequences of pragmatism or practicality—but these rarely inform the practice and policies within our institutions. A real engagement with the fact that people and the planet are dying ought to enable us to resist the temptation of abstractions, to speak clearly and openly about our goals and strategies. But this in itself is a political question: we have to ask who benefits from the abstractions and rhetorical moves of our professional discourse. I hope this book will go some way towards answering that question.

Indigeneity and decolonization are two of the most urgent political issues of the current conjuncture. Understood broadly, they figure into such political manifestations as the rise of the right and right-wing populism, the destabilizing violence of ex-colonial regions, the various refugee and migrant crises, sovereignty in settler-colonial states, and the coming climate catastrophe. Climate change is the ticking clock that underpins the necessity of dealing with these issues, all of which are interlocked, and all of which can be—must be—reconceived from a perspective of indigeneity and decolonization.

Lives and time, then, provide a focus or limiting factor in how we need to think about the politics of libraries. The way we think about political institutions, discourse, values, ethics, work, and identity are all constrained in the current conjuncture by the fact that lives are being extinguished and the planet destroyed. To use a musicological metaphor, lives and time should be heard as the ground note or tonic in the chapters to come, always present even if not specifically sounded. We will address them in more detail in the conclusion. Chapter One lays out the democratic discourse of librarianship, while Chapter Two looks at the structures of oppression, domination, and exploitation inherited by librarianship from broader capitalist society. Chapters Three and Four investigate the question of ideology, first looking at librarianship's inheritance of liberalism and Enlightenment thought more generally, and then laying out a particular history of ideology and social control from a Marxist perspective. Chapter Five attempts to map the history of modern librarianship to changes in the socio-economic conjuncture from 1850 to 2008. Chapter Six opens the positivist, neutral, pragmatic library myth to scrutiny. Chapter Seven looks at the role of information technology in the transition from the society of discipline to the current society of control, while the last chapter explores two potential strategies for resistance to capitalist hegemony and the democratic discourse of librarianship. In the conclusion we will return to the question of lives and time.

Writing a book is precisely the kind of social labor Marxism sees designed to appear as the work of a single person. This particular book owes its existence to many people, not all of whom I will be able to thank. Nevertheless, thanks are due to my colleagues at University of Alberta Libraries, specifically Lydia Zvyagintseva, Peggy Sue Ewanyshyn, Sandra Shores, and Kenton Good. I also want to thank the many past members of the Association of Academic Staff of the University of Alberta, who negotiated to have academic research leave included in the librarian collective agreement.

I also want to thank the many colleagues at the School of Library and Information Science, the Access Conference, the Canadian Association of Professional Academic Librarians, and "Library Twitter" for their support over the years. I especially want to thank Myron Groover, Allana Mayer, John Fink, Gillian Byrne, Jane Schmidt, and Peter Binkley, as well as Rory Litwin for taking a chance on this book. In addition, thanks are due to all of the workers who keep the organizations and systems functioning so that the rest of us can do this kind of work; in my case I want to thank the members of the Non-Academic Staff Association of the University of Alberta, as well as the many precarious, student, and non-unionized staff at the University.

Finally, I want to thank Marie-Claire Simard for her continued love and support throughout this project.

amiskwacîwâskahikan
Treaty 6
March 2018—March 2019

Chapter One

The Democratic Discourse of Librarianship

The connection between libraries and democracy is so widespread, so deeply ingrained in library discourse, that we might be forgiven for thinking there is something almost genetic in the relationship. An arbitrary selection of recent articles and talks makes clear the strength of the link in the popular and professional imagination. In a 2018 *Library Management* article entitled "Democracy and Libraries: Symbol or Symbiosis," Alex Byrne performed a quantitative study using data from the Economist Intelligence Unit and IFLA to test the relationship between libraries and democracy. Byrne concludes that there is indeed a "symbiotic relationship" between libraries and democracy:

> Nations which have well-established systems of government with strong, open and representative electoral systems, well-functioning governmental institutions and processes, widespread political participation and robust civil liberties also tend to have high levels of public library provision and registered users.[1]

---

1   Alex Byrne, "Democracy and Libraries: Symbol or Symbiosis?" *Library Management* 39, no. 5 (2018), 291.

Byrne resists the temptation to ascribe causality—"we cannot say that public libraries create democracy"—but nonetheless reaffirms the connection: "strong public library systems tend to go hand in hand with strong democratic values and traditions."[2] With a study such as this, valuable in its empirical implications, much stands or falls on the definition of "strong, open, and representative electoral systems," "widespread political participation" and "robust civil liberties." Our perspective on these elements is not empirically determined, but is taken in advance, and is dependent on our own experience and subjective position within society. Even the most quantitative research is never purely positivistic.

John Buschman, who has been writing about libraries and politics for many years, wrote "On Democracy and Libraries" for *Library Quarterly*, also in 2018. Buschman begins by analyzing Wayne Wiegand's challenge to the democratic discourse of librarianship in *Part of Our Lives: A People's History of the American Public Library* (2015), in which Wiegand concludes that the connection between libraries and democracy is tenuous. Buschman, while recognizing the importance of Wiegand's work, asks whether we "can… clarify what has long seemed an intuitive relationship between democracy and libraries, or do we abandon the idea as sentimentality?."[3] However, both Buschman and Wiegand begin from the presumption that democracy actually exists in North American society. Wiegand's position is, roughly speaking, that democracy exists, but libraries do not support it, while Buschman's view is more that democracy has been decentralized: "democratic politics now exist in multiple social venues… democracy takes place directly and indirectly in venues not commonly thought of as sites for it but where everyday life is negotiated and played out (e.g. libraries), thereby constructing the culture."[4] The United States, in this

---

2   Ibid., 291.

3   Buschman, John, "On Democracy and Libraries," *The Library Quarterly* 88, no. 1 (2018), 24.

4   Buschman, "On Democracy and Libraries," 34.

view, may not have a democratic *polity*, but it does have a democratic *culture*. Both Wiegand and Buschman see contemporary society as in decline from some period of "good capitalism," in which liberal democratic ideals reigned supreme. For Buschman, this period is that of the welfare state, and neoliberalism is the dismantling of a working public philosophy; Ed D'Angelo sees the golden age of good capitalism as the period of classical liberalism. After 1870, for example, D'Angelo argues that "Western societies developed further and further away from the ideal of a perfectly competitive market of small entrepreneurs which the theory of ethical [that is, classical] liberalism presupposed."[5] A transition, first from "ethical liberalism" to "economic liberalism" and then to "postmodern consumer capitalism" was a moral failing, creating a society "no longer tempered by moral restraints or the imperative to serve the public good."[6] The problems with contemporary society, for Buschman and D'Angelo, are not due to the problems inherent in liberalism or capitalism themselves, but in society's inability to live up to their promise.

Wiegand takes a slightly different position. What is important is less social or collective accounts of libraries in society, but their effect on individuals. "Nowhere in my research did I find evidence that public libraries fostered the major social movements that mark American history," he writes, however, "the changes American public libraries fostered for individuals constitutes their strongest bond with users."[7] While public libraries act as links between individuals and larger communities, Wiegand plays down the structural role they play in the production and reproduction of social relationships themselves. This is because Wiegand holds to the classical view that the individual is the ontological foundation of society (i.e methodological individualism), that society occurs when individuals come

---

5   Ed D'Angelo, *Barbarians at the Gates of the Public Library: How Postmodern Consumer Capitalism Threatens Democracy, Civil Education and the Public Good* (Duluth: Library Juice Press, 2006), 39.

6   D'Angelo, *Barbarians,* 39.

7   Wiegand, *Part of Our Lives,* 268.

together of their own accord. From this perspective, the role of the subject library is to mediate the plurality of individual worldviews. The library "acts as a stage to mediate the parameters of public culture to the satisfaction of most in a relatively peaceful, albeit sometimes messy way. That they do not perceive their public libraries as an appendage of big government may be another reason Americans love them so much."[8] For Wiegand, then, the higher-level socio-economic changes between, say, the welfare state and neoliberalism, are beside the point. Liberal, pluralist, small-government, individualistic American culture maintains its longstanding continuity independent of politics. How far one can subscribe to Wiegand's populist position depends on one's view of American history and society and how far one is willing to characterize the "mediation of public culture" in the United States as "relatively peaceful."

There has never been a period of good liberalism or good capitalism in which the promise of democracy has even come close to being fulfilled, and there has never been a substrate of good, ethical, liberal citizens who simply need their honest differences of opinions to be mediated. The presumption of an actually existing democracy, again, is not an empirical one; it is brought to the research by the researcher. We will see in Chapter Three how far liberalism's "moral restraints" actually went.

More recently, New York University sociologist Eric Klinenberg has argued that libraries "are crucial... for bridging divides and safeguarding the values of democracy."[9] For Klinenberg, the connection between the library and (liberal) democracy is etymologically cemented: "the root of the word 'library' *liber*," he writes, "means both 'book' and 'free'":

> Libraries stand for and exemplify something that needs
> defending: the public institutions that—even in an age
> of atomization and inequality—serve as bedrocks of

---

8   Wiegand, 269.

9   Pearce, Katie, "How Libraries and Other 'Public Palaces' can Bridge Divides, Safeguard Democracy," *Johns Hopkins University Hub* (October 24, 2018), para. 6.

> civil society. Libraries are the kinds of places where or-
> dinary people with different backgrounds, passions, and
> interests can take part in a living democratic culture.[10]

The intimate connection between "library" and "liberty" is a nice, convenient story, but it's wrong. The etymology of the noun "liber" (book) comes from the Indo-European for "the bark of a tree" (pro-to-Italic *lufros*), in other words, the kind of materials words were written on. The *adjective* "liber" comes from the Indo-European word for "people" (proto-Italic *louderos*), and is cognate with the Greek *eleutheria* (freedom). The word "library" comes from the noun, and has nothing to do with the adjective. To argue that the (single) root of the word "library" means both "book" and "free," as Klinenberg does is the equivalent as arguing that "carp" the noun and "carp" the verb mean the same thing("carp" the fish comes from its Old French name "carpe," while "carp" the verb comes from the Old Norse "karpa," "to boast"). What is significant here, however, it not simply etymological point-scoring. The shared root of the words "liberty" and "people" reminds us that "freedom" is a property "we" share; those who are not "us" are by definition "un-free." The distinction between "us free people" and "those other, unfree people" will gain added significance when we look at the way democracy takes particular historical forms based on exclusion and restricted definitions of citizenship in Chapter Three.

The relationship between libraries and democracy is also en-shrined in the core values of the profession as specified by the American Library Association, which remain, despite criticism, touch-stones of professional discourse. The value statement argues that "a democracy presupposes an informed citizenry," silently affirming another presumption: that the societies in which Anglo-American librarianship exists are, in fact, democracies. The ALA core values make three connected claims, that an informed citizenry is a neces-sary condition for a democratic society (the question of whether it

---

10   Eric Klinenberg, "To Restore Civil Society, Start with the Library," *New York Times* (September 8, 2018), para 16.

is a sufficient condition is left unanswered); that the First Amendment protects both free expression and free reception; and that the "publicly supported library provides free and equal access to information for all people of the community the library serves."[11] There is a lot to unpack here.

With respect to the first claim, it seems to me that the argument that an informed citizenry is a necessary condition for a democratic society makes it an easy step to believing that an informed citizenry is a *sufficient* condition. I will argue later that this is precisely the position the democratic discourse of librarianship takes. By making an informed citizenry a sufficient condition, we can effectively ignore everything else that could also be required for a democratic society: political participation, social welfare and social justice, less inequality, exploitation, oppression, etc.

The second claim ties a generalization ("democracy") to a very specific implementation (the First Amendment of the American Constitution). As we discovered in the 2018 debate over the room booking interpretation of the library bill of rights, tying the ALA Core Values to a piece of American legislation causes problems for libraries in other countries which may be closely bound by their relationship to the ALA and its policies. Canadian law, for example, does not have an equivalent to the First Amendment, and indeed the Canadian context must balance the *Human Rights Act* with hate speech provisions in the Criminal Code. Does the lack of First Amendment free speech provisions make Canada less of a democracy than the US?

With respect to the third claim, it is significant that the ALA Core Value becomes very particular on a number of points. In the first place, it refers only to publicly funded libraries. In Canada, where most libraries are publicly funded to some degree, this is perhaps a less significant distinction than in the US. Do private libraries not produce the kind of informed citizenry that creates a democracy? In addition, the value statement restricts the activity

---

11   American Library Association, "Core Values of Librarianship."
     http://www.ala.org/advocacy/intfreedom/corevalues

of the library to "the community the library serves." In practical terms, this often means the community of tax-payers (for public libraries) or faculty, students, and researchers (for academic libraries). In other words, it ties library services to a particular exchange relationship: tax-payers pay for library services through their taxes, university communities by tuition or by their labor. For the ALA, then, democracy and the right/ability to be informed is tied directly to exchange. It also ties democracy to a particular *exclusionary* mechanism: the community can only be defined by those it excludes, those who do not pay for a service. This is a significantly narrow view of democracy, one that equates the *demos* (or people) solely as those who participate in a particular exchange relationship. We will return to the questions of both exchange and exclusion later on.

What is the origin of the connection between libraries and democracy? It is a connection we hear about often—especially in periods when library funding is under attack (which is most of the time)—but it is more often repeated as a cliché, giving no indication of any real consideration of the nature of North American "democracy" or the relationship of libraries to it. Looking at other professions, we don't often hear of an integral relationship between engineering or medicine (as opposed to health services) and democracy; we sometimes hear about it in relation to the law, but the law and politics are so closely intertwined that the relationship cannot simply be repeated as a formula. The other place we hear a lot about the relationship between the profession and democracy is journalism. Significantly, journalism is perhaps even *more* embattled these days than librarianship.

***

A 2018 *Guardian* article on the state of Canada's libraries, held up as an example to the United Kingdom, whose public library budgets have been slashed along with other social services in the name of neoliberal austerity, quotes the Chief Librarian of Toronto Public Library, Vickery Bowles, as saying that "access to information and pathways to learning were the great equalizers of the 20th century."

Bowles, the columnist adds, "sees a vital role of the public library in strengthening civic discourse and enabling political participation."[12] To many people, this perspective is uncontentious; indeed, the intimate connection between libraries, civic education, and democratic participation has a long history within the profession. For her 2000–2001 ALA Presidential Initiative "Libraries: The Cornerstones of Democracy,"[13] Nancy Kranich took her cue from a 1941 letter by Franklin Roosevelt, who argued that libraries are "great symbols of the freedom of the mind,"[14] thus equating political and intellectual liberty. Library historian Sidney Ditzion, who saw libraries as "arsenals of a democratic culture," summarized the views of one of the founders of the early American public library, Francis Wayland, as follows:

> If the intention was to preserve our political democracy and to prevent our government from becoming a farce, the people as a whole must be intelligent, virtuous and—as a by-product of these—religious. The library was an important milestone in reaching this goal.[15]

---

12 Linda Besner, "Risotto, Robotics, and Virtual Reality: How Canada Created the World's best Libraries", *The Guardian* (June 15, 2018), para. 10.

13 American Library Association, "Libraries: The Cornerstones of Democracy."

14 Nancy Kranich, *Libraries and Democracy: The Cornerstone of Liberty* (Chicago: American Library Association, 2001), v; Roosevelt, Franklin D. Letter to Chief Assistant Librarian (1940–1945) of Congress Luther H. Evans, June 13, 1941. Roosevelt Presidential Library, Hyde Park, New York, USA. Evans went on to become Librarian of Congress after MacLeish's retirement in 1945 and was the third Director-General of UNESCO from 1953–1958. This letter is usually cited unsourced in the library literature. The source is identified in Miriam Intrator, "UNESCO, Reconstruction, and Pursuing Peace through a 'Library-Minded' World, 1945–1950," in *The History of Unesco: Global Actions and Impacts*, ed. Poul Duedahl (Basingstoke: Palgrave Macmillan, 2016), 145.

15 Sidney Ditzion, *Arsenals of a Democratic Culture: A Social History of the American Public Library Movement in New England and the Middle States from 1850 to 1900* (Chicago: American Library Association, 1947), 12. Ditzion draws on the same speech of Roosevelt as Kranich.

For Wayland, however, after a failed insurrection in Rhode Island in 1842, "the original issue of political liberty" was "supplanted by the more important question of the stability of the republic."[16] Jesse Shera, perhaps the pre-eminent historian of American libraries, believed that "the modern library in large measure represents the need of democracy for an enlightened electorate."[17] And in an oft-quoted speech given in 1888, Andrew Carnegie—whose philanthropic support for libraries has become eponymous—said that "there is not such a cradle of pure democracy upon the earth as in the Free Public Library, this republic of letters where neither rank, office nor wealth receives the slightest consideration; where all men are equal."[18]

More recently, Ed D'Angelo has claimed that "the notion of the public good is essential to the notion of a public library" and that "modern public libraries were originally conceived as serving the public good by promoting democracy and civil education."[19] These characteristics are now threatened, in his view, by "postmodern consumer capitalism." In her introduction to D'Angelo's *Barbarians at the Gates of the Public Library*, Kathleen de la Peña McCook writes that from the mid-19th century on, "libraries were established in hundreds of US communities as a means to provide people with access to the cultural record and to provide the resources to support an enlightened population for participation in the democratic process."[20] If we are currently not living up to the democratic promise of what D'Angelo calls "ethical liberalism," in McCook's view the solution is simple: "If public librarians can

---

16 Michael H. Harris and Gerard Spiegler, "Everett, Ticknor and the Common Man: The Fear of Societal Instability as the Motivation for the Founding of the Boston Public Library," *Libri* 24, no. 2 (1974), 254.

17 Jesse H. Shera, *Foundations of the Public Library: The Origins of the Public Library Movement in New England, 1629–1855* (Chicago: University of Chicago Press, 1949), vi.

18 Ditzion, *Arsenals,* 154.

19 D'Angelo, *Barbarians,* 11.

20 D'Angelo, *Barbarians,* ix.

re-engage with our foundations of intellectual rigor, commitment to democracy and appreciation for the public record, the gates may be shored up and the barbarians may withdraw."[21]

All of these positions have something in common: they represent a liberal-democratic view of the industrial-capitalist states that form the centers of global capitalism. They believe that the countries of Anglo-American librarianship *are* democracies, even if their democracy is beleaguered or threatened. And they believe in outsiders or others ("barbarians") who are beyond the pale of democratic republicanism. When Vickery Bowles speaks about "great equalizers of the 20th century," she takes for granted the idea that anything like equality existed in the 20th century, a presumption central to a liberal-bourgeois worldview that can only function through the restriction of the idea of equality itself. Only by limiting equality (or the franchise, or democratic participation) to a *subset* of the population could 'equality' be constructed. We will return to this idea later on.

The equation of libraries and democracy, especially in the American context (though the British and the Canadians have no right to be complacent), only makes sense if we uncritically suppose and affirm that the American republic is now or has ever been in any sense democratic. To return to Carnegie's speech, we have to remember that it was made in celebration of union-busting supported by scab labor and Pinkerton violence at one of his steel mills, union-busting that "effectively ended unionism at the Edgar Thomson [steelworks] for decades." In his account of the American steel industry at the end of the 19th century, historian Paul Krause writes that "Carnegie celebrated his victory in Braddock by giving his repentant workers a library and calling it a monument to his partnership with them."[22] Such context not only exposes the hypocrisy of Carnegie's view of a public library "where all men are equal": it exposes a mercenary employment of the ideology of libraries as democratic institutions that borders on the obscene.

---

21   D'Angelo, *Barbarians*, xiv.

22   Paul Krause, *The Battle for Homestead, 1880–1892: Political, Culture, and Steel* (Pittsburgh: University of Pittsburgh Press, 1992), 237.

Even more egregious is the encomium to American values offered by Ditzion:

> The concepts of republicanism, risen from the enlight-
> enment, advertised in the Revolution, strengthened in
> the philosophy of Jeffersonianism, and practiced in the
> era of Jacksonian democracy, were by mid-century deep-
> ly engraved upon the popular mind. The doctrine of hu-
> man rights, political equality, and residence of authority
> in the whole people had become firmly fixed in the pro-
> fessed American credo.[23]

Such a statement can only be construed as fact by denying the existence of slavery. In this passage, Ditzion is describing the United
States in 1850, fifteen years before Emancipation. Only the most
complete ideological submission or the most willful perversion
could allow a librarian—a "guardian of democracy"[24]—to describe
the year of the Fugitive Slave Law (1850) as one in which enlightenment, democracy, human rights, political equality and the authority of the "whole people" held sway. The Fugitive Slave Law, which
"defend[ed] slavery as a property right" is described by Cedric Robinson in *Black Marxism* as one of "two desperate acts in American history", the other being "the desperate resoluteness of John
Brown's final bloody and radical blow against slavery in 1859."[25]

The self-image of American librarians (and *mutatis mutan-
dis* British and Canadian librarians) as making-possible a presupposed democracy, such ideological commitment to the justice and
sanctity of their country, their profession, and their institutions,

---

23   Ditzion, *Arsenals*, 51–52.

24   "Today's information society in which the gap between info-rich and info-
     poor continues to widen needs libraries more than ever and the librarians
     are in a way the guardians of democracy." Christina Tovoté, "Marketing and
     Swedish Libraries: About the Situation Today and the Importance of Visible
     Librarian," in *Adapting Marketing to Libraries in a Changing and World-Wide
     Environment*, ed. Réjean Savard (Munich: IFLA / KG Saur, 2000), 40.

25   Cedric Robinson, *Black Marxism: The Making of the Black Radical Tradition*
     (Chapel Hill, NC: University of North Carolina Press, 2000), 74–75.

is precisely what underpins the notion of the library as *sacred*, as something both to protect (even from criticism) and to venerate. In his 1999 survey of the history of librarianship, Wayne Wiegand summed up the sacred ideology of libraries as one in which "the library would inevitably contribute to the nation's progress and social order" simply by carrying out its professional duties.[26]

Only if we accept the view that democracy, equality, life, liberty, and the pursuit of happiness are *actual* characteristics of the Anglo-American political landscape, could we accept the propositions that underpin the sacredness of libraries. If we accept the alternative, that the US and Canada are countries built on slavery and the extermination of Indigenous Peoples, and the UK one built on colonialism—foundations which are still in full effect today—and that these countries have *never* approached the ideal of democracy that Kranich (following Roosevelt), for example, proposes, then we must also admit that libraries are anything but cornerstones of it. However, if we are to unmask the ideological structures of contemporary librarianship, if we are to desacralize and demystify the library, then we must be prepared to address the white, bourgeois, patriarchal history of librarianship itself.

Exclusion, Resistance, Social Justice

It is ironic that, in the article quoted above, Vickery Bowles should speak about a supposed 20th century equality in a country—Canada—which is still not even a republic, but remains a constitutional monarchy, a political system predicated on a fundamental inequality and social hierarchy. Indeed, the violent dispossession and oppression of Indigenous Peoples through which Canada was founded continued throughout the 20th century (the last residential school closed only in 1998[27]) and its legacy remains, not least in the

---

26   Wayne Wiegand, "Tunnel Vision and Blind Spots: What the Past tells us about the Present: Reflections on the Twentieth-Century of American Librarianship," *Library Quarterly* 69, no. 1 (1999), 4.

27   Truth and Reconciliation Commission of Canada, *Final Report of the Truth and Reconciliation Commission of Canada: Volume 1, Summary* (Toronto: Lorimer, 2015), 70.

epidemic of violence against Indigenous women.[28] As Silvia Federici, Cedric Robinson, and David Harvey have all argued in different ways, what Marx called "primitive accumulation" (= dispossession by violence) was not only something that happened at the dawn of capitalism but has accompanied capitalist development down to the present day.

What emerges from Bowles' view of "20th century equality," however, is not merely irony, but something more strategic that we witness time and again in bourgeois historiography: the substitution of a privileged part for the whole. The "democracy" of a privileged few in New England or Upper Canada erases the slaughter of Indigenous Peoples; the "civilization" of slave-owners denies the bloody reality of slavery; the rising standard of living of white male factory workers after the Second World War ignores the condition of women and other marginalized groups. In the current conjuncture, the prosperity of neoliberalism in the capitalist centers obscures the hyperexploitation and crushing poverty of the periphery.[29] As Federici has written with respect to the history of women in the transition from feudalism to capitalism,

> This history shows that, even when men achieved a certain degree of formal freedom, women were always treated as socially inferior beings and were exploited in ways similar to slavery. "Women", then… signifies not just a hidden history that needs to be made visible, but a particular form of exploitation and, therefore, a unique perspective from which to reconsider the history of capitalist relations.[30]

---

28   National Inquiry into Missing and Murdered Indigenous Women and Girls, http://www.mmiwg-ffada.ca/

29   Nick, Dyer-Witheford, *Cyber-Proletariat: Global Labour in the Digital Vortex* (Toronto: Between the Lines, 2015), 127–28.

30   Silvia Federici, *Caliban and the Witch: Women, The Body and Primitive Accumulation* (New York: Autonomedia, 2014 [2004]), 13.

There is no doubt that the ideology or philosophy of librarianship is equally obscure or hidden: librarians often rail against the fact that the philosophy or worldview is unclear or even lacking. The poet and Librarian of Congress Archibald MacLeish, writing in 1940, argued that "it has proved impossible to arrive at a common agreement as to the social end which librarianship exists to serve."[31] André Cossette, in his 1976 discussion of the philosophy of librarianship, wrote that "contemporary librarianship is characterized by a fight for the full development of its theoretical foundations."[32] Closer to our own time John Buschman, while writing that "the connections between libraries and democracy are more a matter of rhetoric and faith rather than substance", argued that "the profession has yet to come up with real theoretical answers" to the challenges posed by neoliberalism, as evidenced by "a lack of intellectual consensus" and an "intellectual, ethical, and fiscal indeterminacy."[33]

The lack of consensus among librarians interested in political questions is, as we will see, just as much a part of the liberal ideology (of tolerance of "all points of view") as the *invisibility* of political ideology among those who see librarianship either as a value-free practice or as a social science. That mainstream librarianship is divided into these two sometimes overlapping camps is explained by Cossette, who wrote that the development of the theory or *philosophy* of librarianship had to contend with the empiricism of everyday practice of librarianship.[34] In the course of this book, we will analyze the reconfiguring of librarianship as a "value free" social science in the 1930s, dividing the profession into a theoretical component which mystified its allegiance to the military-industrial

---

31   Archibald MacLeish, "The Librarian and the Democratic Process," *ALA Bulletin* 34, no. 6 (1940), 385.

32   André Cossette, *Humanism and Libraries: An Essay on the Philosophy of Librarianship* (Duluth: Library Juice Press, 2009), 1.

33   John Buschman, *Dismantling the Public Sphere: Situating and Sustaining Librarianship in the Age of the New Public Philosophy* (Westport, CT: Libraries Unlimited, 2003), 6–7.

34   Cossette, *Humanism and Libraries*: 8.

complex, and a technical practice which claimed to eschew any theoretical concerns at all. This is not to deny both differing points of view in the early years of the profession, or the division of labor between (primarily male) librarians and (primarily female) library staff, simply to suggest that a single hegemonic perspective reigned despite these variations until the 1930s, when a split occurred. This split led not only to the distinction between theoretical Library Science and empirical practice, but also the rise of a progressive or social justice tendency in librarianship, as opposed to a "value free," pragmatic, or neutralist tendency.[35] From a dialectical perspective, the contradictions within the theoretical unity of theory and practice of the early years of the "library faith" gave rise both to librarianship as activism and as "value-free" social science in the 1930s. Throughout this book, progressive, radical, and critical librarianship will periodically appear as, ostensibly, an antagonist to dominant liberal ideology. I will argue, however, that these movements end up safely recuperated within the hegemonic structures of contemporary capitalism.

To return to the question of the democratic discourse of librarianship, however, we might be tempted to ask why any of this matters. Where is the harm in insisting that libraries are necessary for the flourishing of democracy? Indeed, where is the harm in a view of librarianship that subscribes to idealistic values like liberty and democracy? Without such transcendental values, what reason do people have for continuing to work for a better world? Without them, would we not fall back on the "noble lie" of Plato's *Republic*, the myth of the metals, by which the existing social order is naturalized by the claim that different classes are born with different metals in their souls:

> I wonder if we could contrive one of those convenient stories we were talking about a moment ago... some magnificent myth that would itself carry conviction

---

35 Toni Samek, *Intellectual Freedom and Social Responsibility in American Librarianship, 1967–1974* (Jefferson, NC: McFarland, 2001), 46–47.

> to our whole community... a fairy story like those po-
> ets tell and have persuaded people to believe about the
> sort of thing that often happened 'once upon a time'...
> it should serve to increase their loyalty to the state and
> to themselves.[36]

By positing democracy as an actually existing state of affairs, however, democracy itself becomes precisely this kind of noble lie,
serving to support an unjust, unequal, and exploitative state of affairs. As we shall see in a later chapter, other transcendental values (like "liberty") are also deployed in the same way. Plato's myth
of the metals can only be used to justify and reproduce the status quo. If we want the world to remain the same, to be *conserved*,
then we can leave the purported values of capitalism, liberalism,
freedom (for some) and libraries unchallenged, but this would require us to abandon any pretense that libraries in fact support
such values. If, on the other hand, our purpose is to jettison the
oppressive and tyrannical structures of capitalism itself, to trans-
form and improve the world, then the claims of organizations, social orders, and political institutions must be ruthlessly challenged
and exposed.

     To be more precise, there are two closely connected prob-
lems with not challenging the democratic discourse of librarianship. In the first place, by promoting a vision of capitalist society as egalitarian and democratic (or at least *capable* of equality
and democracy[37]), the democratic library discourse obscures the
very real mechanisms of power and exploitation that are fundamental to capitalist society. Carnegie's provision of a "democratic"

---

36   Plato, *The Republic* (London: Penguin Books, 1955), 181–82.

37   "The current prison-industrial complex contains many examples of injustice,
     but those examples are not necessarily examples of enlightened thinking (far
     from it), and while the panopticon Foucault discusses might metaphorically
     embody the worst aspects of the surveillance society, the treatment of prisoners
     was hardly better before the eighteenth century." Wayne Bivens-Tatum,
     Libraries and the Enlightenment (Los Angeles: Library Juice Press, 2012), 29.

and "egalitarian" public library to placate the workers he had so ruthlessly crushed provides a signal example of the ways in which democratic values are enlisted to support capitalist exploitation and oppression. In this sense, democratic discourse fulfills the same function as the myth of the metals for Plato, or of other naturalizing discourses around various forms of labor, such as housework.[38] By insisting that the mission of libraries is to provide educational opportunities and access to information to support a well-informed citizenry capable of participating in democracy, we tell ourselves and our users that the society we live in *is a democracy*, that their electoral participation matters, and that being well-informed and voting is the correct path for making change in our society, as opposed to, say, revolutionary action. It also makes the library itself resistant to critique and to change: if the library is an "arsenal of a democratic culture," then what we are doing and how we are doing it is valuable in and of itself and should not be changed. Furthermore, to critique libraries and librarianship is itself often seen as lending weight to the neoliberal austerity programs that wish to cut library funding. Libraries must protect their brand while also communicating their value (i.e. supporting the illusion of democratic discourse) because we are so reliant on funding by the capitalist state. Ironically, the democratic discourse of libraries is hegemonic precisely because we have a budgetary gun to our heads. So much for democracy.

***

Libraries have never been autonomous institutions. Today, academic libraries are part of universities, and public libraries are part of municipal corporations. This may seem like stating the obvious, but what is significant is the discourse of autonomy that arose in both academic and public libraries throughout the nineteenth and twentieth centuries and which is still dominant today. Every so often a

---

38   Silvia Federici, *Revolution at Point Zero: Housework, Reproduction, and Feminist Struggle* (New York: PM Press, 2012), 8–9.

librarian will write without irony about the "neutrality" of libraries, or a library organization will insist on their apolitical, independent nature. On the academic side the principle of academic freedom—purporting to mean independence from anything other than academic or intellectual responsibilities—has become, on paper at least, a sacrosanct value of the academy and its libraries. On the public side, the idea of access to information for all citizens, independent of wealth, class, gender, intellectual orientation, etc., is also an avowed value. But how do these values square with the operation and behavior of our parent organizations?

Academic and public librarians, as committed to intellectual independence as we are, are constrained in a double sense: we are both workers and agents of the state. We work for organizations enshrined in and enabled through legislation, but we are also workers in a state-managed relationship to an employer, and that employer is the state itself. What happens to the values and principles of librarians in such an ambiguous role? What happens to intellectual freedom when the very mission of the university or a municipality has become to reproduce the values and ways of thinking of capitalism itself? The library as institution and librarianship as a profession is deeply marked by such contradictions.

All is not hopeless, however. For Marxists, the existence of contradictions is precisely what makes social change possible. Drawing on the work of Hegel, Marx developed an idea of history—social change over time—which saw such change as the process of contradictions coming into being, resolving themselves, and giving rise in turn to new contradictions. This process Hegel and Marx called the dialectic, and in return for providing a theory of how change in the real world works, it requires a different way of thinking about the world as we see it.

Georg Lukács, one of the main figures of Western Marxism, in his 1923 work *History and Class Consciousness*, argued that dialectical thought differed from mainstream science in an important respect. When a contradiction is identified, science (in this case social science) assumes that the contradiction reflects a mistake in our thinking, perhaps caused by a lack of some important piece of information.[39] When the new information is found, our thinking will be corrected, and the contradiction will disappear. Dialectical thinking, in Lukács' view, sees contradictions as present not only in thought but in reality. Contradictions in thought can be dismissed by scientific thinking, but that does not make the contradiction go away in reality. In Marxist terms, the resolution of contradictions is precisely what allows society to change over time.

We therefore have the contradiction between a supposedly independent intellectual profession and a working life in which we all have to pay the bills, with all the attendant compromises and power relationships that go along with this. We also have the contradiction between librarians as agents of the state and employees, that is enforcers of state policy and its subjects. These contradictions are real, they won't go away with better information or wishful thinking.

We are employees, but we are also agents of the state, whose job it is to promote state policy as it exists within the universities and the public library systems. At the same time, we are expected to uphold the sanctity of the values of capitalist society, first and foremost the value of private property. We are complicit in the ideological reproduction of capitalist society through the very work that we do and the very policies that we uphold. A small fraction of us, it's true, have the protection of academic freedom, but an even smaller fraction ever actually uses it. And in public libraries, the commitment to "intellectual freedom" that is enshrined in policy often falls prey to the requirement to protect the brand, because public libraries, like academic ones, are thought to exist at the pleasure or whim of our funding bodies, and we mustn't jeopardize that relationship.

Now, many librarians would argue that through access to information they provide the tools to recognize and counter the spread of capitalist values, perhaps by arguing against corporate presences on campus, for example. But capitalist values are more subtle than that. In the academic world, for instance, the fact that classes always start on time, that assignments have deadlines, that

---

39   Georg Lukács, *History and Class Consciousness: Studies in Marxist Dialectics* (Cambridge: MIT Press, 1971), 10.

work is measured and evaluated through exams and quantitative, competitive grading—all these arose as a response to the requirements of factory work. The fact that desks are all in rows mirrors the factory discipline of early industrial capitalism. This isn't to say that universities aren't providing education, but that at the same time they are also reproducing the subtle ways of being in the world that capitalism requires of all of us. Another contradiction.

One of the problems with approaching these contradictions with scientific thinking, with imagining that more and better information will make the contradictions in our lives disappear, is that when they don't disappear, we can find ourselves at a loss, frustrated, hopeless. The world is alienating and cruel, and when the strategy of finding better information fails, our frustrations increase, and we can find ourselves taking refuge in various things. The safest refuge is simply to stop thinking. The most dangerous is to succumb to an ideology of rage, of racism, fascism, sexism, and other forms of intolerance; the kind of thing which now seems to be enshrined in the presidency of Donald Trump. It is understandable that people fall sway to such ideologies: it is easier to blame the contradictions in our lives on others, and most people have no other way to think about their world. One of the consequences of this–bar the kind of race-war apocalypse predicted by every charlatan from Charlie Manson to David Duke–is that it makes a different world hard to imagine. Fredric Jameson famously remarked that it seems sometimes as if it is easier to imagine the end of the world than the end of capitalism. For the contradictions that I've been talking about, the cruel and frustrating relationships between people that make us either check out or become fascists are not eternal (nothing is)–they are the product of particular ways of engaging with and working in the world that we call by the name of capitalism.

***

To give a sense of the way in which abstract values play a role in the construction of librarianship, I want to take a brief excursion into the realm of intellectual freedom. In 1988 an ALA debate on Intellectual Freedom took place (subsequently published as *The Freedom to Lie: A Debate about Democracy*). As usual in library discussions, the definition of "democracy" is taken for granted; whether or not we truly live in a democratic society must remain unquestioned and unchallenged—the role of the library and librarians is to defend a putative democracy that is presumed to hold in American society. Taking the intellectual freedom side of the debate, John Swan argued that "The commitment of librarians to the truth as an absolute legal defense should never be confused with our basic professional commitment to the flow of all kinds of information without regard to its truth or falsehood... Truth may be, must be, an absolute criterion under the law, but it has no such place in the selection, classification, storage, and weeding decisions made by librarians."[40] Swan quotes from the ALA "Diversity in Collection Development" interpretation of the Bill of Rights in support of his position:

> Intellectual freedom, the essence of equitable library services, promotes no causes, furthers no movements, and favors no viewpoints. It only provides for free access to all expressions of ideas through which any and all sides of a question, cause or movement, may be explored. Toleration is meaningless without tolerance for what some may consider detestable.[41]

Leaving aside what Karl Popper has called the "paradox of tolerance"[42] we find here a classic expression of the hegemonic liberalism of libraries. Indeed, Swan goes on to argue that "as librarians, our cause is, in a very practical sense, not truth but freedom," presuming that such freedom is the default state of liberal society, only deviated from through the actions of extremists on all sides, who must

---

40 John Swan and Noel Peattie, *The Freedom to Lie: A Debate about Democracy* (Jefferson, NC: McFarland, 1989), 2.

41 Swan and Peattie, *Freedom to Lie*, 3.

42 K. R. Popper, *The Open Society and Its Enemies*, volume 1 (London: George Routledge and Sons, 1945), 226.

be resisted. This is, in fact, the position of Eric Klinenberg's 2018 New York Times opinion column entitled "To Restore Civil Society, Start with the Library." What is at stake here is the *restoration* of a period of good capitalism when everyone knew their place and acted like proper, docile, peaceful citizens. Klinenberg claims that "the openness and diversity that flourish in neighborhood libraries were once a hallmark of urban culture," but were they? Referring to the occasional outburst or argument in the library, he writes that "what's remarkable is how rarely these disruptions happen, how civilly they are managed and how quickly a library regains its rhythm afterwards."[43] This ignores, of course, the increased presence of police or private security in public libraries, a presence which is all but invisible to white, middle-class patrons, but all too visible to the identities singled out for oppression by the capitalist state. We are back in the realm of the exclusion of violence identified by Stuart Hall in the Britain of the 1970s. Klinenberg goes on to argue that

> Libraries are the kind of places where people with different backgrounds, passions and interest can take part in a living democratic culture. They are the kinds of places where the public, private and philanthropic sectors can work together to reach for something higher than the bottom line.[44]

This is the liberal library discourse in a nutshell, the discourse which found its highest expression in the period of the welfare state, the period of class compromise and social peace. It bears no relationship to the reality of 21st century public libraries. Despite the argument that "libraries stand for and exemplify something that needs defending: the public institutions that—even in an age of atomization, polarization and inequality—serve as the bedrock of civil society," Klinenberg is seeking a *return* to a period of good

---

43   Klinenberg, "To Restore Civil Society", para. 12.

44   Klinenberg, para. 14.

capitalism—as if inequality did not exist before, say, 2008. "If we have any chance of *rebuilding* a better society, social infrastructure like the library is precisely what we need."[45] We can only rebuild what once existed: the presumption of perfect democracy and freedom, if not today then in some past golden age, runs deep. It is a myth.

Returning to the 1988 ALA debate, Noel Peattie takes the side of social responsibility. He puts the social responsibility perspective concisely:

> In recent years the rise of the social responsibilities movement in library work led many to conclude that the traditional neutrality of library professionals not only tended to neglect the voices of ethnic and left-wing dissent but tended also to weaken the defenses of the profession when faced with authors or speakers whose viewpoints were not simply eccentric, but deliberately fallacious and racist.[46]

We must of course now add to the list of neglected voices those of women, queer and trans people, Indigenous People, and racial and ethnic minorities. Peattie also lays out the fundamental questions of intellectual freedom:

> What is the moral responsibility of librarians for highly controversial materials in their collections? And how do we deal with the person who demands free speech for groups holding theories, which, if they prevailed in the body politic, would diminish or destroy free speech? Are the traditional defenses of intellectual freedom, as they are taught in the profession, adequate to defend us against those who misrepresent historical or scientific fact? Old questions, hashed over by philosophers. Rarely,

---

45   Klinenberg, para 17, emphasis added.

46   Swan and Peattie, *Freedom to Lie,* 35.

however, have they been probed in a library context—
the heart of information and culture in a contemporary
society. When librarians talk about intellectual freedom,
they usually indulge in 'platform speeches' ringing with
well-intentioned (and widely credited) platitudes.[47]

Even when these questions *do* get discussed by librarians, the discussion is not likely to raise the argument above the level of plati-
tude, and rarely reflects back on library practice. Peattie promises
to "probe more deeply into librarianship's most cherished assumptions and defenses,"[48] so we will delve a little more into his argument before moving on. Peattie's argument takes many different—
and valuable—positions on the question of truth (and alternatives
to truth), before coming to a pretty clear statement of the social responsibility perspective on this issue:

I am suggesting that the librarian does have a responsibility to "stay sane": to be able, and to help the community to be able, to distinguish truth from falsehood,
allowable opinion from bigoted manipulation, eccen-
tricity from unworthy ambition. The librarian, like other intellectual workers, has a responsibility to the culture
of her country, beyond passive access.[49]

What I think we can see here in these classic statements of both intellectual freedom and social responsibility—statements and positions endlessly rehashed in forum upon forum—are two distinct
ethical positions. For Swan, "the ethic of freedom is founded on
the belief that knowledge is worth the risk," and "for librarians,
for anyone charged with making the full world of knowledge available and possible," to deny this is a "betrayal of our [librarians']

---

47   Swan and Peattie, 38.

48   Swan and Peattie, 39.

49   Swan and Peattie, 53.

deepest ethical standard."[50] For Peattie, on the other hand, "a society in which the dignity of the oppressed is respected is ultimately more free than a society in which they are insulted or injured."[51] These two ethical perspectives stake out the deontological and the consequentialist positions, respectively. Simply put, deontology can be understood as an ethics of rules and consequentialism as an ethics of outcomes. In the terms of this debate, a deontological ethics claims that there are rules to a free, liberal, democratic society, and that libraries uphold that society best when they follow those rules ("intellectual freedom"), while a consequentialist ethics argues that we must consider the effects on society (e.g. community members, oppressed minorities) rather than simply apply a set of rules ("social responsibility"). Throughout the cycles of this debate since the 1930s, the two ethical positions staked out by both sides have remained largely unchanged. To a certain extent, this is unsurprising. Both the hegemonic, liberal position on intellectual freedom *and* the social justice perspective on social responsibility are partial viewpoints caught within the limits of capitalist society.

In his book *Marxism and Ethics*, Paul Blackledge argues that liberal ethical stances are, in fact, nothing more than the reified expressions of particular bourgeois subjectivities. Marx himself eschewed taking an explicit ethical position, although as Blackledge argues, a particular ethical position is implicit in Marx's work. Because even Marxists are bound by the constraints of bourgeois society, Blackledge—referring to the work of Alasdair MacIntyre and Kelvin Knight—writes that, in their view, "to the extent that Marxists articulate ethical critiques of capitalism they tend to revert to one or other form of modern bourgeois morality: typically either consequentialism or deontology."[52]

---

50   Swan and Peattie, 34.

51   Swan and Peattie, 125.

52   Paul Blackledge, *Marxism and Ethics: Freedom, Desire, and Revolution* (New York: SUNY Press, 2013), 41.

It is for this reason that we can never move beyond the same stale arguments in defense of either intellectual freedom or social responsibility: both stances are bound by the constraints of a partial, bourgeois perspective. This is a classic example of a dialectical contradiction. More information and better arguments will never solve the problem, because the deontological and the consequentialist view are necessarily incommensurable and irreconcilable. The problem of intellectual freedom vs social responsibility in bourgeois society exists not merely in our theory and our perspectives, but in bourgeois reality itself; it is part of the fabric of capitalist society. As a result, the solution to the contradiction between intellectual freedom and social responsibility is insoluble under capitalism; it can only be solved in a future society, one separated from us by revolution, and which can only be reached by way of revolution. That society would not only require us taking a larger perspective on the question, it would *produce that perspective.* Indeed, the future society itself would likely resolve the contradiction between freedom and responsibility as part of the wholesale restructuring of the economy, society, politics, and culture.

Progressive values have long been part of the library discourse, as we have seen, whether that be in support of democracy and civil liberties or, as in the New York Times column, as upholders of civil society. But to have values means we think those values are important enough to actively promote, support, and maintain. The long-standing librarian value of "neutrality", however, imposes an opposing requirement:

> Neutrality, as applied to librarianship, rests on the time-honored principle that librarians on duty, and libraries functioning, base their credibility on avoiding taking sides. Libraries and librarians best protect their freedom, and justify their use of it, by avoiding partisan political activity, by giving equal time and space in groups in conflict, and offering space in their meetings rooms to locals of whatever political persuasion. This

> defense of intellectual freedom is as much an exhibition
> of freedom as a defense of it.[53]

This is not a defense, it is a complete *abdication* of freedom; it is only an exercise and a defense of freedom if we already live in a free society. If, on the other hand, we do *not* live in a free society, then this "neutral" behavior is far from any legitimate conception of neutrality, but instead takes a dishonest, disingenuously partisan position in defense of an unjust and exploitative status quo. We can't be satisfied simply with *saying* we hold progressive values, and yet that is what we do when we give bandwidth, air-time, or oxygen to hateful, corrupt, or reactionary speakers holding vile, violent, and debased values. To claim a set of progressive values but do nothing to uphold them is to not have any values at all—it is a return to the discredited notion of neutrality, and the presumption of democracy and freedom where they do not exist.

One of the arguments in favor of the idea of "intellectual freedom" (which at this point seems like a completely inappropriate term) is that of allowing controversial or despicable ideas to be aired so they can be debated and, in theory, vanquished in the "free marketplace of ideas" (another concept and metaphor whose time has passed). This often comes up in debates around no-platforming, as well as discussions of library speaker series' or conference keynotes. The argument is that we need to hear these perspectives in order to evaluate and challenge them. However, in the 21st century, reactionary perspectives don't *need* libraries to air their point of view; we live in an age of bandwidth abundance rather than bandwidth scarcity. As with our collections, we needed to be comprehensive (as far as that was even possible) when there was no other communications channel, when information could be had through the libraries and almost nowhere else. But this is no longer the case. The Steve Bannons and Jordan Petersons of this world don't need our help getting their message across. The change from communications scarcity to communications abundance is one that the library world

---

has clearly had difficulty adapting to (as, indeed, have the worlds of journalism and copyright law). In a world of limited bandwidth, an attempt at fairness, balance, representing "all sides" might have been achievable, even laudable. We did not have the luxury then, perhaps, of living up to our values. Now that bandwidth is abundant, to pay lip service to progressive values without doing more to uphold them is unconscionable.

The question of values naturally raises the question, yet again, of ethics. What kind of ethics might be appropriate to dealing with this question? Ideally, every library would decide for itself, among the collectivity of its staff, what its role is and what values it decides to uphold. However, we (library workers) are not in charge of our libraries. Our libraries do not serve their publics, they serve the universities and municipalities in which they are embedded; they serve the state; they serve the capitalist mode of production. And they by necessity are busy upholding values different from the ones they (we) profess. But, contrary to neoliberal and neoclassical economic thought, workers do not have the luxury of quitting a workplace that doesn't share their values; the "free market" of labor is an illusion masking a realm of coercion and exploitation.

A focus on values, I think, allows us to avoid both the deontological ethics of rules and the consequentialist ethics of outcomes—not that either practice (rules) or consequences can or should be ignored, but if we are to escape the vicious thirty-year cycle of intellectual freedom/social responsibility debates, we need to look elsewhere. Blackledge argues that, despite Marx's own claims to the contrary—Marxism is consonant with a virtue ethics. Blackledge writes that, "instead of focusing on the intentions of actors or the consequences of actions, virtue ethicists insist that the key ethical question should be 'what kind of person should I be?'"[54] These three ethical stances are not as cut and dried as they might first appear: the rules of a deontological ethics must aim at a particular outcome, and the outcomes of a consequentialist ethics are bound

---

54   Blackledge, *Marxism and Ethics,* 33.

by social custom and practice. However, if we claim to hold progressive values, then we need to live up to those values, not sidestep them—our values are an expression of what we think a good person is. If we want to be moral librarians working in moral libraries for the good of society, then we need to take a perspective broader than both the (partial, bourgeois) positions of intellectual freedom or social responsibility as they have traditionally been framed.

Regarding a proposed Marxist ethics, Blackledge writes:

> Marxist ethics therefore presuppose an unbreakable unity between the facts and the condemnation of exploitation and alienation on the one hand, and the means to an end of socialism on the other. While modern moral philosophy is a reified reflection of our alienated existence under capitalism, Marxism, both as an explanatory account of the dynamics of capitalism and as a condemnation of this system, is rooted in the collective struggle of workers for freedom. Practice does not and cannot follow theory in the way that modern moral theory would have us suppose, for it is universally true that we can theorize only from specific standpoints. Marx thus criticized liberal moralists for being unable to offer an adequate account of human action. By contrast, because he made his own standpoint explicit he revealed not only the limitations of modern moral theory, but also the unity, but not identity, of socialism, social science, and moral realism.[55]

The freedom of a Marxist ethics is not the freedom of liberals: for liberals, freedom exists in the world and must be defended, but theirs is a freedom of the bourgeoisie, of whiteness. For Marxists, for workers, freedom is not yet with us, but must be fought for, struggled for, at every moment. The standard debate on intellectual freedom and social responsibility is insoluble because each position

---

55   Blackledge, 97.

on its own is "unable to offer an adequate account of human action," precisely because the perspectives are limited to a world of alienation and oppression.

It should be clear that I am calling for a *partisan* librarianship, one which decides what a moral profession looks like, and acts according to that decision. But that decision has to be a collective one, a social one, and I'm afraid it will never happen within a capitalist economy, politics, and culture. A partisan librarianship must, therefore, also be a revolutionary librarianship.

This in itself might sound complacent, as if we will need to wait for the revolution before doing anything. Paolo Freire's question—"how is it possible to carry out a pedagogy of the oppressed prior to the revolution"[56]—is a vital one. What we need, in the absence of a socio-economic structure which will allow for collective life, is an "intellectual politics" (in place of a non-existent intellectual freedom). We have to *reject* the rules of liberal society, the rules of an abstract "fairness" and "the marketplace of ideas"; indeed, we need to reject the market itself. And we need to reject the framing of the problem that we inherit from liberalism and from our parent institutions. For example, so many of our intellectual freedom discussions focus on the intellectual freedom of our users, the public; intellectual freedom is outward-facing only. We should reject the exclusivity of that framing and insist on dealing with the huge problem in our profession of the intellectual freedom of public library workers being sacrificed in favour of a liberal hegemony or the market (the library's "brand"). An intellectual politics would insist on trying to live up to our values, even if we fail. We speak a lot about allowing different voices to be heard; we have to include the voices of public library workers, women, librarians of color, or we can never hope to approach the kind of collective action needed for the thorough transformation into the society to come.

---

56 Paolo Freire, *Pedagogy of the Oppressed* (New York: Bloomsbury, 2012 [1970]), 54.

***

Isaiah Berlin famously distinguished between two forms of liberty, positive freedom ("freedom to" do something) and negative freedom ("freedom from" obstruction in exercising my rights and desires). Berlin argued that, for liberals, "if individual liberty is an ultimate end for human beings, none should be deprived of it by others; least of all that some should enjoy it at the expense of others."[57] We will see in Chapter Three, however, that the liberal concept of liberty is based precisely on the deprivation of liberty from certain groups of people, conveniently characterized as non-citizens a priori. Berlin, like all liberals, insists on seeing society as an aggregation of isolated individuals, and his concept of liberty conforms to that presupposition. For Lenin, on the other hand, distinguishing between positive and negative liberty misses the point. Lenin insists that we ask "freedom for whom?"[58] Who is necessarily excluded from any concept of liberty—for as we will see, someone always is. In a 1921 letter about the suppression of newspapers, Lenin writes:

> 'Freedom of the press, from the monarchists to the anarchists, inclusively'... Very good! But just a minute: every Marxist and every worker who ponders over the four years' experience of our revolution will say, 'Let's look into this—what sort of freedom of the press? What for? For which class?' We do not believe in 'absolutes'. We laugh at 'pure democracy'.[59]

For Lenin, 'freedom of the press' was a slogan of the bourgeoisie and expressed the ideas and values of the bourgeois *class* against

---

57   Isaiah Berlin, *Liberty* (Oxford: Oxford University Press, 2002), 172.

58   Raymond Geuss, *Philosophy and Real Politics* (Princeton: Princeton University Press, 2008), 23–29.

59   V. I. Lenin, "To G. Myasnikov," in *Lenin 2017: Remembering, Repeating, and Working Through*, ed. Slavoj Zizek (New York: Verso, 2017), 6.

the ruling classes under feudalism. In this respect, "freedom of the press" was never a neutral proposition, but a political tool for the bourgeoisie to achieve its aims. In this way "freedom of the press" was to the 18th century bourgeoisie what "wages for housework" was to feminists in the 1970s, an idea around which a whole constellation of political ideas and values could circulate. Like the library as an institution, newspapers perform a particular function in bourgeois society. Habermas argues that a *neutral* press only became possible *after* the victory of the bourgeoisie. Prior to that, "the appearance of a political journal and its survival was equivalent to involvement in the struggle over the range of freedom to be granted to public opinion and over publicity as a principle,"[60] on the understanding that "class interest was the basis of public opinion"[61] itself. "Freedom of the press" became a slogan precisely because the press under the *ancien regime* was *not* free. Later on, however,

> With the establishment of the bourgeois constitutional state and the legalization of a political public sphere was the press as a forum of rational-critical debate released from the pressure to take sides ideologically; now it could abandon its polemical stance and concentrate on the profit opportunities for a commercial business.[62]

With the victory of the bourgeoisie after 1848, "freedom of the press" changed from being a radical slogan to be the seal of bourgeois class neutrality. It supported the bourgeoisie in their complacent triumph as it had rallied them in the period of monarchic censorship. From being a challenge, it became a mainstay of the status quo. Lenin remarks that "all over the world, wherever there are capitalists, freedom of the press means freedom to buy up newspapers,

---

60   Jürgen Habermas, *The Structural Transformation of the Public Sphere: An Enquiry into a Category of Bourgeois Society* (Cambridge: MIT Press, 1989), 184.

61   Habermas, *Structural Transformation*, 87.

62   Habermas, 184.

to buy writers, to bribe, buy and fake 'public opinion' for the benefit of the bourgeoisie."[63] Lenin saw that, in the period of his own revolution, "freedom of the press" became once again an element of class struggle:

> The bourgeoisie (all over the world) is still very much stronger than we are. To place in its hands yet another weapon like freedom of political organization (= freedom of the press, for the press is the core and foundation of political organization) means facilitating the enemy's task, means helping the class enemy... We clearly see this fact: 'freedom of the press' means in practice that the international bourgeoisie will immediately buy up hundreds of [opposition] writers, and will organise their propaganda and fight against us. That is a fact. 'They' are richer than we are and will buy a 'force' ten times larger than we have, to fight us.[64]

This position sits uncomfortably for librarians accustomed to a notion of an absolute intellectual freedom. But intellectual freedom, like 'freedom of the press' can never be absolute. When we talk about intellectual freedom, we must ask "freedom for whom"? Who is silently but necessarily excluded from the supposedly universal freedom embodied in this principle? It is commonly understood, for example, that public libraries' commitment to intellectual freedom applies to patrons but not to staff, who are required to "protect the brand" and continue to have their writing and presentations vetted by library administrators. Under conditions of class struggle "intellectual freedom" must be a political, that is a class-based proposition. It cannot be otherwise; "neutrality" in bourgeois society can only mean "supporting bourgeois class interests."

---

63   Lenin, "To G. Myasnikov," 6.

64   Lenin, 7.

***

> What a desecration of the libraries! What an absence of
> the "law and order" we are so justly proud of. Instead of
> *regulations,* discussed and elaborated by a dozen com-
> mittees of civil servants inventing hundreds of formali-
> ties and obstacles to the use of books, they see to it that
> even *children* can make use of the rich collections; that
> readers can read publicly-owned books at home; they re-
> gard as the pride and glory of a public library, not the
> number of rarities it contains, but *the extent* to which
> books are distributed *among the people,* the number of
> new readers enrolled, the speed with which the demand
> for any book is met, the number of books issued to be
> read at home, the number of children attracted to read-
> ing and to the use of the library... These queer prejudic-
> es are widespread in the Western States, and we must be
> glad that those who keep watch and ward over us pro-
> tect us with care and circumspection from the influence
> of these prejudices, protect our rich public libraries from
> the mob, from the *hoi polloi!*[65]

Lenin wrote these words in 1913, in the context of the library's
role in public education, and the targets of his sarcasm, in this instance, were the civil servants—unchanged since the days of Go-
gol and Dostoevsky—who were in charge of the nation's libraries.
These bureaucrats saw libraries as sacred precincts, temples of correct procedure in which they played the part of high priests. Law
and order, correct behavior, procedure, and the conservative values
of the Imperial Russian state held sway in public libraries. Freedom
of inquiry, curiosity, reading for aesthetic or intellectual pleasure,
none of these weighed heavily on the minds of the civil servants. Indeed, to suggest that ordinary people should be allowed to get their

---

65   V. I. Lenin, "What can be done for Public Education?" in *Collected Works*,
      Volume 19 (Moscow: Foreign Languages Publishing House, 1963), 277–79.

grubby hands on the books, should be allowed to remove them from the sacred spaces, amounted to desecration. The spaces and the stock of the public library should be reserved for those gentlemen who had the breeding and sagacity to treat them with the reverence they deserved.

Lenin's counterexample was the New York Public Library which, in 1911, had opened a new main branch on Fifth Avenue. Drawing on an NYPL report from that year, Lenin approvingly notes the number of visitors who used the library in that year, but he goes on to remark that the number of *visitors* is only a partial indicator of the importance of the library; more significant is the number of people who are able to take the books home with them. Lenin contrasts the Russian view of library collections as priceless artifacts to be safely buried beneath layers of bureaucracy with the more properly public mission of NYPL. In fact, Lenin argues that the desacralization of the library from the perspective of the Russian state is necessary if they are to fulfill their educational potential. In this instance, the sanctity of libraries is in direct contrast with their practical mission.

The sacred mission of libraries, as "arsenals of a democratic culture", "cornerstones of liberty", and the rest must be discredited if we want to participate in the creation of a world that is *truly* democratic. True democracy cannot be partial, cannot be exclusionary, and I will argue that this is precisely what "liberal democracy" has always been. The democratic discourse of librarianship, the idea that libraries are sacred to some actually-existing democratic reality, prevents us from working towards the achievement of this radical, total democracy. The focus of this book then, is necessarily negative, thoroughly critical, and by design plays down much of the positive aspects of librarianship, the beneficial role played by libraries in the lives of ordinary people. However, there is plenty of literature on that topic; the current book offers a necessary corrective to the rose-tinted narrative of much library history. A good recent example of a positive history of libraries in the United States which attempts at the same time to challenge the "democratic" view of libraries is Wayne Wiegand's *Part of Our Lives*, and I would refer readers to it not only for its positive narrative, but for the wealth of empirical detail Wiegand brings to the subject.

In the 21st century, American libraries often see their role in much the same way as Lenin's civil servants did, that is the protection of state property and the defense of its values. In September 2016, the Athens-Limestone public library, frustrated at the number of unreturned books and unpaid fines in its system, decided to enforce city ordinance 93–1157, which states the following:

> It is unlawful for any person who has a library card to "fail or refuse to return" any materials borrowed or withdrawn from the public library. Any person who violates the ordinance may receive a fine of up to $100, be sentenced to a jail term of 30 days or possibly both at the discretion of the municipal judge.[66]

Many librarians quickly denounced the strict enforcement of this policy as a violation of the profession's basic principles. The contradiction between library and municipal policy on the one hand and the discourse of librarianship—its basic principles or core values based on community relationships and democracy—mark a tension or contradiction within the profession itself. This tension operates between the objective requirements of the state (itself democratic only in name) and those of its organizations, including the purportedly democratic and enlightening mission of the library as such. The role cultural institutions play within the structure of the state, in this instance, is clear: the protection of private property both as an idea and as a material relationship, and the maintenance and reproduction of a whole suite of values and ideas necessary for the survival of bourgeois capitalist society. As David Graeber notes in his history of debt, the massive bailout of financial institutions during the 2008 financial crisis, the forgiveness of billions of dollars of debt, only applied to the bankers and their cronies.

---

66   Adam Smith, "Overdue Books: Library to Enforce Ordinance," *The News Courier* (August 31, 2016), para 2.

> The bankers were rescued; small-scale debtors—with a paltry few exceptions—were not. To the contrary, in the middle of the greatest economic recession since the '30s, we are already beginning to see a backlash against them—driven by financial corporations who have now turned to the same government that bailed them out to apply the full force of the law against ordinary citizens in financial trouble. "It's not a crime to owe money," reports the Minneapolis-St. Paul *StarTribune*, "But people are routinely being thrown in jail for failing to pay debts."[67]

The strict enforcement of the Athens-Limestone ordinance is a moment of class-struggle, and librarians need to decide what side they are on. The contradiction between democracy and private property is a real contradiction, and not to be overcome simply through more and better knowledge, or a different way of looking at things. In order to make it possible to live under this contradiction without challenging it, ideological domination is required. The cultural work of libraries, including the democratic discourse of librarianship contributes to this ideological requirement. The sacred vision of libraries seeks to resolve in people's minds and thoughts contradictions that exist in the material life of the community itself.

If we were somehow to dismantle the sacred, bourgeois, liberal democratic discourse of librarianship, then we would be faced with the choice between continued complicity—no longer unconscious, however, but fully aware of our complicity—and material resistance to the ideology and logic of capitalism. This goes further than a "counter-hegemonic" project which some librarians on the left have argued for,[68] and must instead constitute actual material resistance to the requirements of our parent institutions. Because these institutions are the ones that fund us, it puts us in a

---

67 David Graeber, *Debt: The First 5,000 Years* (New York: Melville House, 2011), 17.

68 Stephen Bales, *The Dialectic of Academic Librarianship: A Critical Approach* (Sacramento: Library Juice Press, 2015), 131–35.

difficult, if not impossible position. But once again, we must choose between complicity in the name of continued funding, or resistance and risk. Nothing ventured, nothing gained.

The two concrete avenues of resistance I will propose in this book—mathesis and dual power—are by no means the only possible ones. By mathesis, I mean setting up the library—whether academic or public—as a deliberate counterweight to state- and capital-dominated educational systems. The mathetic library supports learning over teaching and is fundamentally connected to the concept of equality of intelligence. Dual power, as the concept comes out of Lenin and Trotsky through such organizations as the Black Panthers and into Fredric Jameson's recent work *An American Utopia*, seeks to leverage the material organizations and networks of library systems as spaces of radical democracy and social services. The two concepts are linked by the deployment of 'utopia' and 'equality' in the work of Paolo Freire and Jacques Rancière. The bulk of the book will clear the way for a discussion of mathesis and dual power that will be addressed in the final chapter. For now, we will turn to an analysis of the interlocking mechanics of oppression within libraries and capitalist society.

Chapter Two

Vectors of Oppression

In 1876, the year of the founding of the American Library Association, the *New York Times* published a column responding to a letter from a woman in Kentucky who stated that "the dawn of women is here begun, because many wives are demanding incomes from their husbands."[1] Silvia Federici quotes from the response to this letter in an epigraph to a 1980 article on housework and social reproduction:

> If women wish the position of the wife to have the honor which they attach to it, they will not talk about the value of their services and about stated incomes, but they will live with their husbands in the spirit of the vow of the English marriage service, taking them 'for better, for worse, for richer, for poorer, in sickness and in health, to love, honour, obey.' This is to be a wife.[2]

For Federici, the idea that women's unpaid work in the home is part of what it means to be a woman is a necessary element in the

---

1   "Wives' Wages," *New York Times* (August 10, 1876), 4.

2   Federici, *Revolution at Point Zero,* 41.

exploitation of (women's) labor by capital, the extraction of surplus value, and the creation of profit. The transcendental, democratic discourse of librarianship (neutral, committed to intellectual freedom, integral to democracy, etc.) serves the same function. The idealized image of what it is "to be a librarian" is much the same as the image of what it means "to be a wife", and both serve as mechanisms by which capitalism continues to operate and reproduce itself, and by which surplus labor can be extracted from workers under the influence of sacredness and mythmaking.

In Federici's view, what differentiates housework from the exploitation of male wage workers in the factories is that "not only has it been imposed on women, but it has been transformed into a natural attribute of our female physique and personality, an internal need, an aspiration, supposedly coming from the depth of our female character."[3] A similarly idealized view of librarians arose along with professionalization after 1876, "the year that Enlightenment scientific principles were finally applied to the organization of information"[4] according to one writer. Shortly thereafter, library education was placed on a more formal footing by the creation of Dewey's School of Library Economy in 1884. Dewey "designed library education to tap the considerable unused energies of educated women" in the nineteenth century, but

> the role he offered women in the library gave them power
> but did not challenge the traditional boundaries placed
> on their activities. The belief of the tender technicians
> in the library that they, as women, had special qualities
> which fitted them for moral reform work and sacrificial
> service was embellished by the touching and persistent
> American faith in the efficiency of education itself.[5]

---

3   Federici, *Revolution at Point Zero*, 16.

4   Bivens-Tatum, *Libraries and the Enlightenment*, 83.

5   Dee Garrison, *Apostles of Culture: The Public Librarian and American Society, 1876–1920* (Madison: University of Wisconsin Press, 2003), 168.

At the 1889 ALA conference in St Louis, Mary Salome Cutler, a library school instructor at Dewey's New York State Library School presented a paper in which she argued for extra pay for working on Sunday. While Dewey, then secretary of the ALA, supported Cutler's paper in general, he opposed any demand for Sunday pay. "Such a spirit," Dewey said, "had nothing in common with the modern library movement, which is nothing if not missionary in character" and he was glad that the ALA was "singularly free from the stigma of being a trades union."[6] Both the religious terminology and the class-snobbery were typical of Dewey.[7]

One hundred years later, in 1992, *Library Journal* ran a cover photo depicting a group of people standing behind a banner that read "Gay and Lesbian Task Force: American Library Association." Despite the progressive, democratic, and liberal discourse of librarianship, the reaction of many readers was "surprisingly virulent and homophobic."[8] It is unnecessary to cite the worst responses here, but two comments in particular are telling:

> I'd like to see the profession cease its endless advocacy of social issues and return to the difficult issues of operating information agencies.
>
> When an organization espouses extreme views, it runs a strong risk of losing credibility and effectiveness in its primary function. The question is not whether gays

---

6 Wayne Wiegand, *The Politics of an Emerging Profession: The American Library Association, 1876–1917* (Westport, CT: Praeger, 1986), 51. That Dewey's class position was reinforced by sexism is well-known by now. See, for example, Anne Ford, "Bringing Harassment Out of the History Books," *American Libraries*, June 1, 2018.

7 Wayne Wiegand, *Irrepressible Reformer: The Life of Melvil Dewey* (Chicago: American Library Association, 1996), 252.

8 Steven Joyce, "A Few Gates: An Examination of the Social Responsibilities Debate in the Early 1970s & 1990s," in *Questioning Library Neutrality: Essays from Progressive Librarian*, ed. Alison Lewis (Duluth: Library Juice Press, 2008), 33.

> or lesbians are discriminated against, but whether this is
> an appropriate or relevant issue for ALA.[9]

In both cases—in 1889 and in 1992—concrete, technical work is opposed to moral values. What is different is that in 1889 moral values (the library mission) were wielded against women's demands for additional pay, while in 1992 a technocratic perspective ("operating information agencies") was wielded against LGBTQ support. These may seem to be opposing examples, but what is common in both is the suppression of demands by marginalized populations (for increased pay, for recognition and support) by the power of the status quo. The fact that those in power in the profession are agnostic when it comes to their choice of weapon should not make us ignorant of the persistence of structural inequality in both examples. The ideology of librarianship in the service of the status quo—capitalist reproduction—is nothing if not flexible; and this flexibility is always in support of continued economic exploitation and social domination.

Dewey's explicit denial that library workers are workers—a denial which also underpins what Fobazi Ettarh has called "vocational awe," down to the use of religious language—also underpins the naturalization of the exploitation of women's work analyzed by Federici. Indeed, his "use of religious terminology and negative inference about unions was deliberately designed to put distance between librarians and other socio-economic groups."[10] And as we have seen, the two processes intersect in the very fact of the feminization of library work studied by Garrison. Additionally, when a Women's Section of the ALA was debated in 1893, ALA Councillor Hannah James wrote in a letter to Dewey, "personally I do not favor [a separate] organization, but only a little gathering to discuss informally any topics that would be interesting to women alone, such as health, hours of work, women's wages, etc."[11] James is careful not

---

9   Joyce, "A Few Gates," 34.

10 Wiegand, *Politics of an Emerging Profession*, 51.

11 Wiegand, *Politics of an Emerging Profession*, 73.

to encroach on the missionary sphere of librarians like Dewey; professional librarianship was founded on this distinction between material work performed primarily by women, and the transcendental missionary work of male librarians, usually characterized as more scholarly and scientific. Both kinds of work were "genteel," and both needed to be protected from the "taint of trade-unionism," but for different reasons. The value of women's work was that it was low-paying[12] and could be framed as care-work; union organization would have changed both these things. The men's work—intellectual, disinterested—had nothing in common with the vulgar concerns of labor organization either. The unequal distribution of library work inscribed a distinction between centre and periphery, a power hierarchy integral to capitalism itself, at the very heart of librarianship, and Ettarh's description rings as true for 1893 as it does for 2018:

> By the very nature of librarianship being an institution,
> it privileges those who fall within the status quo. There-
> fore, librarians who do exist outside librarianship's cen-
> tre can often most clearly see the disparities between the
> espoused values and the reality of library work.[13]

What is especially important here is the fact that the center shifts over time; it is part of a historical process, not just an ideological one. When the center was restricted to upper-class white men in 1893, women were on the periphery, and the appropriate ideological justification was used; in 1992, when LGBTQ struggles "impinged" upon the ALA, a different ideological strategy was deployed. Today, with the resurgence of the far-right as well as militant social justice struggles like #BlackLivesMatter demanding that librarianship take sides, the proponents of neutrality must add new ideological strategies to

---

12 "The presence of women also helped lessen the attraction of educated men to the profession and to keep wages low, thus ensuring continued feminization". Garrison, *Apostles of Culture*, 167.

13 Fobazi Ettarh, "Vocational Awe and Librarianship: Lies we Tell Ourselves," *In the Library with the Lead Pipe* (January 10, 2018): para. 20.

the tried-and-true ones in order to maintain the status quo, the privilege of the center. Indeed, it is precisely the continued (if shifting) differential between the center and the periphery that allows for the continued functioning of the library as a capitalist institution. Just as the accumulation of wealth in the centers of capitalism is predicated on the existence and hyper-exploitation of the global periphery, so too does librarianship require the continued, indeed the *expanded*, exploitation of particular groups in order to sustain and reproduce itself as an institution. This raises the question of the purpose of libraries for capitalism which we will address in Chapter Five.

For Federici, the construction of the home and the family as a sphere supposedly *outside* the system of capitalist relations simply mystifies the structures of domination and oppression that continues to hold in the kitchen and the bedroom: "where women are concerned, their labor appears to be a personal service outside of capital."[14] She argues that the factory-focused Left of the 70s, thinking of the home as a space outside of capitalism, dismissed its position within capitalist relations not only of exploitation and domination, but of the production of value itself. For the Left of the 70s, unwaged workers were not part of the proletariat, the gravediggers proclaimed by Marx, destined to overthrow capitalism and create a new world.[15] Federici argues that for this Left, "women's oppression [is] caused by their exclusion from capitalist relations," the solution to which was "a strategy for us to enter these relations rather than destroy them."[16] She makes the same argument with respect to the global periphery, linking women's struggles with anti-colonial ones:

> In the same way as [the Left] want to bring women to the factories, they want to bring factories to the "Third World." In both cases they presume that the

---

14   Federici, *Revolution at Point Zero*, 28.

15   Karl Marx and Friedrich Engels, *The Communist Manifesto* (London: Penguin Books, 1985 [1848]), 94; Dyer-Witheford, *Cyber-Proletariat*, 13.

16   Federici, *Revolution at Point Zero*, 28.

> "underdeveloped"—those of us who are unwaged and
> work at a lower technological level—are backward with
> respect to the "real working class" and can catch up only
> by obtaining a more advanced type of capitalist exploita-
> tion, a bigger share of factory work.[17]

The democratic, transcendental view of librarianship—compre-
hending both Dewey's "missionary" perspective and the "vocational awe" analyzed by Ettarh—is based on the same idea: that the
library is a space outside of capitalist political, economic, and cultural relations. For Dewey, this allowed for the idea that library
work is sacred, untouched by economic, material considerations
("trade-unionism") and free to go about its work of "salvation" and
"enlightenment" unfettered. For Ettarh, vocational awe is part of
the disciplining of library workers:

> If the language around being a good librarian is direct-
> ly tied to struggle, sacrifice, and obedience, then the
> more one struggles for their work, the "holier" that work
> (and institution) becomes. Thus, it will become less like-
> ly that people will feel empowered, or even able, to fight
> for healthier workspace.[18]

Not only are these dynamics connected, Federici suggests, they are
the same dynamic. The enlightenment and salvation mission of the
library is predicated on (and works through) the continued disciplining of library workers, and the discipline is more severe for
women, LGBTQ people, people of color, and disabled people. In
this way, the disciplining of labor dovetails with other strategies of
oppression.[19] The enlightenment offered by the library to the public,

17 Federici, 29.

18 Ettarh, "Vocational Awe," para. 23.

19 W. E. B. Du Bois, "Marxism and the Negro Problem", *The Crisis,* 40 (5, May
1933): 103–04.

an enlightenment which serves to inculcate bourgeois values and re-produce capitalism socially, politically, and ideologically, requires strict labor discipline within the profession. In this sense, not only is the library an institution of ideological reproduction, it is an institution of *social* reproduction in the same way that marriage and the family are for Federici. It is important to bear in mind, then, that the political demand for wages for housework, far from being a demand for the inclusion of housework within a system of capitalist wage labor (which, in any case, it already was), is a demand to make explicit the domination of unwaged labor. "Wages for housework", Federici writes, could never come about "without at the same time revolutionizing—in the process of struggling for it—all our family and social relations… if we take wages for housework as a political perspective, we can see that struggling for it is going to produce a revolution in our lives and in our social power as women."[20]

The library, then, is put forward by the democratic discourse as an institution outside of capitalist economic relationships, where sharing, curiosity, and intellectual freedom reign. We need to challenge this idea, and so what we need is a political demand akin to "wages for housework" that exposes the reality of library labor, the truth of the library as a capitalist institution, and the necessity of a revolution in our lives and social power as workers.

Gender, Technology, and Library Education

Pierce Butler, in his discussion of the profession of librarianship, argues that by the turn of the 20th century, the profession had seen three transformations of worldview: the initial professionalization of librarianship after 1850, the rapid technological advance of the 1870s, and finally a growing awareness of the social responsibility of librarians at the turn of the century, since which time "Americans, like Europeans, had been becoming ever more 'socially minded.'"[21]

---

20   Federici, *Revolution at Point Zero*, 15–16.

21   Federici, 15–16.

In the 1870s, with the development of new and faster technologies, "librarians, in spontaneous unanimity, began to pay closer attention to their manipulative [i.e. technical] operations."[22] This was the period in which Cutter developed his cataloging rules and when a new focus on technical efficiency developed in tandem with the invention of, for example, new technologies of transportation and communication.[23] These developments led to what David Harvey has called "time-space compression": "processes that so revolutionize the objective qualities of space and time that we are forced to alter, sometimes in quite radical ways, how we represent the world to ourselves."[24] Similarly, Fredric Jameson has characterized our current period as "the predominance of space over time."[25] This technological revolution indeed changed the ways librarians represented the world to themselves: "the librarian came to know himself as being a technician as well as being a bookman."[26] Butler's liberalism prevents him from offering any kind of explanation for these developments. They occurred "spontaneously", "in spontaneous unanimity." By contrast, it is important to insist on the material dialectic of this development as a means to help explain it: the reciprocal exchanges (one might say "metabolism") between technologies and technical work on the one hand and scholarly, intellectual, or socially-minded work on the other. This conforms precisely to Marx's view, not only of the development of productive forces through technical innovation, but also the development of ideology

---

22   Pierce Butler, "Librarianship as a Profession," in *Landmarks of Library Literature, 1876–1976*, edited by Dianne J. Ellsworth and Norman D. Stevens (Metuchen, NJ: Scarecrow Press, 1976), 25.

23   Sam Popowich, "'Ruthless Criticism of all that Exists': Marxism, Technology, and Library Work," in *The Politics of Theory and the Practice of Critical Librarianship*, ed. Karen P Nicholson and Maura Seale (Sacramento: Library Juice Press, 2018), 57.

24   David Harvey, *The Condition of Postmodernity: An Enquiry into the Origins of Cultural Change* (Oxford: Blackwell, 1990), 240.

25   Fredric Jameson, "The Aesthetic of Singularity," *New Left Review* II (92, 2015): 105.

26   Butler, "Librarianship as a Profession," 25.

itself. In the 1859 preface to the *Contribution to the Critique of Political Economy*, Marx explains how these interconnections influence each other:

> In the social production of their existence, men inevitably enter into definite relations, which are independent of their will, namely relations of production appropriate to a given stage in the development of their material forces of production. The totality of these relations of production constituted the economic structure of society, the real foundation, on which arises a legal and political superstructure and to which correspond definite forms of social consciousness. The mode of production of material life conditions the general process of social, political and intellectual life.[27]

If we are to understand the tension between the pragmatic or technical and the transcendent or immaterial in librarianship, then we must understand the material conditions of both. For Butler, the *idea* of professionalism determines certain elements of library history, such as the development of library education:

> The main purpose of the founding fathers was, of course, to provide vocational training. But undoubtedly, they were also influenced by the idea that librarianship should have its professional schools because the other professions have them. These early library schools, however, did not produce the effects that the founders hoped for. They did help some individuals on the way toward professionalism, but they did it almost inadvertently—by their associations rather than their teachings. Unfortunately, they were founded in an age when librarians thought exclusively in terms of library technology. Library education

---

27 Karl Marx, *A Contribution to the Critique of Political Economy* (New York: International Publishers, 1970), 20.

was, therefore, conceived as primarily a training in the niceties of cataloging and classification.[28]

Butler ignores the gendered aspect of library education: from the beginning, library education (focusing on vocational training rather than scholarly engagement) was meant to create a cohort of women library workers to perform the pragmatic work of managing the physical books—what Butler calls the "manipulative operations" of library work. The "founding fathers"—like Dewey and Cutter—could pursue their transcendental, missionary, scholarly, and intellectual work free from the vulgar material considerations of "library economy." Because Butler cannot see the gendered aspect of this process, he ascribes it to a *subjective* response to professionalism and technological development, both of which seem to operate independently and autonomously. We will see later how graduate education in "library science" helped to further cement the gendered distinction between practical and theoretical work, but for now we should look more closely at the gendered nature of the library dichotomy.

In her account of women in librarianship, Dee Garrison argues that women "flooded" into the profession after 1875 for a number of reasons. The rapid growth of librarianship, benefiting from the technological advances of the period, meant that there were plenty of jobs requiring a certain amount of education, and there were enough jobs that "male librarians offered no opposition to the proliferation of women library workers."[29] Partly, however, "women agreed that library work matched presumed feminine limitations":

> Librarianship quickly adjusted to fit the narrowly circumscribed sphere of women's activities, for it appeared similar to the work of the home, functioned

28   Butler, "Librarianship as a Profession," 28.

29   Dee Garrison, "The Tender Technicians: The Feminization of Public Librarianship, 1876–1905," *Journal of Social History* 6, no. 2 (972/3): 131.

as cultural activity, required no great skill or physical
strength and brought little contact with the rougher por-
tions of society.[30]

If we combine this view with that of Silvia Federici on the normalization of housework as a way to exploit women's unpaid labor, we
can argue that librarianship developed as it did, from "bookman"
to "technician", in order to satisfy the demand for cheap (female) labor without giving women the power to break away from "women's
work" completely. The process of feminization of the profession and
the restriction of library education to work that conformed to "feminine limitations" was a way for capitalism to hedge its bets, drawing on a pool of unpaid labor while there were plenty of jobs, while
not giving those workers the opportunity, training, or education to
hold on to those jobs in times of economic crisis (e.g. what we now
call downsizing), such as the one that began around 1873 and lasted until the early 1890s. In a similar, but different, context, Marie
Hicks has written that

> Seen as a 'reserve' labor force whose low cost and elastic-
> ity in times of economic contraction benefited the state,
> women were one of the government's most effective tools
> for keeping the cost of their burgeoning public sector
> under control.[31]

The financial consideration—the ability to pay women less—is an
integral part of the capitalist integration of library work. In an 1886
address to women college graduates, Dewey told his audience that

---

30   Garrison, "Tender Technicians," 132.

31   Marie Hicks, *Programmed Inequality: How Britain Discarded Women
     Technologists and Lost Its Edge in Computing* (Cambridge: MIT Press,
     2017), 91. It is important to bear in mind, however, that "despite economic
     rationalizations… biases that had nothing to do with the bottom line shaped
     managerial conduct". Hicks, *Programmed Inequality*, 10.

> The salary to women for the first year is seldom more
> than $500 and at present few have grown to over $1000,
> though here and there $1,200 to $1,500 are paid to wom-
> en of experience. But there is no reason why a woman
> cannot do that same work for which our leading librari-
> ans receive $3,000 to $5,000 and I have no doubt that as
> women of education, through technical training and ex-
> perience come forward the salaries will rapidly increase.[32]

The continued existence of a gendered pay gap in librarianship
demonstrates Dewey's inability to see beyond the limits of his ideology. Since library education was restricted to the technical aspects
of librarianship, leaving male librarians to occupy themselves with
higher-prestige scholarly and intellectual activity, a gendered pay
gap was more or less assured from the beginning. As Garrison remarks, "the low cost of hiring women was perhaps the most important reason that male library leaders welcomed women assistants."[33]

Marie Hicks's invocation of a 'reserve' labor force brings to
mind Marx's discussion of the 'industrial reserve army' in Chapter
25 of *Capital:*

> If a surplus population of workers is a necessary prod-
> uct of accumulation or of the development of wealth on
> a capitalist basis, this surplus population also becomes,
> conversely, the lever of capitalist accumulation, indeed
> it becomes a condition for the existence of the capitalist
> mode of production. It forms a disposable industrial re-
> serve army which belongs to capital just as absolutely as if
> the latter had bred it at its own cost. Independently of the
> limits of the actual increase in the population, it creates a
> mass of human material always ready for exploitation by

---

32 Melvil Dewey, *Librarianship as a Profession for College-Bred Women*, An
    Address Delivered before the Association of Collegiate Alumnae on March
    13, 1886 (Boston: Library Bureau, 1886), 22.

33 Garrison, "Tender Technicians," 133.

> capital in the interests of capital's own changing valori-
> zation requirements. With accumulation, and the devel-
> opment of the productivity of labor that accompanies it,
> capital's power of sudden expansion also grows...[34]

The analysis of gendered labor as a particular form of reserve army, one which is called into the ranks of waged labor when required, and returned to the ranks of the unwaged (housework, etc.) when surplus to requirements, provides a compelling illustration of the dialectic of gendered labor in librarianship: material, maternal, practical work given to "unskilled" women; scientific, detached, missionary, transcendent work given to men. When librarianship had jobs it needed filled, it filled them with women; increasingly it fills them with precarious workers and people of color, who satisfy the same requirements under neoliberalism as women did in earlier conjunctures. It is easier to dismiss workers considered unskilled or precarious when automation reduces the labor requirements of the profession, as it has steadily been doing since the 1870s.

There is, however, an additional component to the Marxist analysis of gendered work, one which supplements the larger-scale movements of gendered labor in and out of the waged workforce. In his discussion of value at the beginning of *Capital*, Marx starts out with a very simple question: when we exchange two commodities, how do we determine their value? His answer to this is that value is created by human labor; this is the labor theory of value which he took over from, among others, David Ricardo. The labor theory of value states that human labor creates value which is then "embodied" in the commodity. This value is immaterial and not easily measurable, since its measure is really the "socially necessary labor time" embodied in the commodity. Over time, one commodity becomes a "universal measure" of any value, and we end up calling that commodity money. So, we can say that any output of

---

34   Karl Marx, *Capital, Volume 1: A Critique of Political Economy* (London: Penguin Books, 1976 [1867]), 784–85.

production has value through being a product of human labor, and this value can be measured in money.

Money, Marx continues, is not the same as capital. The capitalists have to have a reason to bring labor and raw material together, to advance their own money to set up in industry and produce commodities. This incentive is profit, which returns to the capitalists after they sell the commodities that their workers have produced. The question now becomes, how does the magnitude of value increase during the process of production, so that the commodities are worth more when they are sold than the raw materials and labor costs that went into them? In other words, where does the profit come from? Capital is money that performs this operation of regularly increasing value.

Since the capitalist pays money for raw materials and for human labor, and only human labor can create *new* value, the extra value (what Marx calls *surplus value*) can only come from value added to the commodity *that the capitalist has not paid for*. But how can this be, considering that workers sell their labor to capitalists on the free market? Surely the market will ensure the proper level of wages, as long as the workers simply set the price they want! (See here how the arguments for lower wages for women today are the same as the arguments used to justify worker exploitation at the time *Capital* was written). The price of the commodity "labor power" (what the worker has to sell) is, according to bourgeois economic theory, set by the market the same as everything else: it is the cost of all the commodities that went into its production, so the wages that a worker can command are equal to the amount of money spent on creating them as a worker (this explains why people with degrees are paid more in our society: all the money and time laid out on making them the worker they are goes into the price they can command for their labor power). Let's say the worker asks for $100 per day in wages and in 8 hours of work produces $100 of value–in that case no surplus value is produced and the capitalist receives no profit. The task of the capitalist is therefore to try to get the worker to produce more than $100 worth of value in an 8–hour day.

There are many ways that this can be done. Marx distinguishes between lengthening the working day and increasing the productivity of labor. If the worker produces $100 in 8 hours, they will produce $150 in 12 hours, (even if they've already agreed to be paid only $100); or if, through increased automation, a worker now produces $150 worth of value in 8 hours but are still only paid $100. In both cases $50 of surplus value is produced and pocketed by the capitalist.

But the capitalist can never stop at, say, $50 worth of profit, because all the other capitalists are competing to increase their own profits, making it harder and harder to create surplus value anywhere. So the process continues, with capital constantly seeking new ways to cheapen labor and to increase productivity. Looked at from this angle, any *social* mechanism by which lower pay for *some labor* can be justified (i.e. labor performed by women) is worth it as it increases the amount of surplus labor performed by women, and hence the surplus value derived from their work. These social mechanisms are present as flat-out misogyny, but also operate in less direct ways, for example in the ways that women are subtly disadvantaged during salary negotiations.

Lenin referred on more than one occasion to the bribery of the upper levels of the working class, the raising of their standard of living to bring them around to support the status quo. Another reason for increased exploitation of women with respect to men is that it enables male workers to be bought off by being in a better, more powerful, socio-economic situation (this too manifests itself in insidious social ways, corrosive to both men and women). What has been said here applies to any group (i.e. new immigrants, racial minorities, etc.) which can be exploited to a higher degree and played off against other groups within the working class. One thing to bear in mind (especially among male workers who are happy with their lot) is that, under capitalism, *all* workers are exploited, all workers are forced to produce surplus value. What we have here is a condition in which women are *more* exploited *because* they are women.

Whiteness and White Fragility

When we add race to the question of interlocking vectors of exploitation, we can see how racism and sexism combine to produce a condition of hyperexploitation among women of color; a condition which is not absent from librarianship. Much like Silvia Federici, Patricia Hill Collins argues that separating work and family life is an artificial distinction under capitalism:

> Because African American women have long worked outside the home, their paid labor in the labor market as well as their unpaid labor in their family households do not fit within prevailing understandings of work and family as separate spheres of social organization. Black women's experiences do not simply challenge views of work as a public, male domain, and family as a private, female haven; they also suggest how the framework of a work/family nexus provides new directions for understanding Black women's poverty.[35]

The result of this artificial distinction, in Collins' view, is to focus issues of Black political economy on "public sphere" institutions like the state, the labor market, etc., while confining cultural and social reproduction to the private sphere of the family:

> In this fashion, gender and sexuality as systems of power become coded as private matters; they only emerge into public sphere activities when worn as identity categories by Black women.[36]

The library operates precisely at this nexus of public and private; indeed, many of the dichotomies and contradictions within librarianship can be traced to this position within the structures of capitalist society. The split between masculine "library science" and feminine "library economy", the centrifugal forces operating between

---

35   Patricia Hill Collins, "Gender, Black Feminism, and Black Political Economy," *The Annals of the American Academy of Political and Social Science* 568 (2000), 45.

36   Collins, "Gender, Black Feminism, and Black Political Economy," 52.

cultural center and periphery, as identified by Ettarh, the vectors by which neoliberal capitalism effected the process of turning all work into exploited work, e.g. gendered and racial wage differentials. All of these, it can be argued, are made possible by the library's liminal position between public and private, a position that developed out of the combined material and ideal properties of the book, and the public and private modes of reading itself.

Indeed, the conflict between the practical and the theoretical work of librarianship supports, as David James Hudson has argued, a racial and gendered status quo:

> our very expectations and assumptions about the practical character and value of our field subtly police the work we end up doing and supporting, the kind of questions we ask and conversations we have, our sense of what useful and appropriate conferences, publications, and research look like, and indeed our sense, more generally, of what useful and appropriate political interventions look like from the standpoint of our profession.[37]

The untheorized and untheorizing practicality of library work presumes an unconscious theoretical framework, that of white, bourgeois liberalism. While many library workers and supervisors are willing and able to ignore critical and theoretical questions in favor of "getting the work done" (or are forced to ignore them by our pragmatic professional structures and cultures), I feel that the theory and philosophy of librarianship—equally dominated by whiteness—*also* supports such a status quo. The twofold approach to containing any radical questioning within librarianship, to achieving the social reproduction within the public/private sphere of the library itself, maps on to two different kinds of library work which, as we have already seen, have a gendered history of their own.

---

37   David James Hudson, "The Whiteness of Practicality," in *Topographies of Whiteness: Mapping Whiteness in Library and Information Studies*, ed. Gina Schlesselman-Tarango (Sacramento: Library Juice Press, 2017), 205.

Hudson raises an important point, however, when he argues that

> ultimately, the imperative to be practical in our field
> hinges on a deep (if somewhat paradoxical) individual-
> ism. In spite of overtones of inclusivity, it treats critical
> work as self-contained, suggesting that truly ethical work
> in the library world requires each of us to come up with
> complete sets of questions and complete sets of answers,
> to individually balance what is understood to be theory
> with what is understood to be practice, to ensure that our
> language is always going to be understood by everyone…
> such individualism is, of course, profoundly entangled
> with whiteness… more specifically, it aligns epistemolog-
> ically with the individualism of liberal racial politics.[38]

We will return to the question of bourgeois individualism in a moment, but I want to reinforce the idea that the library sits at the nexus of public and private, housework and wage labor, private reading and public space. The two main trends of library history, the
progressive view of democracy and enlightenment, and the critical view of the library as institution of social control and reproduction, is given motive energy by this set of contradictions: the library
as a social space concerned with the enlightenment of "the masses"
operates through the private activity of reading; tax (i.e. collective-
ly)-funded libraries penalize users via *individual* fines, and so on.
In this the library expresses a fundamental contradiction of capitalist society itself: a society which requires a subjective individualism and the stifling of any and all collective thought or action, but
which is based upon an enormously socialized and cooperative labor process, one which the individualism of modern subjectivity is
designed to mystify and hide. Indeed, for Marx, it is the contradiction between the individual and society, unresolved and unresolv-
able under capitalism, that lays the groundwork for a future society
when, as Ernest Mandel puts it, "both the real unity of the human

---

38   Hudson, "Whiteness of Practicality," 226–27.

race and the real universality of the individual" is "made materially possible by this objective socialization of labor."[39]

This individualistic approach has grave consequences for diversity initiatives in libraries, which paradoxically have the opposite effect to that intended, based on a flawed understanding of the challenges faced by minority librarians—the "pipeline problem" debunked by, among others, Miriam Posner. In her article on the gender imbalance in technology fields, Posner quotes technology historian Marie Hicks, who argues that the "pipeline" of women or people of color into a profession is not the issue: "The pipeline is not the problem; the meritocracy is the problem. The idea that we'll just stuff people into the pipeline assumes a meritocracy that does not exist."[40] In her book *Programming Inequality,* Hicks writes that

> Initiatives to get girls, women, and people of color to train for STEM jobs cannot undo the underlying structures of power that have been designed into technological systems over the course of decades. Despite the rhetoric of meritocracy, patterns like these will not be undone by the individual career choices of workers, especially if they belong to groups that lack the power to participate in the structures of dominance and control that create institutionalized discrimination in a given organization or industry in the first place.[41]

Contrary to the tenets of methodological individualism, a social or collective problem cannot be solved at the individual level.

In an analysis of the role of whiteness in the failure of LIS diversity initiatives, April Hathcock asks, "With minority librarians leaving the profession as soon as they are recruited, what can

---

39   Marx, *Capital, Volume 1*: 946.

40   Miriam Posner, "We can Teach Women to code, but that just Creates Another Problem," *Guardian* (March 14, 2017).

41   Hicks, *Programmed Inequality*, 238.

be done to render our abundance of diversity initiatives truly effective?"[42] Hathcock argues that whiteness refers "not only to the socio-cultural differential of power and privilege that results from categories of race and ethnicity; it also stands as a marker for the privilege and power that acts to reinforce itself through hegemonic cultural practice that excludes all who are different."[43] Such exclusion has been an integral component of the liberal, bourgeois, Enlightenment project from the beginning, and so it stands to reason that it should be a core component of librarianship as well. In Canada, such exclusion has taken violent forms, such as dispossession and expropriation of land as well as cultural genocide[44] inflicted through institutions like residential schools and continued attacks on Indigenous sovereignty (for example, through the federal government's support of the Trans-Mountain pipeline in defiance of First Nations in Alberta and British Columbia[45]), inaction on Murdered and Missing Indigenous Women (MMIW),[46] and astronomical rates of Indigenous incarceration.[47]

Increasing diversity and challenging white supremacy, for both Hudson and Hathcock, involves dismantling the whiteness of librarianship. In terms of diversity initiatives, "the first step is to

42 April Hathcock, "White Librarianship in Blackface: Diversity Initiatives in LIS," *In the Library with The Lead Pipe* October 7, 2015: para. 2; on the demographics of diversity in LIS see Jennifer Vinopal, "The Quest for Diversity in Library Staffing: From Awareness to Action," *In the Library with the Lead Pipe*, January 13, 2016.

43 Hathcock, "White Librarianship in Blackface," para. 3.

44 Truth and Reconciliation Commission, *Final Report*, 1–3, 134, 237.

45 "Indigenous groups lead protest against Kinder Morgan's Trans Mountain pipeline plan," *CBC News* (March 10, 2018).

46 Native Women's Association of Canada, "NWAC Dismayed with Ongoing Issues at National Inquiry," January 11, 2018.

47 Kelly Geraldine Malone, "Nearly half of Canada's incarcerated youth are Indigenous, according to Statistics Canada," *CBC News* (June 24, 2018); Nancy Macdonald, "Canada's prisons are the 'new residential schools'," *MacLean's* (February 18, 2016).

help diverse applicants navigate the whiteness of the profession and make a concerted effort to dismantle whiteness from within."[48] Diversity initiatives in Canada, which tend to focus on Indigenous librarians as part of a larger focus on decolonization and indigenization, are often trumpeted as an example of the progressive nature of Canadian libraries. However, such initiatives fall prey to the same issues as other diversity initiatives identified by Hathcock and others. As Angela Galvan has noted, "For marginalized librarians, the successful performance of whiteness may include integrating aspects of the self which allow White Saviors to feel good."[49] This is made even more problematic when, as in Canadian Indigenous internships, new librarians are made to perform some aspects of professional whiteness, while *also* expressing their Indigeneity in visible ways which allow the library to capitalize on its own supposed progressivity. In this sense, Indigenous interns in Canada are made both to perform whiteness *and* to perform as Indigenous people for the benefit and continuation of white bourgeois capitalism in the institution at large. This indicates an unwillingness or inability on the part of library leadership to understand how oppression continues to work in supposedly enlightened, democratic institutions. As Fobazi Ettarh points out, by compartmentalizing different issues facing oppressed people, "we as librarians fail to fully understand how oppressions work in various contexts."[50] In this regard, I agree with Hudson that a focus on pragmatic work does the profession no favors; however, what theoretical work is being done within librarianship is often unable to overcome this problem. Indeed, in another article, Hudson argues that reliance on the concept of diversity *itself* is an obstacle to anti-racism in LIS:

---

48   Hathcock, "White Librarianship in Blackface," para. 24.

49   Angela Galvan, "Soliciting Performance, Hiding Bias: Whiteness and Librarianship," *In the Library with the Lead Pipe,* (June 3, 2015): para. 26.

50   Fobazi Ettarh, "Making a New Table: Intersectional Librarianship," *In the Library with the Lead Pipe* (July 2, 2014): para 2.

The traditional discourse of diversity that dominated LIS literature of racial difference needs to be understood, then, not as a timeless anti-racist counterweight
to an ahistorically conceived white supremacy, but as
a phenomenon that has emerged as part of the broader adoption of anti-racist rhetoric as a recuperative measure within white supremacy itself: far from over, the
material conditions of racial domination and their read-
ily available (if always precarious) taxonomies of difference persist, even as their reproduction in deracialized
terms has afforded a means of situating a putatively anti-racist present as a foil against which to define racism
as a relic of an unfortunate past.[51]

From a Marxist perspective, I would agree with Galvan's characterization of whiteness as "white, heterosexual, capitalist, and middle
class."[52] From the perspective of the political economy of librarianship, it is clear that particular subject positions are enshrined and
centralized, setting up a hierarchy of class, race, gender, sexuality,
and (dis)ability that serves to reinforce particular power relationships within broader capitalist society. These relationships are structured at least in part through wage/income differentials. While the
hierarchy of librarianship is inscribed by intersectional, interlocking vectors of oppression, it is the wage that provides the ordinali-
ty of that hierarchy; wage difference is perhaps the clearest indicator that other hierarchies are in play. This in and of itself, however,
risks subscribing to bourgeois notions of a depoliticized, objective
wage, the idea that "we are paid for the work that we do", which
connects with the idea of a meritocracy but is distinct from it. In

---

51 David James Hudson, "On 'Diversity' as Anti-Racism in Library and
    Information Studies: A Critique," *Journal of Critical Library and Information
    Studies* 1, no. 2 (2017): 25.

52 Galvan, "Soliciting Performance". In this sense I equate "white" more
    or less with "bourgeois", but with the benefit of reinforcing rather than
    downplaying the racial aspect of the identity.

Marxist theory, the contractual wage is not a fair exchange for labor performed but is rather the *minimum acceptable payment for the reproduction of the worker*. The work actually performed is independent of the wage paid; this is the mechanism by which surplus value is extracted and pocketed by the capitalist. As we have seen, capitalism is often able to get workers to work for free; the struggle over wages is class struggle.

But the hierarchy of librarianship, with white, male, technologically-oriented men at the top, commands higher wages than strictly necessary within the political economy of late capitalism. This is because capitalism is prepared to pay *more* to set up an "aristocracy of labor," a class division within the working class itself, as a means to divide and conquer. W. E. B. Du Bois recognized this in his essay on "Marxism and the Negro Problem," and Keeanga-Yamahtta Taylor sees it in the gap between rich and poor African Americans in the US.[53] Taylor also identifies the reasons for the persistence of the notions of "colorblindness" and meritocracy under neoliberalism. The neoliberal attacks on the institutions of the welfare state, she writes,

> have consequences for ordinary Black people, but they are also a "Trojan horse" shielding a much broader attack against all working-class people, including whites and Latino/as. African Americans, of course, suffer disproportionately from the dismantling of the social welfare state, but in a country with growing economic inequality between the richest and poorest Americans, austerity budgets and political attacks on social welfare come at the peril of all ordinary people. It is an example of how, counterintuitively, even ordinary white people have an interest in exposing the racist nature of US society, because doing so legitimizes the demand for an expansive and robust regime of social welfare intended to redistribute wealth and resources from the rich back

---

53   Keeanga-Yamahtta Taylor, *From #BlackLivesMatter to Black Liberation* (Chicago: Haymarket, 2016): 6–8.

to the working class—Black, Brown, and white. Con-
versely, it is also why the political and economic elites
have such a vested interest in colorblindness and in the
perpetuation of the myth that the Unites States is a
meritocracy.[54]

The myth of a meritocratic US (or Canada) is also the myth of progressive, enlightened librarianship. Elsewhere, Taylor argues that

any serious discussion about Black liberation has to take
up not only a critique of capitalism, but also a credible
strategy for ending it. For Marxists, that strategy hing-
es on the revolutionary potential of a unified, multira-
cial and multi-ethnic working-class upheaval against
capitalism.[55]

Hudson argues that it is precisely the pragmatic approach to library
work that prevents us from even asking questions about race, power, justice, and so forth.[56] And it is definitely the case that our organizational cultures, with their almost exclusive focus on the mechanisms of "operating information agencies" provide no space for
such questioning. Hence the need for theoretical engagement with
these issues in the spaces available. But the division between pragmatic library work, uninterested in and often unaware of theoretical discussions, and scholarly LIS work, sometimes cut off from
day-to-day library work, but also constrained by its own gendered
and racialized history, makes it difficult to see how, to paraphrase
Marx, theory can become a material force by gripping the mass
of library workers. The Canadian novelist Hugh MacLennan once

54 Taylor, *From #BlackLivesMatter to Black Liberation*, 5.

55 Keeanga-Yamahtta Taylor, "Race, Class and Marxism," *Socialist Worker*
(January 4, 2011): para 2.

56 David James Hudson, "Unpacking 'Information Inequality': Toward a
Critical Discourse of Global Justice in Library and Information Science,"
Canadian Journal of Information and Library Science 36, no. 2–4 (2012): 84.

characterized the gulf between French and English Canada as producing "two solitudes." Such a gulf exists in librarianship also, between pragmatic and theoretical work, each with its own unquestioned bourgeois patriarchy and whiteness on the one hand, and critical perspectives and praxis on the other.

In June of 2018, sociologist Robin DiAngelo published *White Fragility: Why It's So Hard for White People to Talk about Racism*. At the very beginning of the book, DiAngelo identifies the liberal ideology of individualism as one of the main obstacles to recognizing the socialized conditions of racism. "A significant aspect of the white script," DiAngelo writes, "derives from our seeing ourselves as both objective and unique."[57] Much as we will see in our discussion of liberalism in Chapter Three, DiAngelo argues that ideologies of individualism and objectivity "make it very difficult for white people to explore the collective aspects of white experience,"[58] This inability to access or think through any kind of collectivity is not accidental: an atomized, fragmented society is built into the very mode of production itself. Liberal, bourgeois, white people who have been uncritically raised under the twin aspects of individuality and objectivity by definition are unable (and unwilling) to see themselves as part of any greater whole—be it of race, class, gender, or sexuality.

More than this, however, the mode of production produces its own subjectivity, based—like Saussure's semiotics—on the relative position within a system. As Marx argues in *Capital*, the "individuality" of the capitalist—his likes and dislikes, his moral code, his manner of dress—does not affect his position *as capitalist* within the system of capitalist relationships. Similarly, the worker is a worker because she has no choice but to sell her labor-power as a commodity in itself. Ideology, in this case, is what obscures one's identity from oneself. Returning to Galvan's characterization of "whiteness" as "white, heterosexual, capitalist, and middle-class",

---

57   Robin DiAngelo, *White Fragility: Why It's So Hard for White People to Talk about Racism* (Boston: Beacon Press, 2018), 9.

58   DiAngelo, *White Fragility*, 9.

then, it makes sense to think of whiteness as equivalent, at least in some respects, to the word "bourgeois" as it has been used in Marxist and communist circles. "Bourgeois" indicates a whole complex of cultural indicators, beliefs, ideologies, etc., which may or may not match up to an objective class position. In this case, we can explain why so many library workers—constrained to sell their labor-power on the market—are in fact culturally or ideologically bourgeois. They subscribe to bourgeois ideologies and aspire to bourgeois values and lifestyles. It is similar with whiteness: being white is composed of a whole network of relationships, values, cultural indicators, and ideologies, all of which—and this is an element typically downplayed or denied within the bourgeois characterization—are built upon particular racialized relations and structures of oppression and exploitation. It doesn't matter whether a worker sees themselves as a worker or not, they are still constrained by the reality of their position within the mode of production. It is the same for the capitalist: he may believe anything at all, have the most progressive values, and be kind to animals *but he is still a capitalist* and benefits from the exploitation of the labor of others. Marx writes that

> Capital therefore takes no account of the health and the length of life of the worker, unless society forces it to do so. Its answer to the outcry about the physical and mental degradation, the premature death, the torture of overwork, is this: Should that pain trouble us, since it increases our pleasure (profit)? But looking at these things as a whole, it is evident that this does not depend on the will, either good or bad, of the individual capitalist. Under free competition, the immanent laws of capitalist production confront the individual capitalist as a coercive force external to him.[59]

White people are in the same position as capitalists, who might be very nice people, but are still benefiting from the oppression of

59   Marx, *Capital Volume 1*, 381.

others; or as the bourgeois workers, who believe in one set of things, but whose material reality is quite another. White fragility, then, arises from two quarters. On the one hand, it is a reaction to pointing out that you are benefiting from systems of oppression that you had no hand in creating and which you do not really comprehend. On the other hand, it is a reaction to pointing out that the values you espouse and hold dear are values of a system which is itself bent on keeping others oppressed.

From a Marxist perspective, any discussion of whiteness or of white people is not necessarily aimed at the personal, unique, individualized guilt of any particular white person; because we already know this to be true of our critique of capitalists. It makes no difference if a given capitalist is anti-worker or not. By dint of his position within the structure of capitalist relationships, he has no choice but to be anti-worker. Similarly, the question of whether a given white person is racist or not is separate from the fact that by dint of their position within a white supremacist society (which we might equate with capitalism without reducing it to capitalism), they have no choice but to be racist, since their lives are structured by a racist framework. White fragility is a reaction to having your comfortable ideology disrupted; again, something Marxists ought to be familiar with—the same discomfort occurs in the challenging or raising of class consciousness.

The fragility of white people can, I think, be explained as yet another manifestation of the psychological and emotional effects of capitalism. The non-institutionalized racism of, for example, the medieval period, did not require its suppression in the minds and discourses of the people who subscribed to it. Like commodity exchange itself in the pre-capitalist world, racism had no need to be obscured or mystified because feudalism did not require its own structures of domination to be obscured or hidden. Exposure to institutionalized racism by white people brings about a "return of the repressed", forces a recognition of the alienation and inequality inherent in capitalism as a totality; add to that the *collective* aspect, structurally absent from the individualist bourgeois worldview, and it stands to reason that the structured subject of capitalism will seek to defend itself by emotional manipulation and aggression—the twin poles of white fragility.

This may help to explain white fragility, but it does not justify it. Just as before the coming of the socialist revolution we have a responsibility to fight against capital's injustices (*pace* the accelerationists), so too do white people have a responsibility to understand the white supremacist structures of capitalist culture and society. If we are to unmask and fight against the capitalist mode of production as a whole, we have to recognize and fight not only against those aspects of it that hurt us, but those aspects that hurt *all* of us. Only in this way—as we will see in the next chapter—can the partial perspectives, desires, and strategies of a particular class or identity be replaced with the communal perspectives of an emancipated human race.

Additional Vectors of Oppression

I haven't spoken yet about sexuality and disability, focusing instead on race and gender, and thereby reproducing the marginalization of sexuality and disability both as intersectional vectors and as oppressed minorities within LIS. It should be clear, however, that the intersectionality[60] (or, in more traditional Marxist language, overdetermination[61]) of vectors of oppression within capitalism interlock. Various excluded identities interact dialectically with the requirements of capitalist production to increase exploitation and reduce the cost of labor. As Roddy Slorach has noted, "disability discrimination is a distinct but complex form of oppression, based on the (negligibly to substantially) greater expense to capital of the labor power of impaired people."[62] Indeed, some adherents of the social model of disability explicitly connect disability discrimination to the mode of production. As disability advocate Mike Oliver has written, "for me

---

60 Kimberlé Crenshawe, "Demarginalizing the Intersection of Race and Sex: A Black Feminist Critique of Antidiscrimation Doctrine, Feminist Theory and Antiracist Politics." *University of Chicago Legal Forum*, 1989: 140.

61 Bales, *The Dialectic of Academic Librarianship*, 114–15.

62 Roddy Slorach, "Marxism and Disability," *International Socialism* 129 (January 4, 2011): para. 51.

our oppression is ultimately due to our continued exclusion from the processes of production."[63] Slorach adds that, with the development of capitalism, "those marginalized or excluded from production, either by injury or already existing impairments, also became marginalized or excluded from wider society. In this way capitalism created disability as a particular form of social oppression."[64]

With the expansion of capitalist relations of production outside the factory into society at large, the capitalist cost-benefit logic replaced other forms of social value. The concept of the "social wage" from autonomist Marxism, familiar to readers of Federici, for example, offers a way of understanding how reducing the cost of social services meets the needs of capitalist production: social services are part of the social wage; reducing the cost of social services reduces the abstract social wage—hence austerity. Cuts to disability services are often the thin end of the wedge for austerity policies precisely because a) such services are often underfunded from a disability perspective anyway and so represent a very small amount of actual budgetary reduction—literally the thin end of the wedge; and b) in the same way that racist structures are obscured and erased in capitalist society, so too are ableist structures. What this means is that cuts to services for disability will not be recognized by mainstream bourgeois ideology as an attack on disabled people. The ability to cut the social wage to various marginalized groups, including disabled people, provides capitalism with a similar kind of flexibility in terms of workforce we have already seen in the case of women. In this case, however, it is backed up culturally by the structural ableism of bourgeois culture.

We can extend this analysis to many if not all vectors of oppression—sexuality, for example—as long as we do not lose the specificity of each mode of oppression. Capitalism searches for, hunts out, and where necessary creates the appropriate structures of

---

63   Mike Oliver, "Defining Impairment and Disability: Issues at Stake," in *Exploring the Divide: Illness and Disability*, ed. Colin Barnes and Geoff Mercer (Leeds: The Disability Press, 1996), 42.

64   Slorach, "Marxism and Disability," para. 14.

dehumanization, humiliation, and exclusion, often through the erasure of specific differences. What is common, however, is the logic of commodity production for exchange—it is that logic, and the fragmented, alienated society it requires—that produces patriarchy, white supremacy, disability, and all the other cruelties of modern life. Librarianship, far from falling back on an ostensible, liberal "neutral" or "objective" pluralism, ought to take a partisan stance in defense of social justice and a utopian project of a free society. Such a utopian project may seem naïve, but only if we "take arms against a sea of troubles", as Hamlet says, will we "by opposing, end them."

***

What kind of utopia is fit for the advanced capitalism of the 21st century? In his 1880 pamphlet on *Socialism: Utopian and Scientific*, Friedrich Engels argued that in the early period of industrial capitalism "crude conditions" led to "crude theories."[65] For the utopian socialists like Saint-Simon, Charles Fourier, and Michael Owen,

> Society presented nothing but wrongs; to remove these
> was the task of reason. It was necessary, then, to discover a new and more perfect system of social order and to
> impose this upon society from without by propaganda,
> and, wherever it was possible, by the example of model
> experiments. These new social systems were foredoomed
> as Utopian; the more completely they were worked out
> in detail, the more they could not avoid drifting off into
> pure phantasies.

Against such utopian socialism, Engels supported the "scientific socialism" discovered by himself and Marx, and much of the Marxist tradition has indeed focused on its "scientific" nature (perhaps finding its fullest expression in the work of Althusser), at the expense of

---

65   Frederick Engels, *Socialism: Utopian and Scientific* (London: Swan Sonnenschein and Co, 1892), 11.

a utopian tendency which, *contra* Engels, may still prove to be some use to us. The theme of utopian imagination is a thread that runs through all of Fredric Jameson's work, most recently in *An American Utopia*, in which he argues that utopian thinking is necessary to reactivate the potential of both politics and society, a potential that has been completely closed by the totalizing logic of capitalism. Jameson connects such a liberatory utopianism with the project of dual power, which can be traced back to Lenin, but can also be found, for example, in the Black Panthers' Free Breakfast for School Children program. As Michael C. Dawson wrote in *Blacks In and Out of the Left*,

> pragmatic utopianism is not new to black radicalism. King's work, and that of the civil rights movement more generally, was based on the utopian imagining of a much different America—one they were repeatedly told was impossible to obtain—combined with the hardheaded political realism that generated the strategies and tactics necessary to achieve their goals.[66]

Indeed, as an example of this kind of "pragmatic utopianism" combined with a realism unavoidable in the situation, during the unrest in Ferguson, Missouri in 2014, the library remained open to serve the community while many other organizations closed. In an article about the role played by libraries in areas of Black resistance, Myron M. Beasley wrote:

> Only a block from the centre of the disruption, the library doors remained open as a place for solace and restoration. The library was a resting place for journalists, and with public school classes suspended, teachers arrived to create programming for children. The library

---

66   Michael C. Dawson, *Blacks In and Out of the Left* (Cambridge: Harvard University Press, 2013), 194.

even provided each child with a 'kit' that included books
for dealing with trauma and a stuffed animal toy.[67]

While it may appear that the library is simply navigating the ugliness and violence of the world as it is, we can see here the utopian principle at work. Just like the Black Panthers, the Ferguson library was operating in a space of dual power. The connection between utopianism and dual power, Jameson writes, can be seen in

> the way organizations like the Black Panthers yesterday or Hamas today function to provide daily services—food kitchens, garbage collection, health care, water inspection, and the like—in areas neglected by some official central government... In such situations, power moves to the networks to which people turn for practical help and leadership on a daily basis: in effect, they become an alternate government, without officially challenging the ostensibly legal structure.[68]

Now, it would be too much to suggest that the Ferguson Municipal Public Library was in any sense sustainable as an institution of dual power, but the example does illustrate a particular dialectical tension between the embattled, reactive institutions of the "real world", and the utopian collective strategies of organizations and communities in crisis. And while Beasley begins his article by repeating the connection between libraries and democracy (quoting the ALA and, once again, Roosevelt), he points out that

> at the time of the ALA's founding, as with that of the United States of America, the concept of democracy was

---

67 Myron M. Beasley, "Performing Refuge/Restoration: The Role of Libraries in the African American Community—Ferguson, Baltimore and Dorchester," *Performance Research* 22, no. 1 (2017): 79.

68 Fredric Jameson, *American Utopia: Dual Power and the Universal Army* (New York: Verso, 2016), 4.

limited to the white colonists; literacy for the enslaves was considered an act of sedition. The foundation of the institution of slavery relied on the premise that black bodies were commodities. Slaves were not given equitable status of being recognized as human and were excluded from the technologies of democracy, including libraries. The library, particularly the public library, for African Americans this inhabits a precarious site: one of performative and transformative possibilities for education and the participation in the democratic process—fraught with exclusionary politics and ensconced in a history of violence and death.[69]

Nothing sums up the dialectic as well as this image of the dual nature of racial capitalism, holding out both the promise of a transformed world and the reality of violence. I have returned to race at the end of this chapter, but capitalism relies on many vectors of oppression to ensure both profit and its own survival. In the next chapter, we will look at some of the hegemonic ideological underpinnings of this system which, Marx wrote, "comes dripping from head to foot, from every pore, with blood and dirt."[70]

69   Beasley, "Performing Refuge", 75.

70   Marx, *Capital, Volume 1*, 926.

Chapter Three

Liberalism and the Enlightenment

Introduction: Marxism, Philosophy, and Ideology

Jean-Paul Sartre understood Marxism's explanatory power in terms of the difference between "philosophy" and "ideology". In *Questions de méthode* (1960), the short text that presaged his monumental *Critique of Dialectical Reason,* Sartre argues that every society is characterized by a single living philosophy which "gives expression to the general movement of society" and acts as a "cultural *milieu*" for its contemporaries.[1] For the mercantilist society of the 18th century, Sartre identifies the liberal philosophy of Descartes and Locke; that of Kant and Hegel for the industrializing bourgeois society of the late 18th and early 19th centuries. For the period following Hegel, Sartre identifies the moment of Marx and Marxism, and writes that since the seventeenth century, these three philosophical moments have provided the "fertile soil for every particular thought and the horizon of all culture":

---

1   Jean-Paul Sartre, *Questions de méthode* (Paris: Gallimard, 1986), 9.

> They are unsurpassable while the historical moment of
> which they are the expression remains unsurpassed. I
> have often noticed that an "anti-Marxist" argument is
> nothing but the apparent renewal of a premarxist idea.
> A supposed "surpassing" of Marxism is nothing but a
> return to premarxism, or at best the rediscovery of an
> idea already contained within the philosophy which we
> thought to have surpassed.[2]

This is not to say, however, that bourgeois society, for example, exists in a period in which Marxist perspectives predominate. Far from it. When we discuss later the idea of a cultural dominant, we will show how, as Marx puts it, "the ideas of the ruling class are in every epoch the ruling ideas."[3] The classical liberalism of the 19th century, the "embedded" liberalism of the postwar period, and the neoliberal ideology of our own age owe much more to Kant than to Marx, but their concrete particularity at any moment in time is determined to a large part by our understanding of Marxism. With this in mind, Sartre distinguishes between the *philosophy* of a historical moment—the "untranscendable horizon"[4] of thought and culture—and the specific ideologies that contend with, but cannot escape, the particular philosophical dominant of their time. Sartre identifies existentialism as one such ideology; indeed, the *Critique of Dialectical Reason* is an attempt to understand existentialism's relationship to Marxism.[5] But just as the particular expression of a dominant philosophy changes over time (giving us the various historical liberalisms and Marxisms, and making it absurd to

2   Sartre, *Questions de méthode*, 12.

3   Karl Marx and Friedrich Engels, *The German Ideology* (Moscow: Progress Publishers, 1976), 67.

4   Fredric Jameson, *The Political Unconscious: Narrative as a Socially Symbolic Act* (Ithaca: Cornell University Press, 1981), 10.

5   Fredric Jameson, *Marxism and Form: 20th Century Dialectical Theories of Literature* (Princeton: Princeton University Press, 1974), 206ff.

speak of "revisionism"[6]), so too do the ideologies that contend with it. The existentialism of Kierkegaard struggles against the dominance of Hegel, while the existentialism of Sartre and Camus engages with the dominance of Marxism. In each case, existentialism sought to support the particular and the individual in the face of a (Hegelian or Marxist) totality. In our time, despite the claims of the "end of history" that accompanied the fall of the Berlin Wall and the USSR,[7] the various postmodern tendencies (poststructuralism, deconstruction, neoliberalism) are still in thrall to Marxism and unable to transcend it. Ahab, consumed by the idea of hatred and revenge against Moby Dick, no longer master of his own fate, but "overdetermined" by the struggle against the whale, might be an appropriate metaphor. Like existentialism, the various postmodernisms "seek to vindicate pure individual subjectivity against the objective universality" of Marxist totalizing. Postmodernism looks to "unmediated life" and "finds weapons to combat the terrible 'mediation'"[8] of Marxist philosophy. Sartre is talking about existentialism, but what he says applies equally to the postmodernism of our own day:

> It discovered in itself the oppositions, the indecisions, the equivocations which cannot be surpassed: paradoxes, ambiguities, the indecisions, dilemmas, etc… In fact [for postmodernism], *subjective life*, to the extent in which it is lived, can never be an object of thought; it escapes knowledge on principle, and the connection between [irrational] belief and transcendence cannot be understood in terms of "surpassing."[9]

---

6   Sartre, *Questions de méthode,* 12.

7   Francis Fukuyama, *The End of History and the Last Man,* 2nd ed. (New York: Simon and Schuster, 2006), xi.

8   Sartre, *Questions de méthode,* 15.

9   Sartre, 15–16.

What postmodernism in general and neoliberal orthodoxy in particular have in common is the insistence that to conceptualize, to critique, to comprehend is an affront to direct lived experience and an invitation to fascism. Ironically, the ideologies of liberalism (classical, embedded, and neo) are, as we will see, themselves reliant on a transcendent, if not totalizing, vision of the human experience defined by the Enlightenment. In this sense, both existentialism and postmodernism challenge liberal orthodoxies and Marxist totalizations, but remain bounded by them nonetheless. Indeed, contemporary Marxist theorists like Fredric Jameson continue to see Marxism as an untranscendable horizon of contemporary thought and culture, opening space to counter both discourses of unmediated specificity (like postmodernism) *and* discourses with claims to transcendence (liberalism).[10]

Liberalism is not only the "cultural dominant" of capitalist society, the ideology that best represents the interests of the ruling class, based on the philosophy of liberal philosophers like Locke and Kant, it is also the unconscious or default ideology of librarianship, sometime explicit and unconscious, in the form of "common sense." This largely unquestioned discourse has always been challenged by minority or peripheral voices in librarianship, those challenges often being dismissed as attempts to "desecrate" the library, to demote it from its transcendental position and to denigrate its cultural mission. However, the transcendental, liberal discourse of libraries allows it to continue to support and reproduce capitalist structures of domination and oppression, even while justifying itself in the name of objectivity, neutrality, and the values of the Enlightenment itself.

---

10 Indeed, I take this to be the main thrust of Fredric Jameson, *Postmodernism, or, the Cultural Logic of Late Capitalism* (Durham, NC: Duke University Press, 1990). Jameson's "claims for Marxism as the 'untranscendable horizon' of any other theory, poststructuralist or other, rest not least on his conviction that Marxist analysis has a greater power to produce... a sense of... the melting away of customary frameworks, than any of its rivals." William C. Dowling, *Jameson, Althusser, Marx: An Introduction to* The Political Unconscious (Ithaca: Cornell University Press, 1984), 40.

"Useful Knowledge"

The dominant model of capitalist liberal democracy is drawn from the Enlightenment. As Wayne Bivens-Tatum writes, the Enlightenment view holds that

> Useful knowledge should improve the lives of the citizens, because in a democratic republic all citizens are supposed to educate themselves to make wise political decisions, and a just society both educates its citizens and seeks to improve their lives. These goals derived from Enlightenment thought motivated the foundation of American public libraries.[11]

However, there is an elision here from "ought" to "is"—the idea that because things *ought* to be this way, then they actually are that way. Simply because the US calls itself a democratic republic, for example, it somehow is a democratic republic, despite its record of imperialist abuses abroad and racist and anti-democratic abuses at home. The view of the "enlightened" capitalist liberal-democracy is dangerously false, as the history of capitalism itself—the finest fruit of Enlightenment thinking—can attest. The Enlightenment itself, far from the triumph of rational truth-seeking divorced from social and political issues, must instead be understood as "part of a properly bourgeois cultural revolution, in which the values and the discourses, the habits and the daily space, of the *ancien regime* were systematically dismantled so that in their place could be set the new conceptualities, habits and life forms, and value systems of a capitalist market society."[12] From the imperial exploitation of non-capitalist countries and the lucrative slave trade which, as Cedric Robinson reminds us, financed capitalist accumulation well into the modern period; to the attempted extermination—both physical

---

11 Wayne Bivens-Tatum, *Libraries and Enlightenment*, xi.

12 Jameson, *Political Unconscious*, 81.

and through "cultural genocide"—of Indigenous Peoples the world over,[13] capitalism is founded equally on the Enlightenment ideology and the violence done towards anyone who is not considered a citizen, those who are *a priori* excluded from democratic participation. But even for citizens, capitalism—justified by the Enlightenment—has brought endless war and repeated economic crisis, all of which increases wealth, luxury, and security for a few while increasing poverty, oppression, and insecurity for the rest. In addition to being an inherently racist process,[14] capitalist accumulation also profits from other forms of inequality. Sexism, ableism, the many injustices perpetrated upon various gender and sexual identities, all give the lie to any thought of a period of "good capitalism" in the 20th century, a perspective which becomes even more perverse when we remember the brutality of that century, which has been called without hyperbole an "age of extremes."[15] Marx described the violent origins of capitalist accumulation as "written in the annals of mankind in letters of blood and fire". If the first twenty-years of the 21st century are any indication, we can only expect the blood and fire to continue, if not to increase.

The standard liberal response to such criticism is twofold. On the one hand, liberals argue, things are better than they were (society is progressive) and, on the other hand, change must be incremental, and cannot be rushed. Revolutionaries must be patient, must avoid extremism, must temper their demands, must be reasonable, responsible, and rely on small reforms. Liberalism tends to see social problems either as technical ones, to be solved by experts and the application of new technologies, or as failures of the social contract, to be solved simply by choosing to be better towards each other. Often these two perspectives are combined, as in Ursula

---

13   Truth and Reconciliation Committee, *Final Report*, 1.

14   Robinson, *Black Marxism*, 3; Robin D. G. Kelley, "What is racial capitalism and why does it matter?" Lecture at Kane Hall, University of Washington, Seattle, November 7, 2017.

15   Eric Hobsbawm, *Age of Extremes: The Short Twentieth Century, 1914–1991* (London: Abacus, 1995), 7.

Franklin's 1989 Massey Lectures, *The Real World of Technology*, in which she argues that

> nothing short of a global reformation of major social forces and of the social contract can end this historical period of profound and violent transformations and give a manner of security to the world and its citizens. Such a development will require the redefinition of rights and responsibilities, and the setting of limits to power and control. There have to be completely different criteria for what is permissible and what is not. Central to any new order that can shape and direct technology and human destiny will be a renewed emphasis on the concept of justice. The viability of technology, like democracy, depends in the end on the practice of justice and on the enforcements of limits to power.[16]

Such idealism—in both its common and philosophical usages—serves to slow the pace of change, making it more easily recuperable by capitalism. Lenin put it succinctly when he wrote in 1913 that "reformism is bourgeois deception of workers, who, despite individual improvements, will always remain wage-slaves, as long as there is the domination of capital."[17] In the face of this perspective, with the weight, power, and inertia of all of Western society on its side, apologists for Enlightenment liberalism can only argue that "the fact that more and better knowledge cannot create a perfect world does not mean that it cannot create a better one."[18] The materialist dialectic argues otherwise. Feeding citizens the message that their history has been one of generalized progress, that they live in a participatory, egalitarian ("post-racial"!) democracy where their

---

16   Ursula Franklin, *The Real World of Technology* (Toronto: House of Anansi, 1999), 5.

17   Lenin, V. I. "Marxism and Reformism", in *Collected Works*, Volume 19 (Moscow: Progress Publishers, 1963), 372.

18   Bivens-Tatum, *Libraries and Enlightenment*, 171.

voice matters, is a falsification of history, an ideological manipulation, and an injustice in itself. Telling library users that their voices matter—in the face of the Trump presidency in the US, the Kinder-Morgan bailout in Canada, and Brexit in the UK, for example—and that the path to democratic participation is education and being well-informed *in itself* puts the lie to libraries as institutions of enlightenment and democracy. It disciplines the very public that libraries claim to serve. Rather than rebelling, we make people docile and complacent. Faced with the unconscionable, horrific separation of families under racist immigration and Indigenous policies, our citizens are made satisfied with gathering more information, being better informed, and voting. In short, by posing *no threat at all* to the capitalist order. Like any other institution that tells citizens that by being better informed and voting they can change society, the library operates as an agency of social control and reproduction, a mechanism by which capitalist society is never challenged, but keeps itself going, generation after generation.

The Dialectic of Liberty and Equality

With its origins in the period of bourgeois triumph following the social upheaval of the 1840s, the modern library is a quintessentially liberal institution. In his "counter-history" of liberalism, Domenico Losurdo writes that in the years following the 1848 revolutions in Europe, Alexis de Toqueville criticized Louis Bonaparte's coup d'état for privileging equality over liberty. According to Losurdo, Tocqueville's criticism

> also encompassed the Enlightenment culture that had prepared and promoted the collapse of the *ancien regime:* in it a sure 'zeal for equality' was matched by a rather 'tepid' 'desire for liberty'. As we know, the first to counterpose liberty and equality and denounce the demand for political equality as an attack on liberty was Barnave, who was nevertheless a defender of slavery. This institution continued to be alive and well in the United States when de Tocqueville held up the transatlantic republic,

together with England, as the model country for love of liberty to a France devoured by the passion for equality. It was precisely here that slavery was justified and even celebrated by southern theorists as an instrument to ensure, along with their liberty, the equality of members of the white community.[19]

One of the presiding spirits of the early public library in Britain, Jeremy Bentham,[20] wrote that "when security and equality are in opposition, there should be no hesitation: equality should give way."[21] It is one of the core claims of this book that modern librarianship has, under the guise of its democratic discourse, always attempted to find a balance between these two abstractions, but that relying on abstract principles is not, in fact, the answer. We will return to this idea in subsequent chapters.

This dialectic tension between liberty and equality was a hallmark of political life in the new republic. During the American Revolution, the colonists and the British government each accused the other of curtailing liberty, in what Losurdo calls a "pitiless demystification" of the material underpinnings of that liberty (i.e. slavery). One of the first acts of the "new liberal monarchy" following the Glorious Revolution—one of the events Wayne Bivens-Tatum identifies with the inauguration of the Enlightenment[22]—was "wresting a monopoly on the slave trade from Spain" while "the revolution that broke out across the Atlantic in the name of liberty involved official consecration of the institution of slavery, and the conquest and prolonged exercise of political hegemony by slave owners."[23]

---

19 Domenico Losurdo, *Liberalism: A Counter-History* (New York: Verso, 2014), 201.

20 Alistair Black, *A New History of the English Public Library* (Leicester: Leicester University Press, 1998): 48–50.

21 Losurdo, *Liberalism,* 201.

22 Bivens-Tatum, *Libraries and the Enlightenment,* 2.

23 Losurdo, *Liberalism,* 14.

Equality, then, was sacrificed in the name of liberty for a few white slave merchants, slaveowners, and their beneficiaries, including some of the great names of liberal philosophy, such as John Locke: "It was these enlightened, tolerant, liberal bourgeois who embarked on colonial expansion; and in this historical period the slave trade was an integral part of it... Locke was a shareholder in the Royal African Company."[24]

Losurdo argues that the surface or imaginary reconciliation of liberty and equality could only be effected by an act of exclusion, one which—ironically—was itself an attempt to overcome an inequality/exclusion, the exclusion of the American colonists from the British "community of the free."

> Quite apart from the problems of [political] representation, the spatial delimitation of the community of the free was perceived as an intolerable exclusion. On the other hand, the colonists, in demanding equality with the dominant British class, widened the gulf that separated them from [Black and Indigenous people]. While in London the zone of civilization was distinguished from the zone of barbarism, the sacred space from the profane, primarily by opposing the metropolis to the colonies, the American colonists were led to identify the boundary line principally in ethnic identity and skin colour. On the basis of the 1790 Naturalization Act, only whites could become citizens of the United States.[25]

The identification of the sacred with the center/metropolis and the profane with the periphery/colonies reminds us not only of Fobazi Ettarh's point about the role of center and periphery in librarianship, but also of Cedric Robinson's argument that the concept of barbarism itself comes out of the Greek and Roman world and into the history of the development of capitalism as a social and political construct:

---

24   Losurdo, 15.

25   Losurdo, 50.

> Prior to the eleventh or twelfth centuries, the use of the collective term 'barbarian' was primarily a function of exclusion rather than a reflection of any significant consolidation among those peoples. The term signified that the 'barbarians' had their historical origins beyond the civilizing reach of Roman law and the old Roman imperial social order.[26]

The movement from a spatial "zone of exclusion" to a racial and ethnic one created the confusion of inclusion and exclusion, freedom and slavery, that still pertains in the Anglo-American world today. Losurdo goes on to write that

> Whites, even the poorest among them, also came within the sacred space; they found themselves forming part of the community or race of the free, albeit situated at inferior levels... the condition of the [B]lack slave deteriorated by virtue of no longer being, as in colonial America, one of several systems of unfree labour... the tendential social rise of poor whites coincided with the consummate dehumanization of [B]lack slaves.[27]

By the time of the Civil War—that is, *after* the founding of the modern public library—what was at stake in the US was not the question of emancipation as such, but of how properly to define the community of the free, that is, how to exclude the "unfree" from the republic of liberty and equality. "For some time Lincoln harboured the idea of deporting [B]lacks... regarded by him as ultimately alien to the community of the free, from the United States to Latin America after their emancipation... what clashed during the Civil War were the causes not of liberty and slavery, but precisely two different delimitations of the community of the free"[28].

---

26 Robinson, *Black Marxism*, 10.

27 Losurdo, *Liberalism*, 50.

28 Losurdo, 55.

Locke and the Enlightenment

For Losurdo, the Glorious Revolution of 1689 and Locke's *Two Treatises of Government*, published in the same year, are formative events in the birth of liberal England. Locke's treatises, indeed, "may be regarded as key moments in the ideological preparation and consecration" of the Glorious Revolution itself. In Locke's work, "we are dealing with texts deeply impregnated with the pathos of liberty, the condemnation of absolute power, the appeal to rise up against the wicked ones who seek to deprive man of his liberty and reduce him to slavery."[29] On the other hand, "every now and then frightening passages open up in this ode to liberty, where slavery in the colonies is legitimized."[30] Losurdo draws an explicit connection between Locke's liberal rationalizations and the founding document of the American republic:

> In Locke... at least in the case of the *Two Treatises on Government*, which were written and published on the eve and at the end of the Glorious Revolution, legitimation of slavery tends to occur exclusively between the lines of the discourse celebrating English liberty. The reticence reaches its peak in the documents that consecrate the foundation of the United States as the most glorious chapter in the history of liberty.[31]

It is in this socio-political context—the celebration of liberty and equality for the few based on exclusion and oppression for the rest—that the modern library was formed, both ideologically and as a concrete institution. The insistence that we live in a democratic society and that libraries are its "cornerstone" is maintained only by the erasure of those who are now and have always been excluded

---

29   Losurdo, 23.

30   Losurdo, 23.

31   Losurdo, 27.

from democratic participation. The "noble lie" of the modern library is the same lie as that on which the American republic is also founded. There was no golden age of liberty, democracy, equality, and justice for all—such a republic never existed. The tensions within librarianship—between how we talk about freedom, equality, and democracy and the real and present elements of exclusion, domination, and oppression in our lives—derive from this broader and deeper contradiction within liberal society. These oppositions reverberate through Locke's political theory. In the *Essay Concerning Toleration*, also published in 1689, for example, Locke wrote:

> I esteem it most important to distinguish exactly the business of civil government from that of religion, and to settle the just bounds that lie between the one and the other. If this is not done, there can be no end put to the controversies that will always arise between those who, on the one hand, have or at least pretend to have a concern for the interest of men's souls, and those who, on the other hand, have or at least pretend to care for the commonwealth.[32]

Bearing in mind his restricted conception of citizenship (i.e. a community of the free that excluded Black and Indigenous People), Locke here sets up a distinction between the jurisdiction of civil government and the religious or spiritual—one might say "moral"—needs and occupations of citizens. "The commonwealth seems to me to be a society of men constituted *only* for procuring, preserving, and advancing their own civil interests… life, liberty, health, and freedom from pain; and the possession of outward things such as money, land, furniture, and the like"[33]. These civil interests are guaranteed "for all the people in general" through "the partial

---

32   John Locke, *An Essay Concerning Toleration* (Peterborough: Broadview, 2013): 48.

33   Locke, *Essay*, 49, emphasis added.

enactment of equal laws," and any citizen who presumes to encroach on the civil interests of another is dissuaded for fear of punishment.

For Locke, punishment by force is inappropriate for the creation of moral or spiritual discipline. Civil society guarantees the *material* rights of citizens, but their moral condition is their own affair. "The whole jurisdiction of the magistrate reaches only to these civil goods, and that all civil power, right, and dominion is exclusively to the promotion of them," and such jurisdiction "neither can nor ought in any manner to be extended to the salvation of souls."[34] With this in mind we can see the establishment of tax-funded, state-controlled libraries as a departure from the liberal ideal. However, Locke's ideal was really only valid for a "community of the free" which included only white, property-owning bourgeois men, who could be expected to share—more or less—a common moral, social, and political outlook. Indeed, the reason that Locke's essay on toleration was required was precisely because gentlemen had differing opinions about religion; they were of a single mind about almost everything else. However, as capitalism developed and extended both the mode of production and the social relations of bourgeois society *beyond* the men of Locke's race and class, the more differences of worldview had to be controlled by the state (in defiance of Locke's views on the role of the magistrate). The working class social unrest of the 1840s, combined with the rising standard of living in the developed capitalist centers by industrial capitalism, meant that classes, genders, and races which had previously been excluded from the political realm gradually had to be incorporated within it. The role of the library was to ensure that those newly franchised constituencies shared the common values and perspectives of bourgeois (liberal) society, and as Terry Eagleton has pointed out, the same was true of the construction of English Literature as a discipline in the same period.[35] Whether we see the library's purpose as public enlightenment or as ideological control, we have to admit that the

---

34   Locke, 49.

35   Terry Eagleton, *Literary Theory: An Introduction* (Minnesota: University of Minneapolis Press, 2008), 15–17.

libraries were founded on a departure from the purity of Locke's ideal. Indeed, this was argued at the time of the Public Libraries Act with respect to using taxes to pay for libraries.[36]

Locke was arguing for a separation between church and state, but there was another larger separation at work, a separation which went back at least to the division in Greek society between economics (οἰκονομία[37]) as the private home life of the citizen, and politics or public life. Hannah Arendt has investigated this question in *The Human Condition*[38] but in short, the private realm of the household was the realm of necessity—biological, economic, religious—while the realm of politics was a realm of freedom. Locke draws on this distinction by positing the jurisdiction of the commonwealth as *solely* those things proper to the free individual (money, land, liberty, etc.), and his arguments in support of this view confirm the original distinction. The most significant for our purposes is his second argument, that "the care of souls cannot belong to the civil magistrate, because his power consists in outward force or compulsion... And such is the nature of the understanding that it cannot be compelled to the belief of anything by outward force."[39] The implication here is that the commonwealth or the civil magistrate should occupy themselves only with what is either *right* or in their power to ensure. The public/private division is split along the lines of those rights which are the *civil interests* of free individuals (again, narrowly construed). Anything not pertaining to free individuals, or anything that properly belongs to the private sphere (where the power of the κύριος or *paterfamilias* is

---

36   Stanley M. Max, "Tory Reactions to the Public Libraries Bill, 1850," *The Journal of Library History* 19, no. 4 (Fall 1984): 509.

37   Joseph Henry Thayer, *A Greek English Lexicon of the New Testament* (New York: American Book Company 1886), 440.

38   Hannah Arendt, *The Human Condition* (Chicago: University of Chicago Press, 1958), 12–17.

39   Locke, *Essay*, 50.

virtually unlimited[40]) is no concern of the government. We should point out at this juncture that we are speaking of course of class society in which the forces of production leading to extensive division of labor and therefore to class-divisions are already well-established.

It is not hard to extend Locke's argument to the technical or operational view of libraries, that the "primary function" is to guarantee the effective and efficient access to information—the civil interest that falls within the library's purview—and that all other matters, social and political, are private responsibilities which the library has no ability to guarantee, and no right to do so even if it could. Indeed, for Wiegand, it is a point of pride that "public libraries have little power to force acceptance of particular ideologies" because this allows individuals to develop alternative values and views."[41] Needless to say, the insidiousness of hegemony allows the spread of ideologies without force; the ideology that people accept from the library is Enlightenment liberalism. However, from the illusion that libraries are non-ideological arises the peculiarly obstinate value of "library neutrality." The clash between the library's *practical* requirement to guarantee "intellectual freedom" and its *ethical* imperative towards social responsibility is one of the most long-standing arguments in library history.

Tolerance and No-Platforming

One current illustration of the problem Locke is interested in is the phenomenon of "no-platforming", the denial of a venue for people who espouse particular views. For Locke, as we have seen, spiritual or moral views fall into the realm of the private. They are no concern of the commonwealth, and the expression of strictly-speaking "political" views (which, again, were very narrowly construed) ought to be guaranteed to the political actor as long as he is in fact a member of "the community of the free" which, for Locke just as

---

40   Giorgio Agamben, *Homo Sacer: Sovereign Power and Bare Life* (Stanford: Stanford University Press, 1998), 55.

41   Wiegand, *Part of Our Lives*, 267.

much as for the Greeks, disallowed white women and people of color by definition. The "toleration" of Locke's essay is, in library terms, the "balance" of library collections and the "all perspectives" pluralism of library policy, the "all sides" rhetoric of the "market-place of ideas" in contemporary politics. In this view, it is not the place of the commonwealth (i.e. the state-funded library) backed up by the use of force, to decide between points of view; it is the right of "gentlemen" to dispute their views in a "genteel" and liberal manner through the use of reason:

> Every man is entitled to admonish, exhort, convince another of his error, and by reasoning try to persuade: but to give laws, receive obedience, and compel with the sword belongs to none but the magistrate. And upon this ground I affirm that the magistrate's power does not entitle him to establish any articles of faith or forms of worship by the force of law. For laws are of no force at all without penalties, and penalties in this case are absolutely inappropriate for convincing the mind.[42]

We can see, then, why Locke-inspired legislation, such as the First Amendment (1791), is concerned only with *state censorship*, and does not concern itself with communal or collective constraints on expression, such as no-platforming. At the time the First Amendment was framed, the "community of the free" was composed, as it was for Locke, exclusively of such reasonable gentlemen who could be expected to "admonish, exhort, or convince" rather than restrain. But as the community has become more diverse, the presumptions of the First Amendment no longer apply; the society in which it was framed no longer exists, and political lines are drawn according to one's opinion of that development. It is a matter of concern to conservatives and many liberals, and a matter of ambiguous, cautious pride to progressives.

---

42   Locke, *Essay*, 50.

The fear of "articles of faith" and "penalties... for convincing the mind", once the preserve of liberal thought and the justification for "neutral" vacillation on the part of libraries and library associations, has been repurposed by right-wing ideologues like Jordan Peterson, Stephen Pinker, and Steve Bannon. The political purpose of this recuperation is to make people believe that the state or some mythical ultra-left cabal is, for example, preventing them from saying "Merry Christmas", or corrupting masculinity, or opening the door to "cultural Marxists" (an anti-Semitic epithet as well as a political one) intent on destroying society's "traditional values." The anti-left strain is often thinly-disguised anti-Semitism, but it is open to all forms of racism and bigotry. The repurposing, indeed the weaponizing, of "free speech" for right-wing purposes is not new, and neither is the sense that Peterson and Pinker, not to mention even more ridiculous figures like Milo Yiannopoulos are not interested in rational argument, despite their appeals to a community of reason and the best argument. Writing about anti-Semitism after the Second World War, Sartre sums up this kind of political theatre:

> Don't imagine that anti-Semites are at all ashamed of the absurdity of their responses. They know that their arguments are lightweight, debatable; but they're having fun, it's their adversary who has to take words seriously because he believes in words; only *they* have the right to take things lightly. They even love this playing with words because, in giving ridiculous reasons, they discredit the seriousness of their interlocutor. They are happily in bad faith, because for them it's not a question of persuading with good arguments, but of intimidating or disorienting...[43]

Complaints of no-platforming on US, UK, and Canadian campuses play on the same fears promoted by the right-wing ideologues mentioned above: that the heavy hand of the state or the irrational

---

43   Jean-Paul Sartre, *Réflexions sur la Question Juive* (Paris: Gallimard, 1954), 22.

mob (manipulated by Jews and/or Communists) is coercively preventing "free speech." The criticism of the state is that it has no business compelling speech or silence "by the sword;" the criticism of the mob, that they—*a priori* since they are controlled by Jews and Communists—can't be reasonable, bourgeois, property-owners ("taxpayers") or "free" (white). In either case, unreason and moral questions (i.e. "private" matters like identity and inequality) are seen as intruding into the realm of politics or public life without warrant. Fundamentally, the likes of Peterson and Pinker want nothing more than to return to the kind of world in which wealthy white men were the only people who mattered, and everyone else (white women, people of color, the disabled) could either be banished to the home, deported, or murdered with impunity. We can see in the responses of liberal bourgeois states in Europe and North America to the various refugee crises (themselves the consequences of Western imperialism) that deportation and exclusion remain the tools of choice for the maintenance of a homogeneous "free," white, bourgeois world.

In librarianship, examples of weak or indefensible responses to such questions are not hard to come by. A good illustration occurred at Toronto Public Library (TPL) in 2017. In July, friends of the lawyer Barbara Kulaszka booked a room at a TPL branch for a memorial service. Among Kulaszka's former clients were the holocaust denier Ernst Zundel, white supremacist Paul Fromm, and former president of the neo-Nazi Heritage Front Marc Lemire.[44] According to one commentator, Kulaszka "was largely responsible… for the fact that Canada has no laws against false news and no human-rights ban on internet hate speech, and for the fact that no Nazi has been convicted in Canada of war crimes."[45] Under fears that white supremacists would use the memorial service as a platform, or that anti-fascist militants might violently disrupt the

44   Sima Shakeri, "Toronto Public Library Allows Neo-Nazi Memorial for Barbara Kulaszka To Go Ahead," *Huffington Post* (July 13, 2017): para. 6.

45   Joseph Brean, "Far-right Extremists Converge at Memorial for Toronto Lawyer," *National Post* (July 12, 2017): para. 3.

proceedings, pressure was put on TPL to cancel the booking. According to Toronto City Librarian Vickery Bowles, "people felt that by upholding the booking we were endorsing the views of the individuals that were organizing the meeting, individuals who have extreme white nationalist views."[46]

Bowles' justification for allowing the meeting to go ahead is firmly in the tradition of Locke's liberalism:

> To deny access on the basis of the views or opinions that individuals or groups hold contravenes the Canadian Charter of Rights and Freedoms and the principles of intellectual freedom, both cornerstones of the library's mission and values. Sometimes in defending freedom of speech, it's very uncomfortable to be put in a situation where we are defending the rights of those whose viewpoints many consider to be offensive. However, it is at those times that we must be vigilant in protecting the rights of all.[47]

Taking offense at someone's views is, from this perspective, purely a private matter, and should not intrude on the state's responsibility to guarantee rights and freedoms. The state—and its institutions—is considered to be "neutral," taking a position above and outside the contending positions of communities. This is the standard "pluralist" view of liberal politics; Locke's theory of a "decentralized, pluralistic" state—as opposed to Hobbes' monarchic power—was the means by which the very freedom of (bourgeois) civil society could be ensured.[48] The state could, indeed must, restrain its own powers in order to maintain the civil interests and civil liberties of its constituents.

---

46   Vickery Bowles, "Update on Last Evening's Event at Richview Library," *Toronto Public Library* (July 13, 2017): para. 2.

47   Bowles, "Update," para. 4.

48   Michael Hardt and Antonio Negri, *Empire* (Cambridge: Harvard University Press, 2000), 7.

By Locke's time the fear of revolt by the many-headed monster which underlay *Leviathan* had diminished: the mob could only riot destructively. So Locke argued in contrast with Hobbes, that the executive may forfeit its rights if it endangers the stability of property, maintenance of which is the reason for the existence of the state. Hobbes thought that any revolution against the authority of the sovereign must dissolve society into anarchy. Locke held that society could continue to exist even if the men of property found it necessary to change the sovereign. 1688 proved him right.[49]

Like all bourgeois political philosophy, Locke's theory of the state ignores, indeed represses, the very idea of classes and class divisions. The state of nature was, for Hobbes, Locke and Rousseau, a condition of competition between individuals. This could not be otherwise, since for Locke and other liberal politicians, the "community of the free" was by definition composed of members of a single class, race, and gender which accordingly faded into insignificance next to the distinct identities of individuals. On the other hand, if we follow Lenin's position in *The State of Revolution*, then the state

> is the product and manifestation of the *irreconcilability* of class contradictions. The state arises where, when and to the extent that class contradictions objectively *cannot* be reconciled.... According to Marx, the state is an organ of class rule, an organ for the *oppression* of one class by another; it is the creation of 'order', legalizing and perpetuating this oppression by moderating the clashes among the classes. In the opinion of petty-bourgeois politicians, order means precisely the reconciliation of classes [Locke's view] and not the oppression of one class

49   Christopher Hill, *The Century of Revolution, 1603–1714* (London: Abacus, 1974), 255.

> by another; to moderate the conflict means to reconcile
> classes and not to deprive the oppressed classes of defi-
> nite means and methods of struggle for the overthrow of
> their oppressors.[50]

The defense of neutrality by libraries or library association, the protection of "intellectual freedom," "free speech," "freedom of expression," is based on a liberal conception of the state and society that is
no longer tenable, or at least no longer goes unchallenged. The promotion of "both sides," the protection of all points of view, no matter how repugnant, is predicated on the view that members of civil
society all have the same class needs, the same (bourgeois) rationality, the same goals and outlooks, and it is the role of state institutions like public libraries to maintain the civil liberties and promote the civil interests of all members. But the world has changed,
the "community of the free" no longer includes only white, male
property-owners who all went to the same schools and universities (as much as they would like to turn back the clock). Subaltern
groups and identities—classes, races, genders, sexualities, disabled
and neuro-atypical people—recognize that "neutral" positions on
the part of libraries is an attempt to "reconcile classes" to their det-
riment, and in fact deprives them of "definite means and methods
of struggle for the overthrow of their oppressors." Library neutrality is a weapon of the dominant class and a tool to maintain (the)
social order.

To return to the Kulaszka memorial—the episode might
have ended with Bowles' supporting the library's "neutral" policy, but a few months later the TPL board decided to revise the
TPL room-booking policy in order to allow staff to cancel bookings
based on fears around the content of the meeting[51] (compare this
Canadian example with the ALA's OIF room-booking debate the

---

50   V.I. Lenin, *The State and Revolution* (London: Penguin Books, 1992), 8–9.

51   Nick Westol, "Toronto Public Library Board Votes to Revise Room-Booking
     Policy after Controversial Memorial," *Global News* (December 11, 2017): para. 2.

following year[52]). While under the Canadian Charter of Rights and TPL's own policies, there were no grounds to cancel the booking, TPL was able to leverage both the Canadian Criminal Code (penalizing hate propaganda) and the Ontario Human Rights Code to revise the room-booking policy. The revision states that

> room bookings will be denied or cancelled when the Library reasonably believes the purpose of the booking is likely to promote, or would have the effect of promoting, discrimination, contempt or hatred of any group, hatred for any person on the basis of race, ethnic origin, place of origin, citizenship, colour ancestry, language, creed (religion), age, sex, gender identity, gender expression, marital status, family status, sexual orientation, disability, political affiliation, membership in a union or staff association, receipt of public assistance, level of literacy or any other similar factor.[53]

What we see here is yet another liberal attempt to reconcile what appears to liberalism to be two antagonistic properties: liberty and equality. From another perspective, on the other hand, it is possible to see these two properties as being in a *dialectical* relationship where the state, rather than reconciling competing interests, instead chooses pragmatic strategies to support the hegemony of the dominant class. As Marx and Engels wrote in the *Communist Manifesto*, liberty and equality do not have to be in opposition—as they are in class societies based on the exploitation of labor with an unequal distribution of private property—they can in fact be mutually reinforcing. They foresaw—and again we have here a utopian moment in the midst of the inequities and criminality of class society—a future society in which "in place of the old bourgeois society, with

---

52   James LaRue, "Library Meeting Rooms for All," *Intellectual Freedom Blog*, July 10, 2018.

53   "Community and Event Space Rental Policy—Revisions," *Toronto Public Library* (December 11, 2017): 5.

its classes and class antagonisms, we shall have an association, in which the free development of each is the condition for the free development of all."[54] Rather than attempt a balance between opposing values, a classless society will be able to combine liberty *and* equality in the form of the free development of each and all. However, since we live in a class-based society, such a reconciliation remains out of reach. In this sense, then, the attempt to balance the abstract values of "liberty" on the one hand and "equality" on the other merely maintains bourgeois hegemony; what we should be looking for instead are commitments to "real politics"[55] rather than abstractions.

Idealism vs. Materialism

The "reconciliation of antagonistic classes" that forms the basis of the (non-Hobbesian) liberal theory of sovereignty[56] raises the question of class compromise or social peace. What, in the end, *are* the social and political gains to be derived from libraries? What, to formulate the question in language more common to librarianship, is the library's *mission*? One of the problems with the hegemonic discourse of librarianship is that it tends to dehistoricize the question. David Lankes' suggestion that "thousands of years of tradition serve as inspiration for our future"[57] elides the many historical changes that have fundamentally transformed libraries as they transformed the societies in which libraries are embedded. A properly dialectical, materialist, historical answer would have to draw distinctions between pre-capitalist, capitalist, and post-capitalist social forms, as well as the inflections of capitalist history itself. Even within capitalist—liberal democratic—society, we have to distinguish between the liberal *ideology* of librarianship—what liberal democracies *think*

---

54   Marx and Engels, *Communist Manifesto*, 105.

55   Geuss, *Philosophy and Real Politics*, 99–101.

56   Hardt and Negri, *Empire*, 7–8.

57   David Lankes, *The Atlas of New Librarianship* (Cambridge: MIT Press, 2011), 2.

is the library's mission—and the role it actually serves within the network of capitalist social relations.

The benefit of the sacred, democratic conception of libraries to bourgeois society is twofold: social peace and social reproduction. We have already looked a little at social reproduction in terms of "women's work", but the idea of libraries reproducing the structures of class society has, in general, only been treated ambivalently—if at all—in library literature. In a 2008 editorial for the *Journal of Librarianship and Information Science* entitled "Libraries and Cultural Capital," Anne Goulding looked at Bourdieu's concept of cultural capital, understood as "a set of cultural competencies needed for the effective understanding of and participation in those cultural activities which are recognized and rewarded by the education system giving access to social and economic advancement and *so reproducing existing class divisions*."[58] Goulding argues that

> libraries could be described as possessing large reserves
> of cultural capital... so it seems that library use is accept-
> ed as a sign of cultural participating and an indicator of
> cultural capital, suggesting that libraries can be regard-
> ed as sites for the production, dissemination and appro-
> priation of cultural capital.[59]

The ambivalent language ("could be described," "seems." "suggesting") could be typical scholarly caution, but is also typical of librarianship's general unwillingness to directly address questions of politics or class (let alone race, gender, or sexuality). And indeed, Goulding's conclusions are just as ambiguous: "We can conclude, then, that the concept of cultural capital is being applied increasingly to cultural institutions, including libraries... it is likely... that we will be hearing more of the term cultural capital as libraries

---

58   Anne Goulding, "Libraries and Cultural Capital", *JOLIS* 40, no. 4 (2008): 236. Emphasis added.

59   Goulding, "Libraries and Cultural Capital", 236.

and other institutions seek to justify the resources spent on them."[60] The question of the reproduction of class society is absent from the conclusion.

A more detailed engagement with Bourdieu can be found in John Budd's response to Wiegand's "Tunnel Vision and Blind Spots". For Budd, as for Wiegand, the problems of librarianship stem from a lack of reflection ("blind spots"), an unconsciousness or lack of awareness of the set of social, political, and cultural networks of power in which librarians are embedded. Budd remarks that

> Professionals may not analyze the social dynamics (and
> I include political dynamics here) of their communities
> and their own role in society. In terms borrowed from
> Bourdieu, librarians tend to be unaware of their own
> habitus... An unconsciousness of habitus can lead to the
> [reproduction of the social order].[61]

Idealism infects librarianship. When Budd concludes that "to avoid some blind spots and tunnel vision, librarians should become more reflective so that we can understand more completely the complex exercises of symbolic power and cultural production that can be imbedded in human action generally and in praxis in librarianship specifically."[62] The prescription, as usual, is to *think differently*, presuming that changing how we think about the world is enough to change the world itself. This ignores the very real structures and constraints of class society on thinking as such; it ignores the reality of *ideology*, the way in which social relations force people—in a very real, material way—to think particular things in particular ways, as well as the material operation of power within society. The focus in so much Black writing on physicality and the body is

---

60   Goulding, 239.

61   John M. Budd, "The Library, Praxis, and Symbolic Power," *Library Quarterly* 73, no. 1 (2003): 30.

62   Budd, "Library, Praxis, and Symbolic Power," 31.

a good example of the very materiality of the social world, for example when Keeanga-Yamahtta Taylor describes the aftermath of Mike Brown's murder by police.[63] Budd's idealism is simply another iteration of Dewey's fear of the "taint of trade-unionism" brought on by women's insistence on the importance of the material conditions of their work. Librarianship represses the physical and material partly because the library is a cultural institution focused on intellectual activity and information, but also because it must serve the dual purpose of social peace and social reproduction. This requires both the *naturalization* of social processes, but also the *mystification* of the processes themselves, a mystification that begins with obscuring the material realities of work and life. As much as Budd argues otherwise, simply becoming "more reflective" cannot challenge the established powers of capitalist society.

Stephen Bales' discussion of the "Modern Capitalist Academic Library" (MCAL) and ideology in *The Dialectic of Academic Librarianship* insists on both the dialectical and the material qualities of librarianship. Bales argues that

> in performing their work as ideological institutions, hegemonic academic libraries help to stabilize social historical structures, with neoliberal capitalism being the current, particularly volatile form of such historical structures. Wittingly or not, those working at the MCALs help to fulfill this function on behalf of the dominant societal class's interests, unless they achieve theoretical consciousness of the underlying circumstances that they are supporting. This contention, that MCALs work as a sort of cultural and intellectual ballast for capitalist societies, does not ignore the fact that there are thousands of well-intentioned academic librarians engaging in good work at their libraries, but that ideology is materially present in the deep structure of Western educational systems, and that because of this the MCAL

---

63   Taylor, *From #BlackLivesMatter to Black Liberation*, 154.

does not fully support the best interests of many people. Instead, as a brace for capitalism, the hegemonic MCAL *qua* ideological apparatus acts as a release valve for tensions found in capitalist societies. The MCAL works to curb capitalism's anarchic tendencies, and it works as an engine for reproducing existing exploitative class structures, thus supporting the social formation's continued survival. This role is mystified in the ideological forms reproduced by the academic library and it may be ignored by those people working in the place. Nonetheless, it possesses a significant material force.[64]

While it may appear as though Bales' subscribes to a similar idealism as Budd, Bales—writing in the Marxist tradition—is instead arguing that workers' consciousness is a necessary but not a sufficient condition for social change. "Concrete material contextualization allows the [librarian] to... engage in theoretically informed and guided praxis."[65] Bales goes on to argue for "counter-hegemonic academic librarianship as a professional practice", a practice which

is very much a normative undertaking that combines librarianship's intuitive altruism with a reasoned political and theoretical stance. Critical reflection upon the academic library... is coupled with a commitment to guide any change that occurs in a direction that hopefully benefits everyone touched by the institution, but particularly those who are marginalized, with the understanding that benefiting those deemed peripheral ultimately benefits all.[66]

While I find Bales' approach perhaps too optimistic, it is a welcome antidote to the liberal idealism of much library discourse. We will

---

64   Bales, *Dialectic of Academic Librarianship*, 94–95.

65   Bales, 123.

66   Bales, 129.

return to Bales' discussion of ideology in Chapter 5, but for now I want to delve more deeply into the question of the dominant class and its interests.

Class Struggle and Social Peace

In the *First Treatise on Government*, Locke argues that the question of power ("who should have it?") must be solved to secure the proper constitution of society:

> For if this remain disputable, all the rest will be to very little purpose; and the skill used in dressing up Power with all the Splendor and Temptation Absoluteness can add to it, without shewing who has a Right to have it, will serve only to give a greater edge to Man's Natural Ambition, which of itself is but too keen. What can this do but set Men on the more eagerly to scramble, and so lay a sure and lasting Foundation of endless Contention and Disorder, instead of that Peace and Tranquility, which is the business of Government, and the end of Humane Society?[67]

Locke here approaches Hobbes' view of the State—recognized, legitimate, sovereign Power—as a means to protect society from the effect of the "war of all against all."[68] However, while Hobbes saw the state as a third party rising above the warring interests, for Locke the proper guarantor of social peace was an authority constituted out of—and held in check by—civil society. Writing in the context of international relations, but applicable to the national context, Hardt and Negri write that for Hobbes,

---

67 John Locke, *Two Treatises of Government* (Cambridge: Cambridge University Press, 1960), 219.

68 Thomas Hobbes, *Man and Citizen (De Homine and De Cive* (Indianapolis: Hackett, 1991), 118

> A new transcendent power, "tertium super partes," pri-
> marily in the hands of the military (the one that rules
> over life and death, the Hobbesian "God on earth"), is…
> the only means capable of constituting a secure interna-
> tional system and thus of overcoming the anarchy that
> sovereign states necessarily produce.[69]

On the other hand, Locke sees the achievement of peace and stability "in more decentralized, pluralistic terms":

> In this framework, just when the transfer towards a su-
> pranational centre is accomplished, networks of lo-
> cal and constitutionally effective counterpowers rise
> up to contest and/or support the new figure of power…
> Whereas the Hobbesian hypothesis emphasized the con-
> tractual process that gives rise to a new unitary and tran-
> scendental supranational power, the Lockean hypothesis
> focuses on the counterpowers that animate the constitu-
> tive process and support the supranational power.[70]

Locke clearly provides the hegemonic model of bourgeois liberal democracy, with its elected representatives nominally responsible to
their constituents and the ability to "change governments" with every election.[71] However, what we have in reality is in fact a *reversal*
of Locke's argument that social peace will be achieved through the
constitution of a legitimate authority ultimately accountable to civil society. Instead of this, we have a situation where the hegemonic
powers of the dominant class *claim* to be a democratically constituted, responsible authority, and that therefore civil society must hold
up its end of the bargain (i.e. keep the peace and stay out of politics).

---

69   Hardt and Negri, *Empire*, 7.

70   Hardt and Negri, *Empire*, 7.

71   "The principle according to which sovereignty belongs to law, which today
seems inseparable from our conception of democracy and the legal State, does
not at all eliminate the paradox of sovereignty." Agamben, *Homo Sacer*, 30.

Instead of the State constituted by civil authority as a guarantor of social peace, social peace is provided in exchange for what we are told is legitimate authority, and backed up by the military power of police violence.

The maintenance of social peace is therefore bound up with the ability of the State to guarantee civil liberties, primarily the maintenance of private property. Locke makes this explicit when he writes:

> For when Men by entering into Society and Civil Government, have excluded force, and introduced laws for the preservation of Property, Peace, and Unity among themselves; those who set up force again in opposition to the Laws, to *Rebellare*, that is, bring back again the state of War, and are properly Rebels.[72]

Leaving aside for the moment the bourgeois idea that individuals choose to enter into society (that is, that there is a concept of "people" outside of society), we must recognize that, in Locke's view, social peace is a particular kind of peace: peace between civil society and those excluded from it. The best example of this in the Western capitalist world is the period of welfare-state prosperity between 1945 and the 1970s, the period of "post-war compromise" predicated on collaboration rather than strife between capital and labour, with the State steering the economy to post-war prosperity through the mechanisms of Keynesianism, Fordism, and Taylorism. In this period, social peace itself became a kind of ideological talisman, as Stuart Hall has argued in "The Birth of the Law and Order Society."[73] Since the neoliberal turn at the end of the 1970s brought an end to class collaboration (and here Thatcher's war on the miners stands in for a whole dynamic of capitalist *revanchisme*), we have seen not only the return of class struggle, but of a transition from

---

72 Locke, *Two Treatises*, 415–16.

73 Stuart Hall, *Selected Political Writings: The Great Moving Right Show and Other Essays* (Durham: Duke University Press, 2017), 158–71.

the Lockean welfare state to a more Hobbesian model of militarized police, ubiquitous State and corporate surveillance, and the data-driven administration of society by an unaccountable and belligerent government.[74]

J. Moufawad-Paul, a Canadian theorist of Marxism-Leninism-Maoism, identifies three states of capitalist society: social peace, anxiety, and emergency. After "thirty glorious years" of post-war prosperity, and another thirty or so of anxiety, we are once more returning to a state of emergency cognate with the period of war and depression between 1914 and 1945. For Moufawad-Paul austerity itself is an attempt, in the state of anxiety known as neoliberalism and which ended, perhaps, in 2008, to recover a sense of the social peace of welfare-state capitalism even while dismantling the institutions that made class compromise possible:

> On the one hand the state of anxiety, on the other hand the state of emergency. The promise of a state of social peace can only be partial; the complete restabilization of welfare capitalism is a never realized delirium… Despite entropy, and because of this promised delirium, the austerity apparatus will find ways to channel its subjects into activities that patch over the holes of a capitalism coming apart.[75]

What is important here is the sense of a cyclical disturbance within capitalism. Those who lived through or inherited post-war peace and prosperity see such a situation as the breakdown of the liberal-democratic norm which ought to constitute properly-functioning capitalism. On the contrary, it is in the nature of capitalism to run

---

74   Hall, *Selected Political Writings,* 180.

75   J. Moufawad-Paul, *Austerity Apparatus* (Montreal: Kersplebedeb, 2017): 157. The idea of the state of exception originates in the work of Carl Schmitt, and has been excavated most thoroughly by Giorgio Agamben, for whom it is bound up with the question, "what does it mean to act politically?" Giorgio Agamben, *State of Exception* (Chicago: University of Chicago Press, 2005), 2.

in cycles of crisis and recovery, which is different from the empirical boom-and-bust of mainstream economics. For bourgeois economists business cycles are empirically explainable without recourse to class, power, or politics. But for Marxists these cycles demonstrate the inherent instability of the capitalist mode of production *as a set of social relationships*. Each cycle produces its own culture, its own politics, its own ideology, and its own contradictions. It is the working out of these contradictions that push the conjuncture towards its own inevitable ruin.

Two aspects of the liberal ideology that gives a sense of continuity to this perennial disruption are the respect for institutions (such the library) and the feeling of constant progress through technological innovation. As Marx demonstrated in *Capital*, technological innovation is one of the core vectors of increased profits and exploitation under capitalism. But culturally, technological innovation *feels* like improvement: labor saving automation, frictionless media consumption, the now-tainted participatory promise of social media—all these contribute to a structure of feeling that our lives are getting better. For our grandparents' generation it was the washing machine or the television; in our own time it is the iPhone and the Internet of Things. Above the purely economic requirement of technological development, we have erected an ideology of progress *as measured by* technological advance. Thus, while periods of rapid technological change can be frightening, destabilizing, and alienating, visible technological progress also gives a sense of hope for the future, a feeling of amelioration, a yardstick against which neoliberalism might not seem like too much of a fall from the years of prosperity and peace after World War II. The highest form of this ideology is the technological solutionism that argues that capitalism can find a technical solution to any problem, from voter fraud to climate change, and which we are more and more recognizing as the self-serving illusion that it is.[76]

---

76 Both Paul Mason, *Post-Capitalism: A Guide to Our Future* (London: Allen Lane, 2015) and Aaron Bastani, *Fully Automated Luxury Communism* (New York: Verso, 2019) promote versions of this idea.

The liberal-democratic discourse of librarianship, however, is not merely ideology for its own sake. In addition to depressing wages and devaluing some library work (e.g. affective labor[77]) while overvaluing other kinds of library work (the scholastic, abstract work performed by predominantly male "library scientists," but also anything that participates in the technocratic ideology of progress), the discourse of librarianship helps to ensure that vocational awe is maintained among library workers and users, so that the library as an institution can resist challenge, attack, or requests to change. This has led to a widespread conservatism within the culture of librarianship, forcing it to react to changes (in the political-economic conjuncture, in technology, in social attitudes, for example) rather than engaging actively with them. We will argue later on that this conservatism stretches back to the beginnings of professional librarianship, in constant tension with a progressive, even radical, minority position within librarianship itself.

In addition to the self-justifying role played by the liberal-democratic ideology, this discourse obscures and mystifies the very real capitalist relationships it both supports and reproduces. The goal of these interlocking—ideological, material—processes is both social reproduction (of library workers as workers, and of library users as respecters of e.g. property rights) and social peace, through the vestigial value of the utopian principle of collectivity and shared use. This utopian principle has long been coopted by capital precisely in order to ensure both the continuation of capital and the dissipation of class antagonisms, but as Jameson reminds us, the utopian principle nonetheless *remains utopian*, even under a more-or-less totalitarian capitalism. As such even the diluted and compromised principles of collectivity and sharing (as opposed to exchange) hold space for the potential reclamation of a real collectivity.

The question remains, however, how does liberal ideology work, how does it maintain itself, spread, and reproduce itself over time through material practice, and how can we demystify or unmask it if we are unable to take up a position outside it? We will address these questions in the next two chapters.

---

77   Lisa Sloniowski, "Affective Labour."

Chapter Four

Ideology and Hegemony in the Marxist Tradition

Introduction: Ideological and Social Reproduction

Given that the focus of libraries is on information and ideas, librarianship is primarily an institution of *ideological* reproduction;[1] it is through ideology that libraries contribute to the socio-economic reproduction of capitalism itself. The information we provide (an activity the democratic discourse sees as neutral) is always politically and ideologically committed, even though that commitment may be unconscious. When it is unconscious and uncritical, its commitment is to the maintenance of inequality, not its reduction; to the support for regimes of private property and labor exploitation. The question then becomes how these ideas arise, spread, and gain the allegiance of either explicit or unconscious commitment. For Stuart Hall,

> The *problem* of ideology is to give an account, within a materialist theory, of how social ideas arise. We need to

---

1 Bales, *The Dialectic of Academic Librarianship,* 114–20.

> understand what their role is in a particular social for-
> mation, so as to inform the struggle to change society
> and open the road towards a socialist transformation of
> society. By ideology I mean the mental frameworks—
> the languages, the concepts, categories, imagery of
> thought, and the systems of representation—which dif-
> ferent classes and social groups deploy in order to make
> sense of, define, figure out and render intelligible the way
> society works.[2]

The intellectual structures of cataloging, classification, and search systems instill in library users the values and perspectives of patriarchal, settler-colonialist, capitalist society. The work of Sanford Berman and Hope Olson, as well as more recent studies by Matthew Reidsma and Safiya Noble all testify to this effect. In addition, through such mechanisms as due-dates, late fines, and municipal property requirements (i.e. proof of taxpayer status), we reinforce in our users the sanctity of property rights, debt-repayment, exchange, and penalties for breach of contract. Althusser sums up this process of material and cultural reproduction as follows:

> It is not enough to guarantee labor-power the *material*
> conditions of its reproduction... the reproduction of la-
> bor-power requires not only that its *qualifications* be re-
> produced, but that is *submission* to the rules of respect
> for the established order be reproduced at the same time.
> This means, for the workers, reproduction of labor-pow-
> er's *submission to the dominant ideology* and, for the
> agents of exploitation and repression reproduction of *its
> capacity to handle the dominant ideology* properly, so as to
> ensure the domination of the dominant class 'verbally'.[3]

---

2   Stuart Hall, "The Problem of Ideology—Marxism without Guarantees," *Journal of Communication Inquiry* 10, no. 2 (1986): 29.

3   Louis Althusser, *On the Reproduction of Capitalism: Ideology and Ideological State Apparatuses* (New York: Verso, 2014), 50–51

In his discussion of the inscription of the debtor-creditor relationship in the current moment of financial capitalism, Maurizio Lazzarato refers to this as a process of "subjectification," that is the creation of a subject (i.e. a person) appropriate to neoliberalism, "a subject capable of accounting for himself as a future subject, a subject capable of promising and keeping a promise" and, perhaps most significantly for the autodidacticism integral to librarianship, "a subject that works on the self."[4]

The first problem with the democratic view of libraries, then, is that it serves the reproduction of capitalist ideology and social relations. If we want the world to change, to break away from the dominance of capitalist oppression, then we must rethink the relationship of democracy and libraries to actually existing society. The second problem is related to the question of the value of work itself. Much energy in libraries goes into "communicating our value," an activity which the democratic discourse of librarianship often supports. However, capitalism doesn't care whether value can be "communicated," only whether it can be realized in profit. This in turn means that value depends on how little we will work for, which the history of women's exploitation, not to mention the current prevalence of unpaid internships and zero-hour contracts shows can and does reach zero. The democratic discourse of libraries expects library workers to put aside practical questions of hours of work, work-life balance, exploitation, etc., and to work instead purely for a (democratic) social good, for the betterment and enlightenment of our neighbors. If, as Bivens-Tatum argues, (public) libraries "were almost always founded as a means of spreading education and enlightenment necessary to the citizens of a democratic republic,"[5] then why should we concern ourselves with questions of wages and working conditions? If our users understand and respect our democratic mission, shouldn't that be enough? Fobazi Ettarh has shown that this argument reaches the level of an ultimately controlling

---

4   Maurizio Lazzarato, *The Making of the Indebted Man: An Essay on the Neoliberal Condition* (Cambridge: MIT Press, 2012), 88.

5   Bivens-Tatum, *Libraries and the Enlightenment*, 93–94.

"structure of feeling" best described as "vocational awe,"[6] serving to discipline workers within the profession, particularly white women and people of color.

As we saw in Chapter Two, a similar vocational awe has traditionally been applied to women's work in the home: that it is proper for a woman to do housework because it is part of her mission to support her husband, to "be a wife." In a sense, the Wages for Housework movement of the 1970s can also be understood as an attempt to "communicate the value" of housework. It is precisely the recourse to supposed transcendental, innate properties of women (lovingness, romance, humility, supportiveness) that entraps women into reproducing labor power for capitalism (and keeps men in thrall to toxic masculinity by denying them those same properties[7]), that keeps women in the position of being exploited through contributing their own labor-power for free:

> By denying housework a wage and transforming it into an act of love, capital has killed many birds with one stone. First of all, it has gotten a hell of a lot of work almost for free, and it has made sure that women, far from struggling against it, would see that work as the best thing in life.[8]

As Ettarh remarks in her essay, the transcendental, religious discourse argues that reward for library work "cannot be a monetary compensation, but instead spiritual absolution through doing good works for communities and society."[9] Challenging such hegemonic

---

6   Ettarh, "Vocational Awe," para. 3.

7   The use of misogyny to control *male* behavior has parallels in racism: "the purpose of racism is to control the behavior of white people, not Black people." Robin D. G. Kelley, "Births of a Nation: Surveying Trumpland with Cedric Robinson", *Race Capitalism Justice* (Boston: Boston Review, 2017), para 1.

8   Federici, *Revolution at Point Zero*, 17.

9   Ettarh, "Vocational Awe,", para. 7.

positions requires concrete political demands, as "wages for house-work" was for radical feminists in the 1970s. However, Silvia Fed-erici, one of the main theorists of the Wages for Housework move-ment, reminds us, the purpose of the movement was not to gain advantage *within* the system of capitalist relations, but to escape and abolish those relations altogether.

Part of the problem here has to do with the idea of "value." In the first section of *Capital*, Marx draws a distinction between the use-value and the exchange-value of a commodity. It is precise-ly the confusion between these two categories that we see not just in the discourse of libraries, but in capitalism at large, a confusion which serves capitalism well. Indeed, while Fredric Jameson has ar-gued that in the current neoliberal conjuncture, "exchange value has been generalized to the point at which the very memory of use value is effaced,"[10] much of the difficulty in discussions of librar-ies comes from the fact that library workers are often talking about use-value, while our administrators, parent institutions, fund-ing bodies, and associated private corporations only care about ex-change-value (except, naturally, when they can leverage the idea of use-value in the service of vocational awe). To be sure, for cultural workers in late capitalism, it often seems as though exchange-val-ue is the only concrete form of value, while use-value is something dreamlike, intangible, opaque, returning to concrete reality only to support the generalized tyranny of commodity exchange itself. So it is understandable that we would want to insist on the transcen-dent, the moral, the usefulness of knowledge, and the value of li-braries and citizenship itself. We hope that by doing so we can avoid the pitfalls and compromises of exchange-value and the commodi-ty-form as such. But in doing so, not only do we tend to ignore the material realities of all these social relations, allowing them to car-ry on undisturbed, but we open up use-value itself as a vector of discipline and exploitation within the profession. By excluding any question of exchange (or exchange-value) from our discourse, we deny or obscure the realities of capitalism, but we do not escape

---

10   Jameson, *Postmodernism*, 18.

them, ironically enough placing our values firmly in the service of capitalist ideology. It is for this reason that the opening of the accounts and the honest discussion of how much we are paying for resources, as well as decisions like not signing non-disclosure agreements with our vendors, is a welcome step forward. Even the fact that the Open Access movement has put costs and financial inequity on the agenda is positive progress. But in general, we continue to exclude questions of exchange and exchange-value (not to mention the institution of property itself) by focusing on the abstract and transcendental, thereby losing the ability to fight a capitalism that excels at paying lip-service to moral values (democracy, for example) while carrying on its corrupt business-as-usual. If library workers insist on believing in libraries as democratic institutions of knowledge, democratic participation, and self-improvement—and this is the message that consistently comes out of the ALA and CIL-IP conferences—then we have no defense against either our role in ideological and social reproduction *or* the austerity measures that are hitting libraries along with other social agencies.

If we lived in a non-capitalist society, if we really lived in a democracy, a society in which use-values took priority, then libraries could perhaps live up to their democratic mission. But we live in a world of austerity, fascism, cruelty disguised as freedom, and a set of economic relationships that no-one controls but everyone is subject to. In the face of this, the positive things that libraries *do* accomplish (which I am not emphasizing, but that we must not lose sight of) are done *in spite of capitalism*, and are always at risk of being mobilized in support of capitalism itself, of being recuperated by the exploitative structures of capitalist domination. As Stephen Bales wrote with respect to class fragmentation in *The Dialectic of Academic Librarianship*, capitalism has an "extraordinary capability to mystify existing social relations as a means of self-preservation."[11] David Harvey put it more forcefully when he remarked in a recent interview that "there's no such thing as a good, moral idea

---

11   Bales, *Dialectic of Academic Librarianship*, 7.

that capital can't co-opt and turn into something horrendous."[12] This includes the "moral idea" of the library itself; the harm of the democratic discourse of librarianship is that it obscures the very real problems with the library as capitalist institution. Given the insistence on the "sacredness" of libraries both in the early "library faith" and in the today's "vocational awe," it appears that in order to transform the library we have to first demystify and desecrate it.

We cannot rely on an idealistic view of the mission of libraries if we truly want to change things. Nor can we try to beat capitalism at its own game, which often seems to be what chief librarians and vendors think we should do. The only way to win is to overthrow the game itself, to change the rules, to bring about a new and just social order. The transformation of libraries must be part of a radical transformation of society as a whole. Until then, adhering to the democratic view of libraries in order to convince people that libraries are *morally* worth saving will not be enough; it is a position that plays into the hands of capitalist restructuring and privatization. In the same interview quoted above, Harvey argues that Marx broke with other, *moralizing*, socialists, despite the moral revulsion to capitalism that was rightly developing in the industrialized and industrializing world precisely because

> the problem with capital is that it's almost *amoral*. To try to confront it with moral reason is never going to get very far, because the system is self-generating and self-reproducing. We've got to deal with the self-reproduction of the system.[13]

In addition, one of the core concepts of historical materialism is that our morality, our sense of right and wrong, is conditioned by the material conditions of our lives; in a very real sense, moral arguments against capitalism are doomed to fail because capitalism produces our morality. Dealing with the self-reproduction of capital

---

12   David Harvey, "Why Marx's Capital Still Matters," *Jacobin* July 12, 2018, para. 39.

13   Harvey, "Why Marx's Capital Still Matters," para. 32.

means dealing with the role libraries play in that reproduction; it means exposing the real injustices and oppressions libraries are complicit in, even while we keep in mind the very real positive role libraries often play in their communities.

The problem with this perspective is that, without giving us something transcendental or moral to work towards, we have to ask why someone should work in libraries to begin with. Why should libraries be defended and saved? On the one hand, it is necessary to bear in mind the subjective importance libraries have to real people; the ideological and reproductive role libraries play under capitalism does not completely erase that importance. On the other hand, under capitalist conditions of labor, where we have no choice but to sell our labor-power to survive, this question can have no honest or unconstrained answer at all. However we choose to answer it, though, at this juncture we cannot simply continue to repeat platitudes about democracy and participation. In the conclusion of this book we will discuss two strategies that might be available to us at the current moment.

Facts and Truth

In contemporary social science, there is often a hard distinction made between "evidence"—empirically gathered, self-sufficient, immediately comprehensible—and "ideology." Those who insist on the social construction of facts, the role of social position, ideology, or structures of power are dismissed as ideological by the responsible keepers of "scientific" objectivity. In a comment on the ALA's Office of Intellectual Freedom blog post regarding the criticism of an amendment to the Library Bill of Rights, one commenter stated that "over the past decade, I've been alarmed to watch my profession go from one of facts to one of feelings, but such is the state of librarianship in 2018."[14] This implies a period when librarianship

---

14   "Alex", blog post comment on "Library Meeting Rooms for All",
      Intellectual Freedom Blog, July 13, 2018. https://www.oif.ala.org/
      oif/?p=14997#comment-562504 Accessed July 14, 2018.

dealt with transparent "facts" in an objective, scientific way; that is, a perspective proper to a realist cultural logic, but inappropriate to the postmodernist one.[15] This has long been the perspective of librarianship as a social science, but it says more about the ongoing challenge to class, race, and gendered power within the profession than about any transparent facts as such. The day after this blog comment was made, Michiko Kikutani wrote a column in the *Guardian* with the headline "The Death of Truth: How we Gave up on Facts and Ended up with Trump." Kikutani's project is "to examine how a disregard for facts, the displacement of reason by emotion, and the corrosion of language are diminishing the value of truth, and what that means for the world."[16] Kikutani's article, like the comment on the OIF blog post, presumes that at one time a regime of truth and reason held sway. This presumption, like so much of the liberal democratic superstructure became naturalized "common sense" during the late 18th century, where truth and reason were opposed to religion and superstition, and has been hegemonic in various ways ever since: "those influenced by Enlightenment thought believe that facts and theories about nature are decided by standards of scientific reasoning theoretically common to all human beings, not just to believers in a particular religion."[17] Enlightenment thought—and the liberal ideology that derives from it—is, as we saw in the last chapter, *not* a universal philosophy, but the partial philosophy of a particular socio-economic class. The role of this philosophy is to construct, maintain, and reproduce the power (social, political, economic) of that class. The belief that the social world is one of rationality, objectivity, transparent language, an individualist epistemology and ethics, and progress is a belief that supports the fragmenting, isolating logic of capitalist

---

15   We might take Nietzsche's dictum that "it is precisely facts that do not exist, only *interpretations*" as the motto of postmodernism. Walter Kaufman, *The Portable Nietzsche* (London: Penguin Books, 1977), 458.

16   Michiko Kikutani, "The Death of Truth: How we gave up on Facts and ended up with Trump", *The Guardian*, July 14, 2018, para. 3.

17   Wayne Bivens-Tatum, *Libraries and the Enlightenment*, 5.

development and obscures the irrationality, violence, and subjectivity of bourgeois society itself. In this view, there is less difference between the realist and postmodernist moments of bourgeois culture; where once "facts" upheld bourgeois class power, now "interpretations" serve the same purpose. Indeed, one of the main claims of Jameson's *Postmodernism* is that what we see now as a decline of the Enlightenment values of truth, reason, etc, is nothing but the latest inflection of the cultural logic of an expanding capitalist world.

What an insistence on a prior "golden age" of truth and reason—"sweetness and light" in Matthew Arnold's formulation[18]—misses is the long tradition of critique: of the Enlightenment project, of bourgeois philosophy and politics, and of reason itself. The "school of suspicion"[19] of the 19th century—Marx, Nietzsche, and Freud—inaugurated a tradition of critique of the Enlightenment project that achieved a certain apotheosis in high modernism before seeming to abandon the field altogether in the postmodernist period.

For Nietzsche the problem was the concept of truth as it came down from Kant. In Deleuze's early book about Nietzsche, he writes:

> Kant is the last of the classical philosophers: he never questions the value of truth or the reasons for our subjection to it. In this respect, he is as dogmatic as anyone else. None of them asks: who is seeking truth? In other words: what does the one who is seeking truth want? What is his type, his will to power? [...] By establishing a bond of right between thought and truth, by relating the will of a pure thinker to truth in this way, philosophy avoids relating truth to a concrete will of its own, to a type of forces, to a quality of the will to power...

---

18   Matthew Arnold, *Culture and Anarchy: An Essay in Political and Social Criticism* (London: Smith, Elder, 1889), 47–49. For a Marxist critique of Arnold's position see Eagleton, *Literary Theory*, 21–23.

19   Rita Felski, "Critique and the Hermeneutics of Suspicion," *MC Journal* 15, no. 1 (2012): para. 2.

Nietzsche does not criticize false claims to truth but truth in itself and as an ideal.[20]

We have always been post-truth, we might say, echoing Latour. For Freud, on the other hand, the problem was not posed in terms of power, but in terms of reason's opposite:

> Freud's Enlightenment is rather suspicious: all because at the same time it is murky, dark, sensual, and analytical. Freud's imagination is inhabited by both "murky" middle-class writers and "dark" denouncers thinking of truth as a "moving army of metaphors"... does it not seem as if Freud were joining back up with a certain classical age or at least with whatever in this age does not determine madness as a psychological illness but as unreason, that is, as something that has to do with reason.[21]

The work of Foucault, of course, combines Nietzsche's problematic with Freud's by linking Enlightenment reason (and unreason) with knowledge (truth) and power.[22]

By the end of his life, Marx's own critique focused primarily upon political economy rather than ideology as such, but articles like Kikutani's, which uncritically ignore the premises of bourgeois

---

20 Gilles Deleuze, *Nietzsche and Philosophy* (London: Bloomsbury, 2006), 88–89.

21 Szymon Wróbel, "Foucault Reads Freud: The Dialogue with Unreason and Enlightenment", *Polish Sociological Review* 171 (2010), 285–6. The phrase "moving army of metaphors" reminds us of Saussure, whose turn of the century linguistic theory paved the way for structuralism and post-structuralism and the theorizing of the postmodern itself. See Fredric Jameson, *The Prison House of Language: A Critical Account of Structuralism and Russian Formalism* (Princeton: Princeton University Press, 1972), 3–39.

22 However, "Michel Foucault has made substantial efforts to diver our attention from the sources of his inspiration which rested in Freud and were underpinning his lines of thinking. Instead, we were encouraged to investigate Nietzsche's influence. For reasons that remain unknown, Foucault preferred to be remembered as a nietzscheanist rather than a feudist. However, Freud's name is always present in Foucault's writings..." Wróbel, "Foucault reads Freud," 272.

liberalism and what had to be hidden in order for the "transparen-cy" of truth and reason to exist, also ignores the work on ideolo-gy which not only appears in Marx but has been a core interest of Marxist theorists ever since. Perry Anderson, while ascribing the importance of ideological theory in Western Marxism to a split be-tween Marxist theorists and real working class activism, "noted the intense preoccupation in these quarters with problems relating to philosophy, ideology and the superstructures."[23] In liberal discus-sions of a "post-truth" world, Marxist theories of ideology are re-pressed. The critique of ideology, which may be said to begin with Marx and Engels' *German Ideology* of 1846, is present even in the later works of political economy (for example, in Chapter 1 of Vol-ume 3 of *Capital*, where Marx explains his own understanding of cost price and profit and *at the same time* explains why capitalists should understand them differently). For Marx, as for Nietzsche, there can be no incontrovertible, ahistorical, eternal "facts," since "in a social order dominated by capitalist production, even the non-capitalist producer is dominated by capitalist ways of think-ing."[24] We might rephrase this as follows: under capitalism even a librarianship predicated on the sharing of resources is dominated by the idea of fair exchange. While Marx is opposed to the German idealists like Fichte and Hegel, insisting on the existence and acces-sibility of the material world in contrast to the social one,[25] he still recognizes the important role ideas and ideologies play in the mode of production as a whole.

In this chapter we will look at the various contributions to a Marxist theory of ideology by Georg Lukács (false consciousness and reification), Gramsci (hegemony), and Althusser (Ideological

---

23   Hall, "The Problem of Ideology," 28.

24   Karl Marx, *Capital, A Critique of Political Economy, Volume 3*
     (London: Penguin Books, 1981), 130.

25   Against contemporary views that nature/society is a false dichotomy, see
     Andreas Malm, *The Progress of this Storm: Nature and Society in a Warming
     World* (New York: Verso, 2018), 15–16, 181–82; on Marx's insistence on the
     distinction, see especially Malm, 161.

State Apparatuses and the reproduction of capitalism), leading into the ideological theory of Fredric Jameson (the political unconscious and the idea of a cultural logic). We will begin our investigation, however, with Marx and Engels.

Historical Materialism

In his introduction to *Social Justice and the City*, David Harvey distinguishes between two kinds of ideology. On the one hand there is ideology as it tends to appear in common usage, "the *aware* and critical exposition of ideas in their social context", which is the kind of ideology often taught in political science classes, and under which we might include the political ideologies of liberals, conservatives, anarchists, communists, libertarians, etc. On the other hand, there is "an *unaware* expression of the underlying ideas and beliefs which attach to a particular social situation," that is the ideas and beliefs that arise from particular social positions.[26] These positions include, but are by no means limited to, socio-economic class. Marx's focus on class stems partly from his preoccupation with economic matters, and partly from the nature of historical materialism itself. In an early statement of historical materialism in *The German Ideology*, we can see how Marx and Engels explained the formation of ideologies (in the second sense) as well as their place within the socio-economic structure.

Marx and Engels begin *The German Ideology* with an attack on the Young Hegelians, a philosophical school that arose in Germany after the death of Hegel in 1831.[27] Marx was close to the Young Hegelians at one time, but by the 1840s he had moved beyond Hegelianism to historical materialism and *The German Ideology* was written to "settle accounts" with the movement. The philosophical polemics contained within *The German Ideology* are too esoteric to be of general interest today, but the book contains the

26 David Harvey, *Social Justice and the City* (Athens: University of Georgia Press, 2009), 18.

27 David Mclellan, *Karl Marx: A Biography* (London: Macmillan, 1973), 25–29.

fullest working out of Marx and Engels' concept of historical materialism and the role of ideas within it. However, the book itself is quite dense, and so perhaps a concrete illustration will help contextualize Marx and Engels' critique of Young Hegelianism and set the stage for the discussion of ideology.

There are many instances of the erasure of labor in archives and libraries. For example, the "discovery" in 2012 of a medical report written by Dr. Charles Leale relating to Abraham Lincoln following his assassination. The report was "discovered" in an archives containing the correspondence of the Surgeon General at the time, "filed alphabetically under 'L' for Leale"—in other words, "right where it was supposed to be."[28] In 2017, a digitized letter by Bertrand Russell, properly described and filed in the Archives and Research Collections of McMaster University in Canada, went viral and was shared by various websites and Twitter accounts with no acknowledgement of the work of archivists who had acquired, described, preserved, and digitized the letter. The letter had made the rounds on the internet several times in the past under similar circumstances, each time without acknowledgement of archival labor and publicly-funded institutional support. This time, the McMaster Archives and Research Collections rightly took issue with this erasure of archival labor and put a few noses out of joint as a result.

The Young Hegelians would argue that ignoring other people's labor is just an idea, a mental behavior or position, something which can be changed simply by changing one's mind (perhaps by acquiring new knowledge). Indeed, in the discourse around the erasure of librarian and archivist labor, we hear similar arguments, often ascribing faculty and researchers' attitudes towards library labor as an ethical and empirical deficiency to be solved by learning more about library work. The Young Hegelians, too, would suggest that we simply need to educate or inform faculty members and researchers about the labor involved in preserving, describing, and making material discoverable. One way to solve the problem, for

---

28   Suzanne Fischer, "Nota Bene: If You 'Discover' Something in an Archive, It's Not a Discovery", *The Atlantic* June 19, 2012, para. 2.

example, might be to "train doctoral students to think interdiscipli-
narily by offering seminars jointly taught by humanities and archival studies scholars."[29] The problem with the behavior of researchers, in this view, is simply that *they have the wrong ideas*; in order
for the problem to be solved, then, researchers simply need to "free
their minds." Marx and Engels respond to this view by laying the
groundwork for historical materialism:

> Since the Young Hegelians consider conceptions,
> thoughts, ideas, in fact all the products of conscious-
> ness, to which they attribute an independent exis-
> tence, as the real chains of men… it is evident that the
> Young Hegelians have to fight only against these illu-
> sions of consciousness. Since, according to their fanta-
> sy, the relations of men, all their doings, their fetters
> and their limitations are products of their conscious-
> ness, the Young Hegelians logically put to men the mor-
> al postulate of exchanging their present consciousness…
> and thus of removing their limitations. This demand to
> change consciousness amounts to a demand to interpret
> the existing world in a different way, i.e. to recognize it
> by means of a different interpretation.[30]

This idealist (in a philosophical sense) perspective, that the problems of the world simply require seeing the world in a new way, ignores the real reasons why the world must be interpreted in a particular way from specific standpoints. Marx and Engels ask "Why
do these ideas exist in the first place? Where do they come from?"
Their answer requires replacing the idealist perspective of the Young
Hegelians with a materialist perspective.

---

29 Michelle Caswell, "'The Archive' is not an Archives: On Acknowledging the
Intellectual Contributions of Archival Studies," *Reconstruction: Studies in
Contemporary Culture* 16, no. 1 (2016).

30 Marx and Engels, *German Ideology*, 36.

The *reason* why faculty members and researchers ignore or erase the labor of librarians and archivists is because the erasure of labor *in general* is a requirement of the capitalist system. Since the dominant philosophy of capitalism is a liberalism descended from Kant, Locke, and others, people are raised to see themselves as individuals and their work as individual labor. But as Marx shows in the three volumes of *Capital*, labor under capitalism is an intensely *social* process, the labor of one person relying on, interacting with, and necessary for the labor of everyone else.

The increasing (and today almost universal) socialization of labor is a product of the division of labor, as in Adam Smith's (in)famous pin factory, reaching such a pinnacle that no worker sees the raw materials they work with, or the retail products they consume, as the products of another's labor. The very logic of capitalist production, the very mystification of the commodity-form itself, leads to what Marx calls "fetishism" (and is often nowadays called reification): mistaking the relations between people for the relations between things. Because we are alienated from the products of our own labor, from each other, and from ourselves,[31] it is impossible for us to see the commodities that we use, work on, produce, purchase, or consume as the products of an almost infinitely complex web of labor relationships. And as long as we cannot see those relationships, we can think of capitalism in ways that allow it to keep functioning, which is the very purpose of ideology. If workers recognized that we constitute the numerically dominant class, producing all the wealth of capitalist society, wealth which lines the pockets of capitalists, then we would be more likely to act to change the situation. As long as we remain caught in the perspective of liberal individualism, as long as we remain unconscious of the socialized labor all around us, then we remain satisfied with the capitalist social and economic structures of domination and oppression. And while I think it's good to try to constantly remind people that all of the artefacts they engage with in their lives, including stacks and

---

31   Karl Marx, *Economic and Philosophic Manuscripts of 1844* (Moscow: Progress Publishers, 1977), 64–70.

books and finding aids and records, are the products of human labor, we mustn't fall into the trap of thinking that one day, if we just convince everyone, if all these misguided researchers would just free their minds, then all will be well. This is the idealist view of writers like Kikutani, who think that a return to a society of "truth" will somehow bring back a period of prosperity and "good capitalism." It is not the view of historical materialism.

Andreas Malm critiques the idealist position strikingly. Against Noel Castree's argument that climate change is not a real process but merely an idea, Malm writes:

> [In Castree's view] the ontological status of global warming is an *idea*. So when the villages in a valley in Pakistan are swept away by a flood, or a monarch butterfly population collapses, or cities in Colombia run out of water due to extreme drought, it is not a real biophysical process but an idea that strikes them. The way to stop climate change would then be to give up that idea. Perhaps we can exchange it for global cooling.[32]

The contradictions of capitalism can only be overcome when capitalism itself is overcome,[33] and this can only take place through organization and resistance. Resistance, if it is to mean anything, cannot simply be the injection of radical examples into teaching sessions; it must include a very real resistance to the forces of commodity logic. And while a critical perspective on how and why the context of library work has changed and is changing for the purposes of increased capitalist exploitation and oppression is necessary, it

---

32 Malm, *Progress*, 24–25.

33 "We have every reason to believe that, in a world in which production is no longer organized on capitalist lines, a sizable share of such bullshit jobs will be rendered, like the human appendix, unnecessary, their residual presence a mystery, a matter for the natural sciences. But in this case, we will have abolished wage-labor altogether." Jason E. Smith, "Jobs, Bullshit, and the Bureaucratization of the World," *The Brooklyn Rail*, July 11, 2018, para. 16.

must be more than this: more material, more physical. Malm concludes his very important critique of various theoretical positions on climate change by saying that "as for theory, it can only ever play a very limited part" in the political movement to deal with climate change, "but at least it should not be a drag on it."[34]

To return, then, to Marx and Engels, what is significant here is that

> definite individuals who are productively active in a definite way enter into these definite social and political relations… The social structure and the state are continually evolving out of the life-process of definite individuals, however, of these individuals *not as they may appear in their own or other people's imagination*, but as they actually are.[35]

Ideology—for example, the suppressing of the sociality of labor manifesting as the ignorance or erasure of the labor of others—develops out of the social and political relationships that arise from the particular mode of production. Under feudalism, for example, the subservient relation of the peasant to the lord appears natural or God-given (like the divine right of kings); under capitalism, the same relationship by which labor-power is appropriated by a ruling class—the wage relationship—also appears natural.[36] The material *reality* of the economic relationship changes over time; so too do the ideas necessary for us to live with them. The immense socialization of labor under capitalism is impossible to really wrap our minds around; if feudal or wage-labor relationships are seen as natural then they might remain unchallenged; both these conditions are necessary for the survival and reproduction of the mode of

---

34 Malm, *Progress*, 231.

35 Marx and Engels, *German Ideology*, 41.

36 Hence the erroneous idea that a wage is money paid in exchange for labor performed.

production itself. As a result, when considering how people see the world (whether or not they are ignorant of the labor that support stheir own work, for example), we have to find out what material realities gave rise to those interpretations, those ideas:

> Morality, religion, metaphysics, and all the rest of ideology as well as the forms of consciousness corresponding to these, thus no longer retain the semblance of independence… it is not consciousness that determines life, but life that determines consciousness.[37]

What is true of morality, religion, metaphysics, etc, is equally true of institutions and the ideas that justify and explain them. Thus the library, for example, arises out of particular social, political, and economic needs, and the transcendental—liberal—discourse of libraries is its ideological support. The insistence on the library as vital to democracy presumes the value of bourgeois "democracy" itself; and all of this is ideology arising from the exigencies of the capitalist mode of production in all its various inflections. In Wiegand's *Part of Our Lives*, he challenges the democratic rhetoric of libraries, but does so by relying on the voices and ideas of individual library users and ends up in more or less the same position: that the library is a vital part of the culture of liberal America. He does not ask where those ideas and opinions come from, how they are formed, and what material structures of exclusion and oppression underpin them.

Marx and Engels sum up their account of ideology by saying that historical materialism

> remains constantly on the real *ground* of history; it does not explain practice from the idea but explains the formation of ideas from material practice, and accordingly it comes to the conclusion that all forms and products of consciousness cannot be dissolved by mental criticism,

---

37   Marx and Engels, *German Ideology*, 42.

by resolution into "self-consciousness" or transformation
into "apparitions", "spectres", "whimsies", etc., but only
by the practical overthrow of the actual social relations
which gave rise to this idealistic humbug; that not criticism but revolution is the driving force of history.[38]

This brings up, however, a long-standing critique of the Marxist
view of ideology: if all ideas are products of the material relationships of society, then how can any thought escape the logic of capitalism? Jameson writes that this criticism

tends to strike one as a strength rather than a weakness.
Marxism is indeed not a political philosophy of the welt-
anschauung [world-view] variety, and in no way "on all
fours" with conservatism, liberalism, radicalism, populism, or whatever. There is certainly a Marxist practice
of politics, but political thinking in Marxism, when it is
not practical in that way, has exclusively to do with the
economic organization of society and how people coop-
erate to organize production. This means that 'socialism'
is not exactly a political *idea*, or, if you like, that it presupposes the end of a certain political thinking.[39]

Because Marxism sees ideas as arising from material practice, it is
true that no ideas can be autonomous or independent of material
reality; but it is also true that ideas that run counter to the status
quo are able to arise precisely through the impossibility of capitalism to control *all* practice. While capitalism may seem totalitarian,
in the sense that its exchange-logic has infiltrated all areas of human
life, there is always space for particular *material* practices beyond
the control of capitalism and the commodity form. It is out of *these*
practices that critical theory can and does arise, feeding back into
practice, each determining the other in a dialectical way.

---

38   Ibid., 61.

39   Jameson, *Postmodernism*, 264, emphasis added.

Lukács: False Consciousness.

After the Bolshevik Revolution in 1917, the European left expected revolution to follow all across the continent. The failure of the revolution to materialize affected socialist thought and spirits for decades. Two of the most significant Marxist theorists of the 20s and 30s in a sense straddle this divide: the Hungarian Georg Lukács theorized what he saw as "the actuality of the revolution,"[40] while the Italian Antonio Gramsci attempted to explain the failure of the European revolution and to construct a Marxist theory proper to the age of "socialism in one country" and the Third or Communist International.

In the "pivotal text of the philosophy of praxis,"[41] *History and Class Consciousness*, a collection of essays which appeared in 1923, the year before Lenin's death, Lukács' concern is to reconstruct a Marxist (dialectical) methodology out of the writings of Marx, Engels, Lenin, and Luxemburg. In the eleventh thesis on Feuerbach, Marx drew a distinction between philosophical contemplation and the need for social and political transformation. For Lukács, then, Marx's materialist dialectic was primarily a method for changing the world rather than a purely contemplative philosophy, and the problem was how to "discover those features and definitions both of the theory and the ways of gripping the masses which convert the theory, the dialectical method, into a vehicle for revolution."[42] If, as bourgeois philosophy imagines, thought and truth are transparent and autonomous, independent of the material relationships of society, then social transformation would indeed simply be a matter of *deciding* to do something differently. But, as Marx wrote in *Capital*, "all science would be superfluous if the form

---

40   Georg Lukács, *Lenin: A Study on the Unity of his Thought* (New York: Verso, 2009), 9.

41   Andrew Feenberg, *The Philosophy of Praxis: Marx, Lukács and the Frankfurt School* (New York: Verso, 2014), viii.

42   Lukács, *History and Class Consciousness,* 2.

of appearance of things directly coincided with their essence."[43] Indeed, for both Marx and Lukács, historical and dialectical materialism *are* sciences. While today we are perhaps more suspicious both of claims of scientificity as well as the progressive assumptions of science itself, it is important to remember that in the period of "the actuality of the revolution," Marxism did appear to have discovered some kind of scientific principle or universal laws.[44] The core of this discovery, in Lukács' view, was "the realization that the real motor forces of history are independent of man's (psychological) consciousness of them."[45]

As we have seen, bourgeois ideology thinks of social relationships—of gender, race, and class, for example—as eternal and natural, thus justifying their continued existence. For Lukács, this is an indication of the thrall in which the independence of consciousness and reality holds bourgeois or common sense thinking: "this independence takes the form of the belief that [historical] forces belong, as it were, to nature and that in them and in their causal interactions it is possible to discern the 'eternal' laws of nature."[46]

Lukács' theory of ideology has two components. On the one hand there is the idea of "false consciousness"—an explanation of how workers come to hold bourgeois values and positions against their own interests—and on the other the more nuanced and productive idea of "reification", the effect of the mystified commodity-form on the way we perceive and experience reality. For Lukács, consciousness was an integral part of the class struggle: "for a class to be ripe for hegemony means that its interests and consciousness enable it to organize the whole of society in accordance with those

---

43 Marx, *Capital,* Volume 3,956.

44 For current scientific claims for Marxism see, for example, J. Moufawad-Paul, *Continuity and Rupture: Philosophy in the Maoist Terrain* (London: Zero Books, 2016), 56–60 and Alex Callinicos, "Critical Realism and Beyond: Roy Bhaskar's *Dialectic*," in *Critical Companion to Contemporary Marxism*, ed. Jacques Bidet and Stathis Kouvelakis (Chicago: Haymarket, 2009), 573–76.

45 Lukács, *History and Class Consciousness,* 47.

46 Lukács, 47.

interests."[47] Indeed, the creation and spread of bourgeois class consciousness was precisely the function of the public sphere, according to Habermas.[48] Lukács argues, however, that the objective problems of a newly-organized society cannot be understood by the hegemonic class so long as it looks at society from its own class-bound, necessarily partial perspective.[49] Lukács offers the example of periodic economic crises, a problem which has a solution (socialism), but which the bourgeoisie, "armed with knowledge of the workings of economics" are unable to grasp because to grasp such a solution is only possible by "observing society *from a class standpoint other than that of the bourgeoisie.*"[50] This is only possible, Lukács goes on to argue, with the abolition of class struggle itself (that is, with the achievement of a classless society):

> No class can [see the world other than from a class perspective] unless it is willing to abdicate its power freely. Thus the barrier which converts class consciousness of the bourgeoisie into 'false' consciousness is objective; it is the class situation itself. It is the objective result of the economic setup, and is neither arbitrary, subjective nor psychological. The class consciousness of the bourgeoisie may well be able to reflect all the problems of organization entailed by its hegemony and by the capitalist transformation and penetration of total production. But it becomes obscured as soon as it is called upon to face

---

47 Lukács, 52.

48 Jurgen Habermas, *Structural Transformation,* 54. Habermas' thinking around the public sphere has been widely adopted by library theorists, see especially Buschman, *Dismantling the Public Sphere,* 41–44.

49 The dominant philosophies that underpin liberalism, that of Kant, for example, formulate an epistemology and an ontology that support the ethical and intellectual requirements of capitalist economic relationships. See Blackledge, *Marxism and Ethics*, 31–32.

50 Lukács, *History and Class Consciousness,* 54.

> problems that remain within its jurisdiction but which
> point beyond the limits of capitalism.[51]

This idea, that the partial perspective of a dominant class can only address problems accessible to that perspective, helps to explain Marx's dictum that "mankind always sets itself only such tasks as it can solve."[52] In Lukács' view, the class which has the historical responsibility of moving society beyond capitalism to a classless society, and which therefore *must* overcome false consciousness, is the proletariat:

> We have now determined the unique function of the
> class consciousness of the proletariat in contrast to that
> of other classes. The proletariat cannot liberate itself as
> a class without simultaneously abolishing class society
> as such. For that reason its consciousness, the last con-
> sciousness in the history of mankind, must both lay bare
> the nature of society and achieve an increasingly inward
> fusion of theory and practice.[53]

The proletariat can achieve this by overcoming the partial perspective not only of bourgeois ideology (the "false consciousness" of the working class), but of *their own class position* as well, thereby seeing society not partially, but entire, as a totality. By relating particular phenomena to the social whole—something which neither the bourgeoisie nor a proletariat limited by class-perspectives can do—the proletariat can overcome the limits of bourgeois-capitalist (liberal) society. Lukács paints an overly romanticized portrait of the proletariat, as when he claims that "the proletariat *always aspires toward the truth* even in its 'false consciousness' and in its substantive

---

51   Lukács, 54.

52   Marx, *Contribution to the Critique of Political Economy*, 21.

53   Lukács, *History and Class Consciousness,* 70.

errors."[54] He nonetheless supports, however, Lenin's contention in *What is to be Done?* that proletarian struggle must not be limited to economic betterment, but must aim at the transformation of the social order as a whole:

> Social-democracy [i.e. socialists] leads the struggle of the working class not only for better terms for the sale of labor-power but for the abolition of the social system that compels the propertyless to sell themselves to the rich. Social-democracy represents the working class not in its relation to a given group of employers alone but in relation to all classes of modern society and to the state as an organized political force. Hence it follows that social-democrats not only must not confine themselves exclusively to the economic struggle but must also not allow the organization of economic exposures to become the predominant part of their activities.[55]

In today's terms, I read this passage as justifying the decentering of economic class from the Marxist or communist political and social program, making space to include race, gender, sexuality, disability, and other marginalized or oppressed identities within the Marxist program of social justice and a new world. But this does not mean that simply being "woke" or paying lip-service to diversity and social justice are enough. Nor does it mean that the ends in all cases justify the means. The "economism" critiqued by Lenin can be ascribed to a risk Lukács identifies whenever proletarian ideology becomes a "banner to follow into battle":

> Every nonprincipled or unprincipled use of tactics on the part of the proletariat debases historical materialism to the level of mere 'ideology' and forces the proletariat to

---

54   Lukács, 72.

55   V. I. Lenin, *What is to be Done?* (London: Penguin, 1988), 123.

> use bourgeois (or petty bourgeois) tactics. It thereby robs
> it of its greatest strength by forcing class consciousness
> into the secondary or inhibiting role of a bourgeois con-
> sciousness, instead of the active role of a proletarian con-
> sciousness.[56]

It is this, I think, that partly explains the existence of capitalist structures of domination and oppression within supposedly progressive (e.g. "democratic") institutions. The working class, especially in "liberal professions" like librarianship, tend to *see themselves* as bourgeois, that is they possess a bourgeois class-consciousness, rather than recognizing that they are workers. Well off—often rich—and privileged workers with a vested interest in maintaining their privilege, but workers none the less. The liberal-bourgeois discourse of librarianship is institutionalized bourgeois class-consciousness, and goes a long way towards explaining the unwillingness of librarianship to engage with social and political realities, to do the real work of diversity, decolonization, and reconciliation, or to champion the causes of library workers over organizational (i.e. economic or practical) priorities. Indeed, the continuation of racism, sexism, ableism, and gender and sexuality intolerance within the working class follows from this logic. W. E. B. Du Bois saw this problem as clearly as he saw so many others:

> The race element was emphasized in order that proper-
> ty holders could get the support of the majority of white
> laborers and make it more possible to exploit Negro la-
> bor. But the race philosophy came as a new and terri-
> ble thing to make labor unity of labor class-conscious-
> ness impossible. So long as the Southern white laborers
> could be induced to prefer poverty to equality with the

---

56   Lukács, *History and Class Consciousness,* 70.

> Negro, just so long was a labor movement in the South
> made impossible.[57]

As long as the proletariat is limited by its own class-position, as long as it sees itself not as working-class but as bourgeois, it cannot achieve that total, universal perspective which is required for the emancipation of all. It will continue to perpetrate injustice and oppression against weaker and more marginalized communities, inscribing and reinscribing hierarchies of oppression necessary for the continuation of the capitalist mode of production.

Lukács: Reification

A more insidious form of ideological conditioning takes place in what Lukács refers to as *reification*. The concept of reification has proved especially productive in the Marxist tradition where, for Jameson, it can be connected to ideas of utopia, and for the Italian autonomists like Maurizio Lazzarato, where it is part of a process of subject-formation within late capitalism. Jameson describes reification, which he connects with Max Weber's theories of rationalization, as

> the way in which, under capitalism, the older traditional
> forms of human activity are instrumentally reorganized
> and "taylorized," analytically fragmented and recon-
> structed according to various rational models of efficien-
> cy, and essentially restructured along the lines of a dif-
> ferentiation between means and ends.[58]

Jameson, following Lukács, argues that in "traditional activity"—that is, pre-capitalist social and economic life, "the value of the

---

57 W. E. B. Du Bois, *Black Reconstruction in America: An Essay Toward a History of the Part Which Black Folk Played in the Attempt to Reconstruct Democracy in America, 1860–1880* (Oxford: Oxford University Press, 2014), 680.

58 Fredric Jameson, *Signatures of the Visible* (New York: Routledge, 1992), 10.

activity is immanent to it," rather than finding its value in some goal or end. As commodity production (production for exchange rather than for use) becomes more generalized, the goal of production becomes more about maximizing efficiency; as the need for expanded profits increase, this logic of increased efficiency (through rationalized control) spreads out of the factory and begins to structure all elements of social life.[59] Rationalization of production takes the form of increased fragmentation of the labor process itself (Fordism, Taylorism), and Lukács writes that

> this fragmentation of the object of production necessarily entails the fragmentation of its subject. In consequence of the rationalisation of the work-process the human qualities and idiosyncrasies of the worker appear increasingly as *mere sources of error* when contrasted with these abstract special laws functioning according to rational predictions. Neither objectively nor in his relation to his work does man appear as the authentic master of this process; on the contrary, he is a mechanical part incorporated into a mechanical system. He finds it already pre-existing and self-sufficient, it functions independently of him and he has to conform to its laws whether he likes it or not.[60]

---

59   This was a common concern in Western Marxism. Horkheimer describes the situation in this way: "Mastery of nature has not brought man to self-realization; on the contrary, the status quo continues to exert its objective compulsion. The factors in the contemporary situation—population growth, a technology that is becoming fully automated, the centralization of economic and therefore political power the increased rationality of the individual as a result of his work in industry—are inflicting upon life a degree of organization and manipulation that leaves the individual only enough spontaneity to launch himself onto the path prescribed for him." Max Horkheimer, *Critique of Instrumental Reason* (New York: Verso, 2013), 4. "Instrumentality" was adopted by librarianship through the "documentation" of Paul Otlet. Ronald E. Day, *Indexing it All* (Cambridge: MIT Press, 2014), 15–25.

60   Lukács, *History of Class Consciousness,* 89.

Lukács based his concept of reification on Marx's analysis of "the fetishism of commodities" in Chapter 4 of the first volume of *Capital*. For Marx, the very structure of commodity-exchange ends in a situation where "the definite social relation [between *people*] assumed here, for them, the fantastic form of a relation between things."[61] For Lukács, "the structure of commodity-relations [can] be made to yield a model of all the objective forms of bourgeois society together with all the subjective forms corresponding to them", and this problem constituted "the central, structural problem of capitalist society in all its aspects."[62]

Lukács's main concern is the effect of reification on the (class) consciousness of the workers, but he also connects it with the bourgeois self-image that is the foundation of the transcendental liberal-democratic discourse of librarianship, expressing a particular class-based, *bourgeois* ideology founded on various political and social presumptions (the existence of democracy, the value of individualism, reason, the Enlightenment, etc). We have seen already how some aspects of bourgeois ideology become naturalized, taken for granted, and it is this that makes for an unconscious ideology even in the most concrete, practical, "non-ideological" library work. For Lukács, "the reified world appears... quite definitively... as the only possible world, the only conceptually accessible, comprehensible world vouchsafed to us humans."[63] As a result, "bourgeois thought bars its own way to a clear view of the problems" that give rise to social phenomena.

---

61 Marx, *Capital*, volume 1, 165. Marx's concept of fetishism drew on Feuerbach's argument that religion was the outward expression of "the relation of man to himself". Ludwig Feuerbach, *The Essence of Christianity* (New York: C. Blanchard, 1844), 84. Between Feuerbach's theory of religion and Marx's theory of fetishism lies the theory of alienation from Marx's *Economic and Philosophical Manuscripts* of 1844, see Ernest Mandel, *The Formation of the Economic Thought of Karl Marx, 1843 to Capital* (New York: Verso, 2015), 33.

62 Lukács, *History of Class Consciousness,* 83.

63 Lukács, 110.

When Marxists insist on drawing connections between seemingly prosaic economic categories, such as the commodity, and social, cultural, or political phenomena, it is not out of a vulgar Marxist insistence on the absolute determinism of the economic (at least not anymore); it is not even because historical materialism tells us that the economic is "in the last instance" a determining feature. The reason for it is precisely to do with reification and the ways in which the commodity form, commodity logic, and commodity exchange have *structured* our way of understanding, experiencing, and being in the world. In his study of Marx and Lukács, Andrew Feenberg writes that

> From a Lukácsian perspective, Marxist theory *explains* the overriding influence of the economy on all sectors of capitalist society rather than simply assuming it a priori on general "materialist" grounds. A specific feature of the capitalist economy, the commodity form, also functions as the basis of the capitalist cultural system. Economic exchange is the paradigmatic order in which rationality emerged from social practice to become the cultural form of society as a whole... This cultural approach is no more reductionist than capitalism itself, a society unique in the cultural significance it assigns the principle of exchange.[64]

However, what is important here is not simply the demystification of obscured social and political processes arising out of concrete economic necessity. Demystification in and of itself—critical theory—can only be the beginning. Unmasking the commodity logic that underpins reification, exposing the "false consciousness" of ideology, is no good if theory does not become a material force, in other words, praxis.

---

64   Feenberg, *Philosophy of Praxis*, 67.

Gramsci and Althusser: Hegemony and the State

The word "praxis" brings us to the ideology theory of Antonio Gramsci. Feenberg writes that Gramsci's *Prison Notebooks* "offer a striking complement to Lukács's theory of class consciousness" in which "Gramsci elaborates precisely the least developed sides of that theory within a generally similar framework."[65] My own reading of Lukács and Gramsci indicates that while Lukács begins at the level of production and work (e.g. the commodity) and sees reification as spreading outward, Gramsci takes as his starting point the relations of politics and the class struggle and brings the question of hegemony down from the level of sovereignty to the level of individual life.

In his seminal article, "Gramsci, Hegemony and International Relations," Robert Cox introduced Gramsci into the study of international relations. Cox argued that Gramsci's concept of hegemony was derived from the experience of the Bolshevik Revolution and, later, the Third (Communist) International, or Comintern. For the Comintern, class relationships were divided between enemy classes, over whom the working class exercised dictatorship, and allied classes over whom the working class exercised hegemony. The Comintern Programme of 1929 refers to the "hegemony of the international proletariat" which it characterizes as "an alliance of workers and peasants... under the intellectual and political leadership of the former."[66] One of the weaknesses of this view was that hegemony was something only wielded by the working class in its leadership role over an alliance of workers, peasants, and other allied groups. In other words it was not a *general* theory of hegemony, only a theory of hegemony as it applied to the particular situation of the dictatorship of the proletariat. It had nothing to say about non-socialist contexts. In Cox's view, Gramsci's original contribution was to modify this view of hegemony by applying it to the bourgeoisie, that is "to the apparatus or mechanisms of hegemony

---

65   Feenberg, *Philosophy of Praxis,* 241.

66   "Programme of the Communist International, Comintern Sixth Congress," 1929.

of the dominant class"[67] in non-revolutionary situations (i.e. to situations other than the dictatorship of the proletariat), such as the world of the triumphant bourgeoisie.

Gramsci's understanding of hegemony—a term already in use by Lenin and the Comintern—was influenced by his reading of Machiavelli, particularly "the image of power as a centaur: half man, half beast, a necessary combination of consent and coercion."[68] Gone was the simple dichotomy of allied and enemy classes, and the corresponding strategies of dictatorship (coercion) or hegemony (leadership). For Gramsci, political activity required a "dual perspective" which, while complex, was reducible to

> two fundamental levels, corresponding to the dual nature of Machiavelli's Centaur—half-animal and half-human. They are the levels of force and of consent, authority and hegemony, violence and civilisation, of the individual moment and of the universal moment ("Church" and "State"), of agitation and of propaganda, of tactics and of strategy, etc.[69]

Gramsci warns against a mechanical view of these two perspectives alternating in time, first the carrot and then the stick: "In actual fact, it often happens that the more the first 'perspective' is 'immediate' and elementary, the more the second has to be 'distant' (not in time, but as a dialectical relation), complex and ambitious."[70] Rather than alternating, then, hegemony and domination must be understood as "strategically differentiated forms of a

---

67 Robert Cox, "Gramsci, Hegemony and International Relations," in *Gramsci, Historical Materialism and International Relations,* ed. Stephen Gill (Cambridge: Cambridge University Press, 1993), 50–51.

68 Cox, "Gramsci", 52.

69 Antonio Gramsci, *Selections from the Prison Notebooks* (New York: International Publishers, 1971), 169–70.

70 Gramsci, *Selections*, 169–70.

unitary political power."[71] But while seeing hegemony and domination as two alternative choices is risky, there is another risk from the opposite side where, in common usage, hegemony is *equated* with domination, and the aspect of leadership, of taking on the struggle of allied or subaltern classes or identities as one's own, is lost. This too is part of the dialectical relationship between coercion and consent. For Lenin, from whom the Comintern and Gramsci adopted the concept of hegemony, it was incumbent upon the revolutionary proletariat to support the needs of allied classes—particularly the peasantry—in its struggle for revolution. "The proletariat is the only class that is constantly revolutionary," Lenin wrote in 1918, "the only class that can unite all the laboring and exploited people in the struggle against the bourgeoisie, in its complete overthrow."[72]

But leadership, in this case, must not be understood as something tyrannical or necessarily authoritarian. As Paul Blackledge points out in *Marxism and Ethics*, if we avoid the "'Leninist' caricature of Lenin's politics,"[73] then we can reclaim Gramsci's insistence on workers' direct control (as opposed to the 'capitalist managerial pseudo-expertise'[74] of the Stalinist period), and the direct relationship between party and factory "cells":

> Concretely, these party cells were designed not merely
> to reflect the consciousness of the workers around them,
> but aimed at real leadership of the class struggle... Importantly, this concept of leadership escapes the common conflation, originating with Weber, of leadership
> with domination.[75]

---

71   Peter D. Thomas, *The Gramscian Moment: Philosophy, Hegemony and Marxism* (Chicago: Haymarket Books, 2011), 163.

72   Lenin, *State and Revolution*, 23.

73   Blackledge, *Marxism and Ethics*, 131.

74   Blackledge, *Marxism and Ethics*, 1.

75   Blackledge, *Marxism and Ethics*, 131–32.

What is important here—the lesson we can learn from Gramsci—
is that hegemony is an aspect of bourgeois society just as much as
of the proletarian society as imagined by Lenin and the Comintern.
Gramsci's concern was with the capitalist countries of Western Europe which had emerged by the skin of their teeth from the period of war and revolution between 1914 and 1923. The failure of the
revolution to spread from Russia to Western Europe required an explanation, and the explanation Gramsci developed was the hegemony of the European bourgeoisie over the working class in situations
where direct coercion was rarely employed. In these cases,

> the bourgeoisie had attained a hegemonic position of
> leadership over other classes... In Northern Europe, in
> the countries where capitalism had first become estab-
> lished, bourgeois hegemony was most complete. It nec-
> essarily involved concessions to subordinate classes in
> return for acquiescence in bourgeois leadership, con-
> cessions which could lead ultimately to forms of social
> democracy which preserve capitalism while making it
> more acceptable to workers and the petty bourgeois.[76]

We have seen this before: institutions and ideas which are meant to
preserve capitalism, to sustain it, to allow it to reproduce itself. This
is the function of the ideology of married love for Federici, as well
as the liberal discourse of librarianship: hegemonic in the Gramscian sense, and not only as an idea, but as a set of materially structuring practices.

Althusser and Ideological State Apparatus

In his valuable discussion of many of these issues in *The Dialectic of
Academic Librarianship*, Stephen Bales argues that

> there is a mythology surrounding libraries that has been
> built on political, religious, and philosophical founda-

---

76   Cox, "Gramsci," 51.

tions stretching back to the ancient civilisations. Libraries continue to reflect a mythological narrative that evolves with the social formation, even though many of the institution's basic ideas remain sublimated…. The capitalist social form is based on and persists because of [a] convergence of ideas regarding a ceaseless positive expansion reinforced by some underlying mythical idealist permanency. The volume of eulogistic rhetoric concerning libraries suggests that people connect the institution with progress in a way that puts them squarely in line with this dominant capitalist ideology.[77]

Drawing from Louis Althusser, Bales identifies the "modern capitalist academic library" or MCAL as an Ideological State Apparatus, the means by which subjects are created. Althusser argues that the school system is the dominant agent of ideological reproduction under capitalism, and his description fits the academic library perfectly:

The relations of production of a capitalist social formation, that is, the relations of exploited to exploiters and exploiters to exploited, are primary reproduced in this process of acquiring what comes down, in the end, to a handful of limited types of know-how, accompanied by a massive inculcation of the ideology of the dominant class… An ideology which depicts the school as a neutral environment free of ideology… where teachers respectful of the 'conscience' and 'freedom' of the children entrusted to them (in complete confidence) by their 'parents'… set them on the path to adult freedom, morality and responsibility by their own example, and provide them access to learning, literature, and the well-known 'emancipatory' virtues of literary or scientific humanism.[78]

---

77   Bales, *Dialectic,* 112–13.

78   Althusser, *On the Reproduction of Capital,* 146.

For Althusser, ideology "'acts' or 'functions' in such a way as to 're-cruit' subjects among individuals (it recruits them all) or 'trans-form' individuals into subjects (it transforms them all) through the very precise operation we call 'interpellation' or 'hailing.'"[79] In other words, individuals are "called" to be the appropriate subject for the conjuncture; in our current conjuncture that subjectivity must be capable of performing intellectual and affective labor, and thereby to participate in the "mass intellectuality" of the system itself. How-ever, as Dyer-Witheford points out in reference to Marx's "Frag-ment on Machines," the ruling class and its administrators open up new grounds of class struggle through the creation of this cognitive workforce. The change in socio-economic conjuncture that created this cognitive workforce was based on the transition (as yet incom-plete) from a regime privileging industrial labor to one that privi-leges immaterial labor. In Maurizio Lazzarato's article on immate-rial labor in the 1996 collection *Radical Thought in Italy* he writes:

> The worker is to be responsible for his or her own control and motivation within the work group without a fore-man needing to intervene, and the foreman's role is rede-fined into that of a facilitator. In fact, employers are ex-tremely worried about the double problem this creates: on one hand, they are forced to recognize the autono-my and freedom of labor as the only possible form of co-operation in production, but on the other hand, at the same time, they are obliged (a life-and-death necessity for the capitalist) not to 'redistribute' the power that the new quality of labor and its organization imply... Once again, this phase of transformation succeeds in conceal-ing the fact that the individual and collective interests of workers and those of the company are not identical.[80]

79   Althusser, *On the Reproduction of Capital,* 190.

80   Maurizio Lazzarato, "Immaterial Labor," in *Radical Thought in Italy:
     A Potential Politics*, ed. Paolo Virno and Michael Hardt (Minneapolis:
     University of Minnesota Press, 1996), 136.

We must be clear, however, that we are speaking both about library workers who find the library as organization already in existence, who are forced to conform to the culture of the library and the broader university—but also about patrons, students, staff, and faculty, all of whom learn *from us* what it means to be intellectual workers, citizens in the new regime of immaterial labor. When we value the digital over other kinds of library work,[81] when we fetishize the latest technologies (through makerspaces or digital scholarship centres), when we prioritize automation over workforce, or e-resources over print materials, or student space over collections space, all of this helps to create a workforce for whom these things are priorities also. We can think of how library fines for late or lost material reinforces in the user the primacy of private property and the financial hierarchy of the organization over the individual to see how this process of reification and ideological construction continues outside the library.

The question of ideology becomes, then, how we are able to *interpret* the concrete activities and behaviors libraries and librarians are engaged in. I have been arguing that the real history of libraries and librarianships betrays a different social role and a different set of concerns, not to mention a different hierarchy of power and oppression, than the democratic discourse of librarianship—itself an interpretation—would have us believe. If we are dealing with a difference of interpretations, how are we to choose between them?[82] To discuss the connection between ideology critique and interpretation, I want to turn now to the work of Fredric Jameson.

Jameson: Hermeneutics and the Political Unconscious

If what libraries "really" do is different from what they "claim" to do, in other words if the transcendental discourse of librarianship is an ideology that serves to obscure and mystify the true role played by libraries under capitalism, then understanding that role becomes

---

81 Lisa Sloniowski, "Affective Labor, Resistance, and the Academic Librarian," *Library Trends* 64, no. 4 (2016): 649.

82 Moufawad-Paul, *Continuity and Rupture*, 56.

an act of interpretation or hermeneutics. The philosophical approach of hermeneutics has a long history, originating in the interpretation and analysis of biblical texts. In the twentieth century, however, the phenomenological hermeneutics of Heidegger—who, following Nietzsche, essentially argued that "there are no facts, only interpretations"—gave rise to a whole series of ontological, epistemological, and methodological approaches such as Hans-Georg Gadamer's *Truth and Method* (1960) and the current of Italian Theory known as "weak thought" (*il pensiero debole*).[83] As such, Heidegger's philosophical hermeneutics can be seen as inaugurating and supporting a particular line of postmodern thinking.[84]

In contrast to Heideggerian anti-foundational hermeneutics, I want to investigate the Marxist hermeneutics proposed by Fredric Jameson in *The Political Unconscious* of 1981. In a way, choosing between a Marxist and a Heideggerian hermeneutic requires taking sides in a long-standing debate between Frankfurt School critical theory and the conservative tendencies of Heideggerian hermeneutics. One moment in this polemic, the Habermas-Gadamer debate, took place in the late 1960s, and involved a critique of Gadamer's insistence on "tradition" as the horizon of interpretation.

> For Gadamer, to understand is to understand from within a tradition. The task of understanding cannot be performed by stepping outside of the tradition—by ridding oneself of 'prejudices'—but must be performed by remaining within it… It is tradition that shapes our 'prejudices,' our expectations, with which we approach a particular experience.[85]

---

83   Peter Carravetta, "What is 'Weak Thought'? The Original Theses and Context of *il pensiero debole*," in *Weak Thought*, ed. Gianni Vattimo and Pier Aldo Rovatti (New York: SUNY Press, 2012), 1–37.

84   Michael Brint, William G. Weaver, and Meredith Garmon, "What Difference does Anti-Foundationalism Make to Political Theory?" *New Literary History* 26 (1995): 225.

85   A. T. Nuyen, "Critique of Ideology: Hermeneutics or Critical Theory?" *Human Studies* 17, no. 4 (1994/5): 420.

In contrast, Habermas argued that without an exterior perspective, tradition simply becomes another unquestionable foundationalism. "Without being able to stand outside and look back on tradition, hermeneutics will fail to reveal what may be wrong with tradition itself."[86] Habermas himself had critiqued earlier Frankfurt School theorists for avoiding hermeneutics as a critical approach. As Jack Mendelson has argued, "one of Habermas' basic goals has always been to rethink the concept of critique and critical theory in the hopes of renewing the theory's original emancipatory intentions."[87] Part of this reconception involves bringing in competing philosophical traditions to critique critical theory itself. The incorporation of hermeneutic concepts was part of Habermas' project of renewal. As a corrective to the deterministic tendencies of Orthodox Marxism, Mendelson writes, Habermas

> attempts to reintroduce categories of intersubjectivity [communication, language, etc] which are no longer mere epiphenomena of production, and which permit the development of a non-objectivistic theory of history and the reconceptualization of the possibilities of radical transformation... Habermas believes that these same categories can be unfolded so as to yield... a vision of a domination-free society that links the overcoming of the capitalist economy to political freedom and democracy.[88]

Despite recognizing the significance of hermeneutic approaches, however, Habermas remained critical of Gadamer's view of tradition as the horizon of interpretation. The debate boils down to a difference of opinion on metaphysics or transcendentalism. In arguing that hermeneutics required some kind of stable, external standpoint

---

86   Nuyen, "Critique of Ideology, 420.

87   Jack Mendelson, "The Habermas-Gadamer Debate," *New German Critique* 18 (Autumn 1979): 46.

88   Mendelson, "Habermas-Gadamer", 48.

from which to judge tradition, Habermas seemed to be arguing *against* the hermeneutic approach of Heidegger and Gadamer, while still insisting on the value of hermeneutics. For Gadamer, who argued that "no critique of ideology can stand outside hermeneutical understanding, and that an external reference point is an illusion,"[89] Habermas' assumption of the possibility of a transcendental point of view was anathema:

> All our theoretical reflections, all our ideological critiques, must necessarily be conceived within tradition and conditioned by the theoretician's preconceptions and prejudgements, i.e. his or her prejudices. For Gadamer, what Habermas [demands] is an unacceptable (and unavailable) transcendentalism, a demand motivated by the foundationalist desire to ground justification.[90]

Such a hermeneutic would obviously have grave consequences for Althusser's project of an objective Marxist science, as well as his stance on ideology. Indeed, *The Political Unconscious* can be understood as attempting to think through Althusser's approach from the standpoint of hermeneutics itself.

One of the main points made by Althusser against Lukács' notion of "false consciousness" was that ideological structures—like Gadamer's "tradition"—are not false, but true. They may be mystifying, they may obscure for reasons of power, etc, but our experience of them is as a *true* state of affairs (since there is no external standpoint from which to offer an alternative). Following from Lukács' concept of reification, Althusser recognized that such mystification "was not simply a by-product of the market economy but one of the primary ways capitalism perpetuates itself."[91] Ideology, in Althusser's view,

---

89   Nuyen, 423.

90   Nuyen, 423.

91   Dowling, *Jameson, Althusser, Marx,* 82.

is simply the way this same process of self-occultation occurs at the level of collective consciousness or thought, not illusion merely but *necessary* illusion produced by the operations of the system itself. Thus ideology, in Althusser's famous formulation, expresses not the relation between men and their real conditions of existence but *the way men live in the relation* between themselves and their real conditions. So ideology, far from being false consciousness merely, expresses its own kind of truth.[92]

Jameson begins by addressing a strain of anti-interpretation theorists, notably Deleuze and Guattari, whose *Anti-Oedipus* attacked the Freudian interpretive strategy. In Jameson's view "hermeneutic or interpretive activity," whether of Freud, Heidegger, or Gadamer, constituted "one of the basic polemic targets" of post-structuralism in France. Interestingly, Jameson claims that such anti-interpretive positions are "powerfully buttressed by the authority of Nietzsche"[93] despite Nietzsche being one of the main inspirations of Heidegger's own anti-foundationalist hermeneutics. In fact, what French post-structuralism critiques is not hermeneutics as such, but interpretation as allegorical interpretation according to a "totalizing" master key. For Deleuze and Guattari, what is "denounced" in their critique of (Freudian) interpretation is "a system of allegorical interpretation in which the data of one narrative line are radically impoverished by their rewriting according to the paradigm of another narrative, which is taken as the former's master code or Ur-narrative and proposed as the ultimate hidden or unconscious *meaning* of the first one."[94] In this sense, what is at stake is the richness and plurality of life and experience; a richness which post-structuralism (and postmodernism in general) seeks to guarantee against

---

92   Dowling, *Jameson, Althusser, Marx,* 82–83.

93   Jameson, *Political Unconscious,* 21.

94   Jameson, *Political Unconscious*: 22.

the supposed reductiveness of "strong thought."[95] For Deleuze and Guattari, what is called for to avoid such reductiveness is the exclusion of meaning—the possibility of interpretation itself—from the literary text itself. It doesn't matter what a text *means* as long as it *works*.[96] For Jameson, however, Deleuze and Guattari's prescription "amounts less to a wholesale nullification of all interpretive activity than to a demand for the construction of some new and more adequate, immanent or antitranscendent hermeneutic model."[97]

Jameson insists that such a hermeneutic must be Marxist and engage with Althusser's "powerful objections to traditional models of interpretation,"[98] which were based on two modes in which reality can be understood as being expressed within a text. Althusser calls these modes of expression: 1) mechanistic causality, a kind of transitive, "billiard ball" understanding of cause and effect; 2) expressive causality in which "elements of the whole are no more than the phenomenal forms of expression" of an "inner essence." Interpretation by means of expressive causality is the realm of allegory and master narratives, as in Deleuze and Guattari's critique of Freudianism.[99] In place of these, Althusser argues for a structural causality, in which a structure like those found in Saussure's structural linguistics or Levi-Strauss's structural anthropology is recognized, understood, and known solely and precisely through its effects. For Althusser, such structural causality is necessary to solve the "epistemological problem posed by Marx's radical modification of Political Economy," in other words, to explain the ways in

---

95 Lorenzo Chiesa and Alberto Toscano, "Introduction," in *The Italian Difference: Between Nihilism and Biopolitics*, ed. Lorenzo Chiesa and Alberto Toscano (Melbourne: Re.press, 2009), 3–4.

96 Jameson, 22.

97 Jameson, 23.

98 Jameson, 23.

99 I take this also to be the realm of postmodernism's critique of master narratives more generally. See Jean-Francois Lyotard, *The Postmodern Condition: A Report on Knowledge* (Minneapolis: University of Minnesota Press 1979): xxiii-xxiv.

which capitalist society produces and reproduces a particular (ideological) subjectivity over time *through* the relations of production themselves.

Jameson's response to Althusser's critique of the first two modes of expression is to recuperate them in local terms. In the first place,

> I would want to argue that the category of mechanical effectivity retains a purely local validity in cultural analysis where it can be shown that billiard-ball causality remains one of the... laws of our particular fallen social reality... It must therefore be objected to Althusser's ideological analysis of the 'concept' of mechanical causality, that this unsatisfactory category is not merely a form of false consciousness or error, but also a symptom of objective contradictions that are still with us.[100]

In other words, the relationship of effect to a cause outside itself is both an objective one *and* the reflection of alienated capitalist social relations. Interpretation by mechanical causality remains valid because sometimes an internal effect can only be explained by an external/extrinsic cause.

Similarly, Jameson argues that interpretation by expressive causality reflects an objective reality about our texts and cultural phenomena: "if interpretation in terms of expressive causality or of allegorical master narratives remains a constant temptation, this is because such master narratives have inscribed themselves in the texts as well as in our thinking about them."[101] The conclusion Jameson draws from this is that Althusser's famous characterization of history as a "process without a *telos* or a subject" is incomplete. In Jameson's view, Althusser "does not at all draw the fashionable

---

100   Jameson, *Political Unconscious,* 25–26.

101   Jameson, 34.

conclusion that because history is a text, the 'referent' does not exist."[102] Rather, Jameson argues that "history is *not* a text, not a narrative, master or otherwise, but that as an absent cause, it is inaccessible to us except in textual form, and that our approach to it and to the Real itself necessarily passes through its prior textualization, its narrativization in the political unconscious."[103]

Only Marxism, for Jameson, can provide a philosophy which can make sense of this textualized History:

> Only Marxism can give us an adequate account of the essential *mystery* of the cultural past, which, like Tiresias drinking the blood, is momentarily returned to life and warmth and allowed once more to speak, and to deliver its long-forgotten message in surroundings utterly alien to it. This mystery can be reenacted only if the human adventure is one; only thus—and not through the hobbies of antiquarianism or the projections of the modernists—can we glimpse the vital claims upon us of such long-dead issues as the seasonal alternation of the economy of a primitive tribe, the passionate disputes about the nature of the Trinity, the conflicting models of the *polis* or the universal Empire, or, apparently closer to us in time, the dusty parliamentary and journalistic polemics of the nineteenth century nation states. These matters can recover their original urgency for us only if they are retold within the unity of a single great collective story; only if, in however disguised and symbolic a form, they are seen as sharing a single fundamental theme—for Marxism, the collective struggle to wrest a realm of Freedom from a realm of Necessity; only if they are grasped as vital episodes in a single vast unfinished plot... It is in detecting the traces of that uninterrupted narrative,

---

102   Jameson, 35.

103   Jameson, 35.

in restoring to the surface of the text the repressed and
buried reality of this fundamental history, that the doctrine of a political unconscious finds its function and its
necessity.[104]

At this point, then, History is no longer one interpretive master-code
among many, but becomes "the ultimate ground as well as the untranscendable limit of our understanding."[105] However, as Jameson
admits, critiques of this Marxist position tend to argue that History itself has here become reified, objectified, turned into a weapon,
and therefore is to be rejected as simply another contingent, partial
(but "totalitarian"), and partisan perspective. Rather than attempting to champion History against other master-codes (language, say,
in the period of the linguistic turn[106]), Jameson suggests we would
do better to ask "how History as a ground and an absent cause can
be conceived in such a way as to resist such thematization or reification, such transformation back into one optional code against others?"[107] His answer is, in some respects, similar to Heidegger's and
Gadamer's hermeneutics: History is something other than *just another* interpretive strategy because we are *always already* born into it.
History is what has happened, how things came to be the way they
are. Or, as Jameson puts it History is the experience of Necessity:

> History is what hurts, it is what refuses desire and sets
> inexorable limits to individual as well as collective prax-
> is, which its 'ruses' turn into grisly and ironic reversals
> of their overt intention. But this History can only be ap-
> prehended through its effects, and never directly as some
> reified force. This is indeed the ultimate sense in which
> History as ground and untranscendable horizon needs

---

104 Jameson, 19–20.

105 Jameson, 100.

106 Jameson, *Prison House*, vii.

107 Jameson, *Political Unconscious*, 101.

no particular theoretical justification: we may be sure
that its alienating necessities will not forget us, however
much we might prefer to ignore them.[108]

Jameson's project, then, is to provide a hermeneutics that overcomes
Habermas' objections to Gadamer, placing Jameson at odds with
scientific or realist tendencies within Marxist thinking, such as J.
Moufawad-Paul's or Roy Bhaskar's. History is, for Jameson, the
"immanent" required by hermeneutics, which for Gadamer is provided by tradition. But it is an objective ground—even if not directly apprehendable or even representable—from which any given
interpretation may be critiqued, thus satisfying Habermas' concern
that hermeneutics maintain a critical perspective. In the context of
the political unconscious, then, it becomes easier to explain Jameson's concept of postmodernism as "cultural logic" of contemporary
capitalism.

Postmodernism as Cultural Logic

Marxism, with its combined interest in historicity and ideology, has
produced many cogent analyses of both the current political-economic conjuncture (including Ernest Mandel's *Late Capitalism* and
David Harvey's *New Imperialism* and *Brief History of Neoliberalism*)
and the cultural sphere that developed within it (the two most important, I think, being Terry Eagleton's *The Illusions of Postmodernism* and Harvey's *The Condition of Postmodernity*). The relationship within Marxist theory of economic forces and relations on one
hand and culture on the other means that both neoliberalism (or
"late capitalism") and postmodernism do not exist independently
of one another.

Eagleton sees postmodernism as "politically oppositional
but economically complicit," that is, it puts forward a cultural theory that only *appears* to oppose the norms of late capitalism. But Eagleton argues that "postmodernism usually fails to recognize that

---

108   Jameson, 102.

what goes at the level of ideology does not always go at the level of the market."[109] For Eagleton, postmodernism is ambivalent or even contradictory, but he sees this as an error at the heart of postmodernism itself. Harvey, on the other hand, explicitly connects postmodernism with a transition from a Fordist to a post-Fordist flexible "regime of accumulation," and sees postmodernism as the theory required by this change in the space-time structuration of the new (neoliberal) regime.

For Jameson, it appears as though the transition from welfare-state capitalism to (what we now call) neoliberalism engendered many different "competing formulations," depending on the disciplinary vantage point of the theorist. Thus for philosophers, the neoliberal conjuncture was marked by poststructuralism, for economists it was described as "postindustrial society," while media theorists adopted "this or that McLuhanite nomenclature."[110] Jameson sees the ideological requirements and cultural dynamics of the new conjuncture to be more far-reaching, and thus requiring a broader underlying conception:

> The fundamental ideological task of the new concept... must remain that of coordinating new forms of practice and social and mental habits... with the new forms of economic production and organization thrown up by the modification of capitalism—the new global division of labor—in recent years.[111]

As a result, and as we will see in the next few chapters, "postmodernism" is the "cultural dominant" by which the appropriate workers (subjects) are created and structured for use within the neoliberal labor/capital relationship (or regime of accumulation). "The postmodern," Jameson writes, "is to be seen as the production of

---

109   Terry Eagleton, *Illusions of Postmodernism* (Malden, MA: Blackwell, 1996): 132.

110   Jameson, *Postmodernism*, xiii.

111   Jameson, xiv.

postmodern people capable of functioning in a very specific socio-economic world indeed, one whose structure and objective features and requirements—if we had a proper account of them—would constitute the situation to which 'postmodernism' is a response."[112]

Postmodernism in all its forms—poststructuralism, postmodern art and architecture, etc—is, then, the narrative in which we can read the "political unconscious" of neoliberalism. It is the reification—in Lukács' sense—of the particular forces and relationships of the neoliberal economy. The hegemonic (Gramsci) and ideological (Althusser) structures necessary to neoliberalism are different from those required by the welfare state, just as the kinds of workers and the kind of work they perform is different. In the cultural sphere, this difference is seen as "postmodernism" as against the high modernism appropriate to the postwar decades, and the realism appropriate to the period of classical liberalism and industrial/bourgeois capitalism in the 19th century. The library as an institution of hegemony/ideology participates in postmodernist culture (its relativism, its absence of absolute values, etc), and thereby replicates that culture not only among library workers, but among our users and patrons as well, despite the persistence of vestiges of the realist and modernist moments of library ideology.

***

The relevance to libraries of Jameson's concepts of the political unconscious and postmodernism as cultural logic lies in the subtle ways the ideologies of late capitalism inform library theory and practice. We must understand libraries and librarianship not (or not only) through the discursive struggle within liberal democracy. I see such a struggle in the long back-and-forth between the social justice and mainstream wings of librarianship. The social justice wing has taken many forms: social responsibility, progressive librarians, #critlib; while the mainstream line of librarianship—liberal, practical, "neutral"—modulates according to the socio-economic

---

112   Jameson, xv.

moment, but only within very narrow limits. In order to break out of this back-and-forth struggle, we have to look at the political unconscious of library work, especially as it relates to the particular "cultural logics" of the different periods of library history. We will turn now to a high-level analysis of library history and its cultural logic from 1950 to 2008.

Chapter Five

Three Hegemonies of Library History

Introduction: History, Continuity, Disruption

To support the claim that both the form and the content of librarianship can be mapped to socio-economic changes in capitalist society, we must first understand this historical terrain, the sequences of conjunctures into which the entire period from 1850 to 2008 may be divided. As Fredric Jameson has noted, the question of the continuity or discontinuity of a historical period is not an empirical one;[1] it doesn't arise out of the evidence itself but is a theoretical position taken in advance.[2] Indeed, for Foucault, the distinction between continuity and discontinuity marked a division between history and other human sciences. Rather than focusing on the long periods of seemingly unbroken human activity which became a dominant historical methodology with the *longue durée* of Braudel

---

1   G. W. F. Hegel, *The Philosophy of History* (New York: Dover, 1956), 11.

2   Fredric Jameson, *Late Marxism: Adorno, or the Persistence of the Dialectic* (New York: Verso, 1990), 3. This is not to suggest, as some have done that history is a purely textual phenomenon; real history can be known because we can see its effects (Malm, *Progress*, 20–23).

and the Annales school, social scientists instead turned their attention to thresholds, interruptions, "displacements and transformations of concepts."[3] Indeed, Foucault's position can be seen as an engagement with Braudel's view that

> nothing is more important, from our perspective, at the center of social reality, than that lively, intimate opposition, indefinitely repeated, between the instant and slowly unrolling time. Whether we are speaking of the past or the present, a clear consciousness of this plurality of social time is indispensable for a common methodology in the human sciences.[4]

However, to look at history dialectically (or, to use Braudel's phrase, employing "the dialectic of duration") requires seeing continuity and discontinuity not as mutually exclusive, either ontologically or analytically, but as contradictory productive moments in an ongoing process. As J. Moufawad-Paul has written in a Maoist context, "rupture does not emerge from a vacuum but in direct and continuous relation to the tradition of which it is a part, a tradition that it upholds (with which it possesses continuity) by *the very fact of its rupture*."[5]

On the other hand, we live in a conjuncture cut off from history in many ways, and suspicious of any kind of "totalizing" agenda lurking underneath the act of periodization itself. Jameson describes his book on postmodernism as offering "a periodizing hypothesis... at a moment in which the very conception of historical periodization has come to seem most problematical indeed."[6] Jameson reminds us that the postmodern suspicion of periodization

---

3   Foucault, *Archaeology of Knowledge*, 4–5.

4   Fernand Braudel, "Histoire et Sciences Sociales: La Longue Durée," *Annales* 13, no. 4 (1958): 726.

5   Moufawad-Paul, *Continuity and Rupture*, xxv.

6   Jameson, *Postmodernism*, 3.

(a suspicion exemplified but also subverted by Foucault), is due to the fear that "periodizing hypotheses... tend to obliterate difference and to project an idea of the historical period as massive homogeneity."[7] In other words, to argue for the division of a history into different periods, assigning particular characteristics, properties, or structures of feeling to each period, erases the differences present *within* each period while overstating the differences *between* each period.

In another work, Jameson connects the suspicion of periodization with the suspicion of interpretation itself[8] out of a concern that the abstraction required to characterize a specific period is overly reductive, erasing the inexhaustible variety of life as it is lived and replacing it by something homogeneous. In this way, Jameson connects the postmodern loss of historicity with hermeneutics and the crisis of representation itself.

> The construction of a historical totality [it is feared] necessarily involves the isolation and the privileging of one of the elements *within* that totality... such that the element in question becomes a master code or 'inner essence' capable of explicating the other elements or features of the 'whole' in question.[9]

He concludes, however, that "individual period formations always secretly imply or project narratives or 'stories'—narrative representations—of the historical sequence in which such individual

---

7   Jameson, *Postmodernism*, 3–4.

8   "Totalization is itself numbered among the approaches stigmatized by [expressive causality], which range from the various conceptions of the world-views or period styles of a given historical moment... all the way to contemporary structural or post-structural efforts at modelling the dominant epitome or sign-system of this or that historical period." Jameson, *Political Unconscious,*: 26–27.

9   Jameson, *Political Unconscious,* 28.

periods take their place and from which they derive their signif-icance."[10] We can draw connections here between the idea of narra-tive representations of history with Roy Bhaskar's transitive and in-transitive objects of science[11] as well as Althusser's "thought object and real object of a science":[12] the narrative representation of history must be distinguished from history itself. The division of a stretch of time into periods, then, is a theoretical construction, which raises the question of how best to divide the history of the modern library, and what is the historical sequence that gives the resulting periods their significance? What story are we trying to tell?

We could start, as Jesse Shera did, with the early libraries of the pre-Independence colonies, but it seems to me that, alongside the circulating and Mechanics' Institute libraries of the early 19th century on both sides of the Atlantic, the colonial libraries form part of the pre-history of the modern library in the West. For the purposes of this investigation, I start with the years around 1850, partly for their political and economic significance, but mainly be-cause these years mark a significant turning point in the history of public libraries: the Boston Public Library was founded in 1848 and opened in 1854, and the Public Libraries Act of Great Britain was passed in 1850. However, even the very beginnings of the pub-lic library are mystified by ideology. As Michael Harris wrote in his landmark "revisionist" history of the public library in America,

> American librarians have been generally convinced of the truth of a warm and comforting explanation of the origins and consequent growth, of the American pub-lic library. They believe that although the first public li-brary was founded in a small town in New Hampshire in 1833, the public library movement really was launched in the 1850s, when the Boston Public Library was

---

10   Jameson, *Political Unconscious,* 28.

11   Roy Bhaskar, *A Realist Theory of Science* (Leeds: Leeds Books, 1975), 21.

12   Callinicos, "Critical Realism and Beyond," 573.

> established by an intelligent middle class led by a group
> of enlightened civic leaders. In those early years, so the
> story goes, the library movement was in danger of being
> captured by an aristocratic intellectual class designing to
> make the public library an elitist center for scholarly re-
> search... This attempt was countered by a group of hu-
> manitarian and liberal reformers led by George Ticknor,
> who insisted that the public library be dedicated to the
> continuing education of the "common man."[13]

Be that as it may, this starting point coincides with the beginning
of what Ernest Mandel has identified as a sequence of "revolutions
in power technology" which, while not deterministic in any technological sense, will have a major impact upon the remarks to follow. Indeed, while these moments may not be crudely determinant
upon society as a whole, Mandel does argue that they are "determinant moment[s] in revolutions of technology" under capitalism.
Mandel's three technological revolutions are "machine production
of steam-driven motors since 1848; machine production of electric
and combustion motors since the 90s of the 19th century; machine
production of electronic and nuclear-powered apparatuses since the
40s of the 20th century."[14] For Mandel, the history of capitalism
"appears not only as a succession of cyclical movements every 7 or
10 years, but also a succession of longer periods, of approximately
50 years."[15] Four such "long waves" can be identified:

1. From the end of the 18th century to 1847;
2. From 1847 until the beginning of the 1890s;
3. From the 1890s to the Second World War;
4. From 1945 to 1972 (when *Late Capitalism* was written).

---

13   Michael H. Harris, "The Purpose of the American Public Library in Historical
     Perspective: A Revisionist Interpretation," (ERIC Clearinghouse, 1972), 4.

14   Ernest Mandel, *Late Capitalism* (New York: Verso, 1999), 118; Jameson,
     Postmodernism 35.

15   Mandel, *Late Capitalism*, 120.

Combining stage 2 and 3 into a single socio-economic period, Mandel describes three phases of capitalism between 1750 and the 1970s: "freely competitive capitalism," 1750–1850; "monopoly capitalism,"1850–1940; and "late capitalism,"1945–1972. Mandel's three technological revolutions therefore operate as pivots or inflection points in the history of capitalist accumulation. From the benefit of another 45 years on Mandel, we can see that the early 1970s in fact inaugurated a new phase in the history of capital accumulation, one which puts a different perspective on the periodization offered so far. With the advent of neoliberalism (culturally, from the early 1960s; economically from the early 1970s; and politically from the early 1980s), we can adjust our evaluation of the previous moments of inflection, in the end proposing the following for the period of the modern library (i.e. from 1848 on):

1. 1848–1914: Classical liberalism, industrial technology, factory work, bourgeois library;
2. 1914–1945: War and depression;
3. 1945–1973: Embedded liberalism[16], welfare state, mass work, mass library;
4. 1973–2008: Neoliberalism, postmodernism, post-Fordism, neoliberal library.

This schema has the advantage not only of carrying us more or less to the present (I see the financial crisis of 2008 as marking yet another moment of social, political, and cultural inflection, the nature of which is as yet unclear[17]), but also of mapping fairly precisely to the shorter epicycles which compose the period of British and

---

16 David Harvey, *Brief History of Neoliberalism* (Oxford: Oxford University Press, 2005), 10–11.

17 Some theorists set the end of the neoliberal/postmodern period even earlier. Romano Luperini writes that "with September 11, the stage of postmodernity has ended. A new period has begun which still has no name and which requires different commitments and responsibilities". Romano Luperini, *La fine de postmoderno* (Rome: Guida Editori, 2005: 20.

American capitalist hegemony in the theoretical model constructed by Giovanni Arrighi. Before turning to the major text of Arrighi's on the topic of the three hegemonies of historical capitalism,
I want to pause briefly to discuss Jameson's account of the significance of Arrighi's model.

Rumours of Death

In 1897, Mark Twain "tried to preserve his obscurity in London,
but it was a losing battle; he may no longer have been interested in
the world, but the world was interested in Mark Twain". Rumors
abounded, including rumors that he and his family were living in
poverty. The New York *Journal* sent a young reporter to find Twain,
bearing two telegrams. The first read: "If Mark Twain dying in poverty in London, send 500 words," the second: "If Mark Twain has
died in poverty send 1000 words." Twain's response to this ghoul-
ish inquiry became a famous example of his wit: "The report of
my death was an exaggeration."[18] Capitalism's demise, like Mark
Twain's, has been almost constantly predicted, to the extent that
Marxism has been described as millenarian in its imminent expec-
tation of salvation.[19] The imminence of the revolution was a common perspective among 19th century socialists, which explains the
psychological effects of, first, the betrayal of the revolution by the
German Social Democratic Party in 1914, and then the embrace of
the successful revolution in Russia in 1917. The failure of the revolution to spread, the European revolutionary impulse finally being extinguished in 1923, drastically affected socialist thinking until the
fall of the Soviet Union in 1991. The moments of significance in a

---

18   Ron Powers, *Mark Twain: A Life* (New York: Free Press, 2006), 584–85.

19   Ernest L. Tuveson, "The Millenarian Structure of *The Communist Manifesto*,"
     in C. A. Patrides and Joseph Anthony Wittreich, eds., *The Apocalypse in
     English Renaissance Thought and Literature: Patterns, Antecedents, and
     Repercussions* (Manchester: Manchester University Press, 1984), 323–41; and
     David T. Byrn, "The Victory of the Proletariat is Inevitable: The Millenarian
     Nature of Marxism," *Kritike* 5, no. 2 (2011): 59–67.

historical sequence—even at the level of a life—are often obscured and become "predictable" only in hindsight. Thus the death of capitalism, too, has often been exaggerated, making Mandel and Jameson's adoption of the term "late capitalism" appear naïve if not dishonest. However, as Jameson notes in *Postmodernism*, not only can the true nature of a historical inflection point only really be understood retrospectively, but the joins are often obscured, with many of the cultural manifestations of the break prefiguring the transition as such.[20] This fact expresses itself in two connected phenomena: the fact that theorizations of a transition may appear at "the wrong time," and that those same theorizations may posit the latest stage as the "last" or "highest," a culmination or end-point or *telos*. We can see this both in Mandel's adoption of the adjective "late" to describe the most recent stage in his model of capitalist development, though Jameson effectively recuperates the idea of "late capitalism" as marking a moment of "continuity and rupture" with what came before. In this case, the word "late," Jameson argues

> Rarely means anything so silly as the ultimate senescence, breakdown, and death of the system as such… What "late" generally covers is rather the sense that something has changed, that things are different, that we have gone through a transformation of the lifeworld which is somehow decisive but incomparable with the older convulsions of modernization and industrialization, less perceptible and dramatic, somehow, but more permanent precisely because more thoroughgoing and all-pervasive.[21]

This teleological temptation can also be seen in Lenin's pamphlet on *Imperialism: The Highest Stage of Capitalism* which on the face

---

20   Jameson, *Postmodernism*, xix-xx.

21   Jameson, *Postmodernism*, xxi. Jameson remarks elsewhere that his use of the term "late capitalism" "is meant as a homage to Mandel, and not particularly as a prophetic forecast" (Fredric Jameson, *The Cultural Turn: Selected Writings on the Postmodern, 1983–1998* (New York: Verso, 1998), 139).

of it seems discredited by the continued development of capitalism since Lenin wrote it in 1916. Indeed, Jameson argues that such "historical descriptions" as Lenin's "do not do us much good; and here the teleological ('highest stage') does seem fully to merit all the opprobrium called down upon it in recent years."[22] The problem which needs solving, then, is how to reconcile the idea of transition—of the localized ending of one period and the beginning of another—with the impossibility of historical teleology. This is the problem that, in Jameson's view, Arrighi solves:

> Arrighi's luminous insight was that this peculiar kind of telos need not lie in a straight line, but might well organize itself in a spiral… It is a picture that unites various traditional requirements: capitalism's movement must be seen as discontinuous but expansive. With each crisis, it mutates into a larger sphere of activity and a wider field of penetration, of control, investment and transformation.[23]

Jameson traces this model of capitalist accumulation back through Mandel's *Late Capitalism* to Marx's *Grundrisse*, arguing that this model allows us to reconcile or "co-ordinate" the historical, economic, and narrative requirements. With that in mind, we can turn now to the three periods in which the history of the modern library may be divided.

Three Hegemonies, 1850–2008

It has been remarked many times that one of the characteristics of the neoliberal period is the explosion of financialization: the deregulation of banking, a proliferation of new financial instruments, a

---

22   Jameson, *The Cultural Turn*, 138.

23   Jameson, 139.

deepening of the capitalization of risk and debt, etc.[24] In his work on postmodernism—the "cultural logic of late capitalism" or neo-liberalism—Jameson has argued that we were unable to compre-hend the financialization of capitalism while it was taking place:

> No doubt it swarmed around our heads in the form of vague perplexities, quizzicalities that never paused long enough to become real questions: Why monetarism? Why are investment and the stock market getting more attention than an industrial production that seems on the point of disappearing anyway? How can you have profit without production in the first place? Where does all this excessive speculation come from?[25]

Early commentators on the neoliberal turn, such as Daniel Bell, tried to make the case for a "post-capitalist," "post-industrial society" which was to be celebrated rather than condemned, and such interpretations remain popular. For example, Bell argues that "it is post-capitalist so-ciety, in short, because relation to the instruments of production no longer decides dominance or power or privilege in society. Econom-ic or property relations, while still generating their own conflicts, no longer carry over or become generalized as the major center of conflict in society."[26] Jameson critiques this view in *Postmodernism* as both too-easily recuperable by the right, and as overemphasizing the idea of a radically new society, rather than the continuity of neoliberalism with the capitalism of the previous period.

What is important here is to note that the characteris-tics of neoliberalism, such as postmodernism, only became clear

---

24   Harvey, *Brief History of Neoliberalism,* 161–2; Harvey, *The Condition of Postmodernity,* 160–166. This deregulated financialization of capitalism led directly to the crisis of 2008, see David Harvey *The Enigma of Capital and the Crises of Capitalism* (Oxford: Oxford University Press, 2010), 54.

25   Jameson, *The Cultural Turn,* 136.

26   Daniel Bell, *The Coming of Post-Industrial Society: A Venture in Social Forecasting* (New York: Basic Books, 1976), 51.

in hindsight. Arrighi's *Long Twentieth-Century* (1994) is a significant contribution to this clarification—as indeed was Jameson's *Postmodernism* (1991)—precisely because it "produce[d] a problem we did not know we had, in the very process of crystallizing a solution to it: the problem of finance capital."[27]

Naturally the problem of finance capital did not arise with neoliberalism: Marx discusses it in Volume 3 of *Capital* and elsewhere, and it was a significant part of Lenin's analysis of imperialism. What is new in Arrighi is the idea that instead of a linear, teleological trajectory of expansion, "capitalism has known any number of false starts and fresh starts; any number of new beginnings, on an ever larger scale."[28] Arrighi's model of capitalist development—bearing in mind the critique of eurocentrism offered by Samir Amin, among others—begins in the financial centres of Northern Italy, then moves in an expanded form first to Holland, then Great Britain, and finally (so far) the United States. In each case, the ruling class of the dominant power holds political (and often cultural) hegemony over an ever-larger system of nations participating in capitalist accumulation[29]. Along the way, there are false starts, as in the case of Spain:

> We knew that Spain had an early form of capitalism, of course, which was disastrously undermined by the conquest of the New World and the fleets of silver. But Arrighi stresses the way in which Spanish capitalism is to be understood in close functional and symbiotic relationship to Genoa, which financed the Empire and which was thus a full participant in the new moment. It is a kind of dialectical link to the earlier Italian city-state

---

27 Jameson, *The Cultural Turn,* 136.

28 Jameson, 140.

29 Giovani Arrighi, *The Long Twentieth Century: Money, Power and the Origins of Our Times* (New York: Verso, 2010), 14.

moment, which will not be reproduced in the later discontinuous history.[30]

Jameson sees Arrighi's expansionary model of capitalist development as following to a certain extent the dialectical model laid out in the *Communist Manifesto*: in the case of Genoa, "the political form, here, the city state itself, stands as an obstacle and a limit to development."[31] This dialectic produces the historical sequence of capitalist hegemony as such: the Dutch, the British, and the American, bringing us up to our own time where, however, "Arrighi's model has touched the limits of its own representativity, and the complex realities of contemporary globalization perhaps now demand something else of a wholly different synchronic mode."[32]

But the sequential model is not, for Jameson, the most significant aspect of this theory, which is instead that "the internal stages of the cycle itself, the way in which capitalist development in each of these moments replicates itself and reproduces a series of three moments... modelled on the famous formula of *Capital*: M-C-M'."[33] This circuit, which Marx analyzes in the opening chapters of *Capital*, essentially identifies three phases of the circulation of capital: Money (M) is exchanged by the capitalist for commodities (C; raw materials, means of production, and labor power)

---

30   Jameson, 140. This characterization of events either falling into a world-historical sequence because they offer something new, or being outside the sequence, conforms, I think, to the discussion of what constitutes a world-historical revolution in Moufawad-Paul, *Continuity and Rupture*, 21–26. For the concept of "world-historical" see Hegel, *Philosophy of History*, 29ff.

31   Jameson, *The Cultural Turn,* 140.

32   Jameson, 41. Jameson rarely, if ever, uses the term "neoliberalism" in his writing on postmodernism. In the 1990s, "globalization" was a common term used to denote the still-unclear contours of the neoliberal turn.

33   Jameson, 141. Considerations of space require leaving out a full discussion of Marx's circuit, but see the opening chapters of *Capital*, volume 1; for an introduction this element of Marx's economics, see Michael Heinrich, *An Introduction to the Three Volumes of Karl Marx's* Capital (New York: Monthly Review, 2012), 85ff.

and, after the process of production which is hidden within this circuit, the commodities are again sold, this time for more money (M'; M+ΔM), that is, the capitalist makes a profit.[34] Much of the three volumes of *Capital* is devoted to demystifying, explaining, and expanding upon this basic model. Arrighi maps this circuit to internal cycles or transitions within larger periods of capitalist development. In the first phase, corresponding to the capitalist's acquisition of money capital, we have a period of primitive accumulation[35] which "brings into being a quantity of money for eventual capitalization."[36] In the second phase the money acquired in phase one is converted into capital and put to work (M-C), leading to a period of intense productivity such as that seen in Britain during the Industrial Revolution and in the United States after the Second World War. This phase, however, reaches its limits in the tendency—identified by Marx and subject to considerably controversy even within Marxist circles[37]—of the rate of profit to fall. In Arrighi's words, "profits are still high, but it is a condition for their maintenance that they should not be invested in further expansion."[38] Arrighi's theory is born out in empirical events. In his discussion of the 2008 financial crisis, Harvey writes that in the US,

> Profits began to fall after 1990 or so in spite of an abundance of low-wage labor. Low wages and low profits are a

---

34 It is important to note here that, for Marx, money is distinct from capital (capital includes things which are not money, and money does not always function as capital). This is different from either the common usage of capital (= money) as well as, for example, Piketty's view of capital "defined as the sum total of nonhuman assets that can be owned and exchanged on some market," Thomas Piketty, *Capital in the Twenty-First Century* (Cambridge: Harvard University Press, 2014), 58. For Marx, the designation of capital is always *functional*.

35 Marx, *Capital*, Volume 1, Part Eight, "So-Called Primitive Accumulation." But see also Federici's critique in *Caliban and the Witch:* 61ff.

36 Jameson, *The Cultural Turn,* 141.

37 Andrew Kliman, *Reclaiming Marx's Capital: A Refutation of the Myth of Inconsistency* (Lanham, MD: Lexington Press, 2006), 32–38.

38 Arrighi, *The Long Twentieth Century,* 95, emphasis removed.

peculiar combination. As a result, more and more money went into speculation on asset values because that was
where the profits were to be had. Why invest in low-prof-
it production when you can borrow in Japan at a zero
rate of interest and invest in London at 7 per cent?[39]

In terms of the problem of finance capital identified by Jameson,
Arrighi sees it as the third phase in the life a hegemonic power:

Arrighi's treatment of the recurrent moment of cyclical
finance capitalism is inspired by Braudel's remark that
'the stage of finance capitalism' is always 'a sign of autumn'. Speculation, the withdrawal of profits from the
home industries, the increasingly feverish search, not
so much for new markets (these are also saturated) as
for the new kinds of profits available in financial transactions themselves and as such—these are the ways in
which capitalism now reacts to and compensates for the
closing of its productive moment.[40]

According to this model, the neoliberal conjuncture, what library
theorists like Ed D'Angelo and John Buschman see as a corruption
of a previous golden age of good capitalism, is simply the period of
finance capital at the end of the current (American) period of hegemony. Arrighi's model, when laid out schematically, looks like this:

	Hegemony	
M: Primitive Accumulation	C: Production	M: Financialization

---

39   Harvey, *Enigma of Capital*, 29.

40   Jameson, *The Cultural Turn*, 141–42.

Periods of hegemonic dominance are interrupted by periods of struggle for supremacy within the (always expanding) system of nations concerned with capitalist accumulation. Arrighi connects the construction of the Westphalian system of European states with the achievement of Dutch hegemony, though "the Dutch never governed the system which they had created."[41] The chaos of the Thirty Years War (1618–1648) opened space for the Dutch to propose a new model of inter-state relations based on something *other* than medieval power and dynastic relationship. The Peace of Westphalia which ended the war in 1648 had both social and economic consequences. Politically, it isolated the remnants of the Habsburg Empire (Spain) and "liquidat[ed]... the medieval system of rule."[42] Socially it "placed under international guarantee the principle of religious equality,"[43] important for the Dutch since their Protestantism had been a significant factor in their struggle against Catholic Spain, as well as generally being the main issue for which the war was fought. However, "beside religious tolerance, the most important application" of the Westphalian settlement "was in the field of commerce":

> In the treaties that followed the Settlement of Westphalia a clause was inserted that aimed at restoring freedom of commerce by abolishing barriers to trade which had developed in the course of the Thirty-Year War. Subsequent agreements introduced rules aimed at protecting the property and commerce of noncombatants. An international regime was thus established in which the effects of war-making among sovereigns on the everyday life of subjects were minimized... The systemic chaos of the early seventeenth century was thus transformed into a new anarchic order.[44]

---

41   Arrighi, *The Long Twentieth Century*, 48.

42   Arrighi, 44.

43   Arrighi, 44.

44   Arrighi, 44. Note that "anarchy" in international relations refers to a system of states without a clear political sovereign. Cf. Arrighi, 30–31.

Dutch hegemony did not last long, however. A struggle for power broke out almost as soon as the Peace of Westphalia was concluded and "for the next century and a half—from the outbreak of the Anglo-Dutch Wars in 1652… to the end of the Napoleonic Wars in 1815—the inter-state system came to be dominated by the struggle for world supremacy," first between the Dutch and the British, later between the British and French. British hegemony after 1815 relied heavily not only on its naval and industrial superiority, but on three particular mechanisms: "settler colonialism, capitalist slavery, and economic nationalism… all three components were essential to the reorganization of world political-economic space, but settler colonialism was probably the leading element in the combination."[45] It is important to point out that we are speaking here of the period following the French Revolution, that is the period in which liberalism became the dominant ideology, in which bourgeois "democracy" was ostensibly victorious, and the period in which the public library was invented. This is also the period of "classic" or "ethical" liberalism to which D'Angelo turns for his golden age; a presumption of "good capitalism" which underpins his critique of consumerism in libraries, which he sees as a corruption, fall, or desecration of librarianship's bright shining principles, summed up under the headings of democracy and liberalism. This presumption is untenable; the public library is inextricably linked to the structurally oppressive components of capitalist hegemony (settler colonialism, slavery, and nationalism). It is not an institution that exists in spite of those things, but *because* of them; they are part of the fabric of the society that produced the modern public library. As Arrighi points out, "under British hegemony, non-Western peoples did not qualify as national communities in the eyes of the hegemonic power and of its allies, clients, and followers… At the same time, the nations that had become the constituent units of the interstate system under British hegemony were as a rule communities of property holders from which the propertyless were effectively excluded."[46]

---

45   Arrighi, 50.

46   Arrighi, 64–65.

Following yet another round of economic crisis (the depression of 1929–1939) and power-struggle (the First and Second World Wars, 1914–1945), the period of British hegemony closed and the American began. American hegemony can be said to have begun with the Bretton Woods accords (1944) and the Marshall Plan (1948), with its productive period ending sometime around the end of Bretton Woods (1971) and the OPEC oil crisis (1973), inaugurating a period of neoliberal financial capitalism that lasted until 2008. The closing financial period of American hegemony which is neoliberal in its politics and economics and postmodern in its "cultural logic" seems to have come to an end with the global financial crisis of 2007–8. Whether American hegemony is in the process of ending (perhaps being transferred to China) is difficult to say. It seems safer to end our periodization with the 2008 financial crisis rather than carrying on up to the present day.

In the years leading up to the Public Libraries Act, Great Britain inaugurated a period of deregulation not unlike the neoliberal deregulation which began in the 1970s:

> In the 1830s and 1840s the liberal crusade for free markets resulted in a series of legislative Acts aimed at repealing restrictive regulations. The key measures were the Poor Law Amendment Act of 1834, which subjected the domestic labor supply to the price-setting mechanisms of the market; Peel's Bank Act of 1844, which subjected monetary circulation in the domestic economy to the self-regulating mechanisms of the gold standard more strictly than it already was; and the Anti-Corn-Law Bill of 1846, which opened up the British market to the supply of grain from the entire world. These three measures established the core of a self-regulating world market system centred on Britain.[47]

As with neoliberal deregulation, this legislation was also guaranteed to ensure increased profits for industrialists and increased

---

47   Arrighi, 265.

misery for the proletariat, and indeed such measures did pro-
voke reactions on the part of radicals. Alistair Black identifies the
years between 1839 and 1842 as "the peak of Chartist agitation".
Chartism was

> the first avowedly independent working-class politi-
> cal movement... a movement largely free from the fet-
> ters of middle-class leadership or aristocratic patron-
> age... Although its aims were not out of keeping with
> those of previous reform campaigns, its methods were
> sometimes new; at times little different from those in-
> surrectionary movements which in recent genera-
> tions the British ruling classes had observed sweeping
> through Europe...[48]

We will see when we look at neoliberalism in detail how such deregulation in the 1970s was part of a coherent plan to reassert class
power following the compromises of the post-war settlement. In
any event, it was in this deregulating context that the Public Libraries Act was passed in 1850, and the "social control"[49] thesis gains
credence when we recognize the context of class struggle in which
the Public Library was constituted by the state.

To summarize, then, the period of library history in question—1850 to 2008—can be divided between three phases of
capitalist hegemony and economic expansion, four if we include
the struggle for power during the "second thirty years' war" of
1914–1945:[50]

---

48   Black, *New History*, 37.

49   Alistair Black, *New History*, 220–24; For the American context, see Harris
     and Spiegler, "Everett, Ticknor and the Common Man".

50   Charles De Gaulle, "Discours prononcé à Bar-le-Duc, 28 juillet 1946."

	British Hegemony, 1850–1914	International Struggle, 1914–1945	American Hegemony (Productive)	American Hegemony (Finance)
Economic phase:	Finance capital (Britain)	Primitive accumulation (US)	Production (US)	Finance capital (US)
Political phase:	Classical liberalism	Struggle between liberalism, fascism, and communism	Embedded liberalism	Neoliberalism
Cultural logic:	Realism	High Modernism and heterodoxy	High Modernism and postmodernism	Postmodernism
Labor regime:	Industrial	War economy	Mass / Fordist	Precarious / post-Fordist
Library regime:	Bourgeois library	"War library"	Mass library	Neoliberal library

As David Harvey has pointed out, such transformations are always indicative of changes in social relationships, often taking the form of antagonism and struggle. "During phases of maximal change, the spatial and temporal bases for reproduction of the social order are subject to the severest disruption."[51] The role of the library in the social reproduction of capitalism requires that such "disruption" be visited on libraries and the profession as the social relationships of capitalism themselves develop.

The Bourgeois Library

At the beginning of the bourgeois period, the ideology of the architects of the early public library like William Ewart and

---

51   Harvey, *The Condition of Postmodernity*, 239.

Edward Edwards drew first upon a utilitarian and later an idealist philosophy:

> Elements of the two philosophical stances coalesced in
> the public library context throughout the period. For
> example, utilitarians and idealists supported the estab-
> lishment of public libraries out of respect for their so-
> cial harmonizing effect: idealists in search of a commu-
> nal, organic past; utilitarians peering into a future of
> unbounded progress shared by all. Further, both utili-
> tarian and idealist motivation focused on the public li-
> brary's material role, as is evident in the institution's per-
> sistent concern to produce, in the context of the quest for
> social stability, better educated, more efficient workers; a
> confident, enterprising middle class; and individual and
> economic success.[52]

What is important here is to distinguish between what public library activists thought and said and what the material reality of the
development of public (and academic) libraries really was. Samir
Amin argues that, prior to the development of capitalism, the trans-
parency of economic relationships meant that the dominant ideology of feudal society did not need to mystify or obscure them; the
complexity and fundamentally exploitative nature of capitalist economics, on the other hand, requires just such an obfuscatory ideology.[53] It is no small part of mainstream library discourse to uphold
rather than challenge the appearance (neutral, civilizing, enlightening) of libraries and librarianship. In this sense, then, the narrative
of the origins of the public library forms what Black calls a "fictitious narrative." Black characterizes this narrative as one of 'sweetness and light', the phrase referring to Matthew Arnold's *Culture*

---

52   Black, *New History*, 16.

53   Samir Amin, *Eurocentrism: Modernity, Religion, and Democracy: A Critique of
      Eurocentrism and Culturalism*, Second Edition (New York: Monthly Review,
      2009), 155–56.

and Anarchy, a collection of essays first published in 1869. There, Arnold writes that

> Plenty of people will try to indoctrinate the masses with the set of ideas and judgments constituting the creed of their own profession or party. Our religious and political organisations give an example of this way of working on the masses. I condemn neither way; but culture works differently. It does not try to teach down to the level of inferior classes; it does not try to win them for this or that sect of its own, with ready-made judgments and watchwords. It seeks to do away with classes; to make all live in an atmosphere of sweetness and light, and use ideas, as it uses them itself, freely,—to be nourished and not bound by them.[54]

Dewey, of course subscribed to a similar position when he devised a motto for the American Library Association in 1879: "the best reading for the largest number at the least cost."[55] Dewey's motto was more concrete—not to say materialist—than Arnold's formulation, reflecting the practical, technical work of librarianship as the early professional librarians saw it (e.g. in the idea of financial responsibility). But Dewey's idealistic view of the role of culture—generally the view of the ALA as a whole—was not very different from Arnold's.

However, Arnold's project was neither neutral nor apolitical, as the fictitious narrative of the library would have it. To paraphrase Terry Eagleton, culture "in the meaning of the word we have inherited, is an ideology."[56] For Eagleton, it was the decline of religion as a unifying, pacifying force in England that by the 1870s led to the construction of "English Literature" as an alternative unifying cultural phenomenon:

---

54   Arnold, *Culture and Anarchy*, 52.

55   Wiegand, *The Politics of an Emerging Profession*, ix.

56   Eagleton, *Literary Theory*, 19.

> As religion ceases to provide the social 'cement', affec-
> tive values and basic mythologies by which a socially tur-
> bulent class-society can be welded together, 'English' is
> constructed as a subject to carry this ideological burden
> from the Victorian period onwards. The key figure here
> is Matthew Arnold…[57]

In the decades following the construction of Habermas' bourgeois
public sphere, Arnold saw the triumphant bourgeoisie as "unable
to underpin their political and economic power with a suitably
rich and subtle ideology"[58] and proposed the dissemination of an
English literary culture in order to bolster middle-class hegemony. Boosting the bourgeoisie, however, was not the only benefit of
such a project: "The true beauty of [Arnold's plan], however, lies in
the effect it will have in controlling and incorporating the working
class."[59] In Eagleton's view, Arnold is "refreshingly unhypocritical"
compared with other ideologues of his day:

> There is no feeble pretense that the education of the
> working class is to be conducted chiefly for their own
> benefit [i.e. the library myth], or that his concern with
> their spiritual condition is, in one of his most cherished
> terms, in the lease 'disinterested'… If the masses are not
> thrown a few novels, they may react by throwing up a
> few barricades.[60]

It is in this context that Black's "new history" is situated. "It be-
hooves cultural investigation in search of reality," he writes, "to challenge, wherever possible, accepted cultural 'truths' and myths… the
more 'accepted' an institution or mode of behavior, the more likely

---

57   Eagleton, 21.

58   Eagleton, 21.

59   Eagleton, 21.

60   Eagleton, 21.

it is to be the product of powerful, dynamic cultural forces."[61] Black characterizes the fictitious narrative of the early public library as one of "unbounded social progress, of emancipation and of self-realization," acting "as an enabling institution, providing individuals and society with cultural enrichment, for the purpose of civilized development."[62] Mainstream library historians like John Buschman consider it "perverse to hold that libraries cannot or should not be one of the educative institutions that help to shape citizens and citizenship,"[63] but in Black's view—and as we shall see, Harris's view as well—the "educating mission" of the early public library was bound up in struggles over class power and ideological hegemony within English culture more broadly. Indeed, the core of Black's book is to propose "that those who encouraged free access to knowledge in municipal libraries did so for both practical and aesthetic social ends."[64] The practical and the aesthetic, Black argues, each independently contributed to the stabilization of industrial society and the defusing of working class discontent, but when they were combined, as in the early library they constituted a "civilizing project" that "is not to be viewed as unproblematically progressive… they were not premised on the 'liberation' agenda of the emergent working class."[65]

The situation for academic libraries is a little different, but only because of their long history as intellectual institutions. Because the municipal, tax-funded public library was new in 1850—its precursors in the subscription libraries and Mechanics' Institutes were genuine bourgeois public sphere institutions focusing on the construction of a bourgeois self-identity rather than on social control—it could not benefit from a traditional perception as an institution of enlightenment and disinterested scholarship. The ideology of public libraries had to be constructed, while the ideology of

---

61   Black, *New History*, 1.

62   Black, 2–3.

63   Buschman, "On Libraries and Democracy," 30.

64   Black, *New History* 4.

65   Black, 4.

academic libraries proved ready to hand. Between the 1850s and the 1880s British universities came under state control, primarily by way of funding. "Their role in the education of a national elite was too important to escape political attention."[66] Just as state-established schools were a core part of Arnold's cultural project, so state-funding for universities and their libraries brought academic culture firmly under the control of the bourgeois state as well.

In the mid-1970s Michael Harris embarked upon a project of "revisionist history", an attempt to dislodge "the myth of public library origins" in American librarianship. In Harris' view,

> American librarians have been generally convinced of the truth of a warm and comforting explanation of the origins, and consequent growth, of the American public library. They believe that although the first public library was founded in a small town in New Hampshire in 1833, the public library movement really was launched in the 1850's, when the Boston Public Library was established by an intelligent middle class led by a group of enlightened civic leaders. In those early years, so the story goes, the library movement was in danger of being captured by an aristocratic intellectual class designing to make the public library an elitist center for scholarly research.[67]

Harris admits that librarians' adherence to such a myth is understandable, given its idealistic and humanitarian perspective, but argues that such a myth is contrary to facts of library history. Besides the fact that public libraries were "elitist institutions from the beginning", their pretensions to egalitarian democracy is undercut by the fact that "everyone knows that historically only a very small portion of the eligible users have ever crossed the threshold of a public library."[68]

---

66   Robert Anderson, "University Fees in Historical Perspective," *History & Policy*, February 8, 2016.

67   Harris, "Purpose," 4.

68   Harris, 5.

Harris' focus is on the supposedly progressive reasons behind the founding of the Boston Public Library. Despite the long-standing idea that the founders—who came from Boston's aristocratic upper class—were concerned with creating a "people's university" free for all, in fact they "were especially unhappy about the flood of ignorant and rough immigrants" into the city.[69] Such immigrants, in the words of George Ticknor, "at no time, consisted of persons who, in general, were fitted to understand our free institutions or to be intrusted with the political power given by universal suffrage."[70] Indeed, Ticknor "saw an urgent need to 'assimilate the masses' and bring 'them in willing subjection to our own institutions.'" The mechanisms for such assimilation was "education through schools, through the church, and any other institution that might be effective in this important crusade."[71] We should bear in mind here Althusser's characterization of the institutions of the Ideological State Apparatus (see Chapter Four).

Harris sees the origins for the public library myth in Ticknor's own authoritarianism and elitism, providing the framework for "a philosophy which was to dictate the 'purpose' of the public library for more than a century."[72] The goals of the Boston Public Library reflected this philosophy:

> To educate the masses so that they would follow the 'best men' and not demogogues; to "stabilize the Republic and to keep America from becoming another Carthage."
>
> To provide access to the world's best books for that elite minority who would someday become leaders of the political, intellectual, and moral affairs of the nation.[73]

---

69   Harris, 14.

70   Harris, 14.

71   Harris, 14.

72   Harris, 19.

73   Harris, 19.

For such a "stabilizing" and "civilizing" mission to succeed, the public libraries had to convince people to use them. As in England, literature was envisioned as a means to inculcate the masses into the values and behaviors of American life. "The most sensible way to entice the 'middling classes' into the library was to provision one's shelves with numerous popular works, especially fiction."[74] The inclusion of popular fiction in library collections proved contentious for many years, as it contravened Dewey's injunction for libraries to provide "the best reading" which, for the elitist leaders of the profession, disqualified popular fiction from the outset.[75] The inclusion of popular fiction, however, filled certain needs that outweighed, to a certain extent, their a priori exclusion. On the one hand, librarians believed that "if the common man could be induced to read the 'best' books, he would be more inclined to be conservative, patriotic, devout, and respectful of property."[76] Additionally, "even the most desultory reading of fiction was preferable to the 'vicious' entertainments designed to satisfy the 'lower impulses in human nature.'"[77] Such considerations tipped the scales in favor of the inclusion of popular fiction, but only under strict control:

> Being thus convinced of the value of good books, librarians were also quick to see the potential danger that 'bad' books held for the nation. Consequently they were careful to select only those books best suited for the purpose they had in mind. The word 'censorship,' now considered taboo by librarians, was frequently used in the pages of the professional literature. It connoted the idea that the librarian was responsible for keeping certain books from the public... Thus, the so called 'recreational function'

---

74   Harris, 24.

75   Wiegand, *Politics,* ix, 9–10.

76   Harris, "Purpose," 24–25.

77   Harris, 24–25.

> of the public library was introduced as one means of im-
> proving and controlling the people.[78]

Harris details the strict authoritarianism of the early public library, from providing areas for patrons to wash before being allowed to touch library materials,[79] to pressing charges against a sixteen-year-old student for stealing books from New York Public Library, "after all, the boy had to be taught respect for the law."[80] "Men would learn to treat property with respect," if they wanted to use the library.[81]

In the 1890s, a new wave of immigration provided a fresh challenge to American librarians, who promptly began to develop "programs designed to 'Americanize' the immigrant, and thus render him harmless to the American way."[82] Such programs, however, were often "repressive and autocratic," and librarians

> seemed to feel that they enjoyed a mandate from God to
> enlighten the immigrant and went about their various
> tasks in a spirit of authoritarianism that reminds one of the
> 'moral stewardship' of an earlier generation of librarians.[83]

By the turn of the century, in a society rocked by financial crisis and depression, and increasingly reliant on the munificence (and therefore the demands) of private philanthropists like Andrew Carnegie, librarianship increasingly lost its way. Few Americans used the public library: "discouraged on the one hand by their inability to

---

78 Harris, 25.

79 Alistair Black describes a similar situation in Britain in "The Library as Clinic: A Foucauldian Interpretation of British Public Library Attitudes to Social and Physical Disease, ca 1850–1950," *Libraries & Culture* 40, no. 3 (2005): 416–34.

80 Harris, "Purpose," 26.

81 Harris, 26.

82 Harris, 30.

83 Harris, 32.

increase library use significantly, and on the other by their seeming failure to elevate those who did use the library, American public librarians began slowly, almost imperceptibly, to abandon their mission as originally defined by the founders."[84] For Harris, such discouragement led American librarians to become even more authoritarian and elitist. To hide such a state of affairs, "afraid to make an open proclamation of their covert design to concentrate on the elite because they feared it would cost them public support,"[85] librarians began to rely even more on the myth of democracy and enlightenment. Such a "rhetorical smokescreen" was only partially successful: "The American public library had become a bureaucracy; a social institution without a purpose—except perhaps to preserve itself."[86] It was not until the very concept of democratic civilization was cast in doubt with the rise of Fascism and Nazism that public libraries regained a sense of social purpose. Such a social purpose was bound up with the system of class collaboration known as the postwar consensus.

The Industrial Library

British hegemony was challenged primarily by Germany, but it was America that emerged from the Second World War as undisputed leader of a new system of capitalist states. It is no accident that Hardt and Negri begin their discussion of Empire with the United Nations. American industry, technological advances, and sheer volume of money (which circulated through Europe as Marshall Plan aid from 1948 to 1952) were qualitatively *different* from either Britain's or Germany's before and during the war. In 1941, Time publisher Henry Luce coined the phrase "American century" to characterize what he believed would be the result of the end of American isolationism. In *The New Imperialism*, David Harvey writes that

---

84   Harris, 37.

85   Harris, 38.

86   Harris, 39.

> Luce, an isolationist, considered that history had con-
> ferred global leadership on the United States and that
> this role, though thrust upon it by history, had to be
> actively embraced. The power conferred was global
> and universal rather than territorially specific, so Luce
> preferred to talk of an American century rather than
> an empire.[87]

The "American century" saw a restructuring of capitalist states and international relations for the purpose of stabilizing the capitalist system after 30 years of war and depression. International agreements and organizations—for example, the United Nations and the Bretton Woods accords, which created the World Bank and the International Monetary Fund in 1944, were set up to ensure the smooth functioning of a reconstructed international capitalist order. "To ensure domestic peace and tranquility," in contrast, "some sort of class compromise between capital and labor had to be constructed."[88] Keynesian economics and a Fordist labor regime were dominant within the industrialized capitalist states, and in order to ensure the Keynesian goals of "full employment, economic growth, and the welfare of its citizens" it was understood that "state power should be freely deployed, alongside of or, if necessary, intervening in or even substituting for market processes to achieve these ends."[89] A class compromise between labor and capital was recognized as a key element in postwar economic growth, and "states actively intervened in industrial policy and moved to set standards for the social wage by constructing a variety of welfare systems."[90]

Following John Gerard Ruggie, Harvey calls the hegemonic political and economic worldview of the welfare state "embedded

---

87   David Harvey, *The New Imperialism* (Oxford: Oxford University Press, 2003): 50.

88   Harvey, *Brief History of Neoliberalism*, 10.

89   Harvey, 10.

90   Harvey, 10–11.

liberalism." For Ruggie, embedded liberalism was a compromise, "a framework which would safeguard and even aid the quest for domestic stability without, at the same time, triggering the mutually destructive external consequences that had plagued the inter-war period."[91] Harvey describes the situation as one where "market processes and entrepreneurial and corporate activities were surrounded by a web of social and political constraints and a regulatory framework that sometimes restrained but in other instances led the way in economic and industrial strategy."[92] The institutions of the welfare state—nationalized health care, state-provided education, etc.—were what the capitalist class "gave" a working class that had just fought to save "civilization" in exchange for social peace: "One condition of the post-war settlement in almost all countries was that the economic power of the upper classes be restrained and that labor be accorded a much larger share of the economic pie."[93]

In the 1930s, the aimlessness and frustration of librarians was curtailed by a call to a new social mission. We have seen how Archibald MacLeish, in 1940, enjoined librarians to "do more" in defense of democracy against fascism. During the war "free access to information on social and political matters suddenly took on a new significance,"[94] as mass propaganda took center stage on both sides of the conflict. As a result, the mission of the library began to change:

> The library was now portrayed as an institution which could play a vital role in promoting and preserving democracy in America by assisting the successful working of self-government. This was to be done by giving all the

---

91   John Gerard Ruggie, "International Regimes, Transactions, and Change: Embedded Liberalism in the Postwar Economic Order," *International Organization* 36, no. 2 (1982): 393.

92   Harvey, *Brief History of Newliberalism*, 11.

93   Harvey, 15.

94   Harris, "Purpose", 40.

> people free and convenient access to the nation's cultur-
> al heritage and the day's social intelligence. In accept-
> ing this conception of the library's role, public librarians
> were forced to drop, publicly at least, their commitment
> to authoritarianism.[95]

It is here that we find the origin of the view that the purpose of
the library is to support democracy through the creation of an informed citizenry. It is also where we find the origin of librarianship's commitment to "neutrality." Prior to the war, librarians did
not consider themselves neutral, but as active moral educators of
the masses. Now, however, and in parallel with the move towards
value-neutrality in the social sciences, "the librarian was suddenly
asked to become completely neutral on social, economic, and political questions... and was expected to provide ample information
on both sides of the issue in order to enable the user to make an informed decision."[96] We will return to the idea of "both sides" in a
later chapter, as it informs contemporary thinking around intellectual freedom. Harris argues that the new "neutral" library philosophy was welcome to librarians, despite requiring them to give up
their authoritarian views. In the first place, the new philosophy af-
firmed librarians' faith in the importance of education to a democratic society; second, the mission seemed achievable:

> As most librarians interpreted the library as a guardian
> of the people's right to know, the principle task was to
> acquire and organize information on all sides of social,
> political, and economic issues. This, reasoned many li-
> brarians, should not be too difficult, and it would allow
> librarians to continue to indulge their penchant for tech-
> nical and organizational matters.[97]

---

95   Harris, 40.

96   Harris, 41.

97   Harris, 42.

The third reason this philosophy was acceptable was that it allowed librarians, "who were not noted for possessing aggressive and extroverted personalities, to continue their passive approach to library service."[98] In other words, neutrality and impartiality became shields for passivity and a tacit support for the status quo. Finally, it allowed librarians to abdicate responsibility for library use:

> The librarian need only provide access to the information; the user was responsible for coming to the library to acquire it. The emphasis was on the library as guardian of the information; very little attention was devoted to the dissemination of this information once acquired by the library. Librarians no longer need worry about their inability to interest large numbers of people in their services. All of their attention could be focused on acquiring, organizing, and preserving the library materials. This, of course, was simply more business as usual, but now librarians had a rationale for their action.[99]

Here, too, is the origin of that "whiteness of practicality" identified by Hudson. In this sense, librarians achieved a sense of mission through understanding their place in the postwar labor/capital compromise. For librarians and for library users, social peace became the watchword, and the self-improvement of citizens went hand in hand with their pacification, giving up radical demands in exchange for the institutions of the welfare state in a society they believed they had a say in running.

But as we saw in the chapter on liberalism, bourgeois democracy is built upon exclusion, and the ideology that supports such "democracy," whether it be classical liberalism or embedded liberalism, can only justify such exclusion, not overcome it. In the case of the welfare state, such exclusions—based on interlocking factors

---

98   Harris, 42.

99   Harris, 43.

of race, gender, ability, poverty, and sexuality—were justified by the improved standard of living gained by those *not* excluded. The growth of the "middle class" (really middle income) during the 30–year postwar boom allowed those who benefited from it to ignore the structural oppressions of capitalism by arguing that things were better than they were and would continue to improve. The postwar labor/capital compromise—supported by the cultural role of libraries—saw the standard of living rise for many Americans, but only at the cost of the continued exclusion of marginalized, excluded, and oppressed populations both at home and abroad.

In the end, then, the new library philosophy, while it required abandoning librarianship's authoritarianism, left the elitism of the profession untouched. Imagining that "the audience for the book is self-limiting," the library's clientele remained middle and upper class. "This suited librarians, for they felt much more comfortable with the middle class patrons who made up the majority of the library's clientele, than they did with the rough, inarticulate, poorly educated, and unappreciative masses of the country."[100] Even though today's public libraries—especially main or downtown branches—provide spaces and services for marginalized populations, many library workers are uncomfortable with them, and the class structure is immediately apparent when one considers the demographics and locations of suburban library branches. Indeed, the Little Free Library movement, as Schmidt and Hale have argued, is very much a bourgeois phenomenon, often most widely used in wealthy, suburban locations.[101]

The Neoliberal Library

Throughout the postwar period, as part of the mechanism of class collaboration, a larger share of industrial profits went to labor,

---

100   Harris, 43–44.

101   Jane Schmidt and Jordan Hale, "Little Free Libraries®: Interrogating the Impact of the Branded Book Exchange," *Journal of Radical Librarianship* 3 (2017): 30.

resulting in a rising standard of living among some sections of the working class. As David Harvey argues, as long as growth continued apace, the capitalist class was prepared to accept a smaller share of profits in return for stability and social peace. At the end of the 1960s, however, profit rates that had remained high since the capitalist restructuring after 1945 began to fall, with growth collapsing in the early 1970s. In order to restore capitalist power in the welfare state countries, deregulation, precarious labor, austerity, and an increase in job loss through automation became part of the economic programme of recovery. However, still fearing unrest and revolution, especially after the revolts of May 1968, capitalism sought to sweeten the deal by recuperating the desire for individual personal freedom from the collective constraints of welfare capitalism that informed the counterculture and exploded in the late sixties. As Harvey explains, "an open project around the restoration of economic power to a small elite would probably not gain much popular support. But a programmatic attempt to advance the cause of individual freedoms could appeal to a mass base and so disguise the drive to restore class power."[102] The cynical harnessing of a desire for more personal freedom to a project of the restoration of class power illustrates how good capitalism is at coopting resistance movements to its own cause.

Neoliberalism—the economic programme that promised a return to profitability—found its ideological justification in the student and worker demands for individual freedoms, recuperating these demands and putting them to use in furthering the capitalist agenda. Thus we have, in the early 1970s, a younger generation anxious for "freedom" from the constraints demanded by social solidarity under the welfare state, and a socio-political project that seeks to harness this desire in order to restore class power.

By directing the desire for individual freedoms against state regulation at home and interventionist policies abroad, capitalism could seek to pressure policy makers into adopting deregulationist policies designed to free up space for capitalism to increase the rate

---

102   Harvey, *Brief History of Neoliberalism,* 40.

of exploitation and thereby the rate of profit. And while the neoliberal economic program was appropriate for the practical requirements of policy, it still needed to emphasize individual liberty, re-
packaged as liberty of consumer choice, lifestyle differences, and a
plurality of cultural practices. It is in this sense that neoliberalism is
a "new liberalism" and not fundamentally at odds with either classical liberalism or the embedded liberalism of the postwar period.
The next two chapters will investigate two aspects of the neoliberal library in detail: the question of epistemology and "library science" under postmodernism, and of library labor in the age of in-
telligent machines.

Chapter Six

The Library Myth

Antinomies of Library Science

In 1975, the philosopher of science Roy Bhaskar saw a paradox in the distinction between knowledge and the objects of knowledge.

> Any adequate philosophy of science must find a way of grappling with this central paradox of science: that men in their social activity produce knowledge which is a social product much like any other, which is no more independent of its production and the men who produce it than motor cars, armchairs or books, which has its own craftsmen, technicians, publicists, standards and skills and which is no less subject to change than any other commodity. This is one side of 'knowledge'. The other is that knowledge is '*of*' things which are not produced by men at all.[1]

---

1   Bhaskar, *A Realist Theory of Science,* 21.

This paradox echoes Marx's own epistemological position, which is that "the mode of production of material life conditions the general process of social, political and intellectual life,"[2] and which underpins historical materialism in general and Marx's theory of ideology in particular. This contradiction—between the material basis of knowledge and theoretical knowledge itself—is inscribed in librarianship in the tension we have already seen between practical, concrete library work, and the discursive formations that attend that work. For Bhaskar, the empirical objects, causes, and effects that populate the real world are "intransitive" in that their existence and behavior are independent of human presence or activity. In contrast,

> the *transitive* objects of knowledge... are the raw materials of science—the artificial objects fashioned into items of knowledge by the science of the day. They include the antecedently established facts and theories, paradigms and models, methods and techniques of inquiry available to a particular scientific school or worker... The intransitive objects of knowledge are in general invariant to our knowledge of them: they are the real things and structures, mechanisms and processes, events and possibilities of the world; for the most part they are quite independent of us[3]

What Bhaskar is proposing is a theory of knowledge based on the strict separation between knowledge about the world (which is often based on *other* knowledge) and the real mechanisms and processes that occur in the world. Such a separation is the cornerstone of Jameson's political unconscious as well, since the "real ground" of history is unavailable to us except through narrative representations. The space between knowledge and reality, or between narrative and history, is precisely the space in which both science and ideology thrive. Indeed, the contradiction—not to mention the

---

2   Marx, *Contribution to the Critique of Political Economy,* 20–21.

3   Bhaskar, *A Realist Theory of Science,* 21–22.

difficulty in perceiving the difference—between science and ideology is one of the main concerns of the Marxist project.

Librarianship—like the world itself—is full of contradictions or antinomies, tensions, productive or causal, non-static dichotomies, dialectical "unities of opposites," such as that between enlightenment and social control, between concrete library work and the more intellectual labor of library science, or between men's and women's work, the center and the periphery, etc. Such productive tensions have existed at least since the founding of the American Library Association. In the first issue of *Library Journal*, founded to coincide with the ALA itself, Dewey writes that—"at last"—librarianship may be considered a profession. The dating of "professional" librarianship to 1876 fits with much of what we have already discussed in terms of periodization: the development of what seems like a new stage of industrial technology and a new expansion of "democratic" procedures, either in good faith (expanding the franchise) or in bad (to manage the unruly lower classes). In addition to his usual transcendent language—librarians stand "in the front rank of the educators of their communities, side by side with the preachers and the teachers"[4]—Dewey draws another point of historical contrast, between an oral and a literary political culture:

> The people are more and more getting their incentives and ideas from the printed page. There are more readers and fewer listeners, and men who move and lead the world are using the press more and the platform less... The largest influence over the people may be wielded most surely and strongly through our libraries.[5]

The mark of professionalization, in Dewey's view, is the transformation of the librarian from "his" role simply as keeper and preserver

---

4 Melvil Dewey, "The Profession" in *Landmarks of Library Literature, 1876–1976*, ed. Dianne J. Ellsworth and Norman D. Stevens (Metuchen, NJ: Scarecrow Press, 1976), 21.

5 Dewey, "The Profession," 21.

of materials to educator and molder of the consciousness of society. It is here, I think, that the curious dichotomy between the pragmatics of library work and its transcendental, missionary character—born, possibly, from Dewey's own ambition and arrogance—first comes to light. Dewey's professional librarian is himself one of the "men who move and lead the world":

> Such a librarian will find enough who are ready to put themselves under his influence and direction and, if competent and enthusiastic, he may soon largely shape the reading, and through it the thought, of his whole community.[6]

The early profession had no illusions about "neutrality"—it saw itself as engaged with influencing and giving direction to society; and while the profession saw *itself* as doing altruistic and missionary work, some library historians have pointed out the social control function inherent to the work of the early modern public library. In their analysis of the social control thesis as it applied to the founding of the Boston Public Library, Harris and Spiegler concluded that

> One reason the public library has proven so inhospitable and cold for the man on the street is that it was designed to control him and not to liberate him. The authoritarian nature of early public libraries has been amply documented, and yet librarians seem confused and frustrated at their failure to reach the 'masses.'[7]

In many ways, the history of modern librarianship is nothing more than the dialectical working out of the contradiction between competence—technical, pragmatic, concrete library work which served through technical means to reproduce capitalist property and social

---

6   Dewey, "The Profession," 22.

7   Harris and Spiegler, "Everett, Ticknor and the Common Man," (264)

relations—and enthusiasm (vocational awe, missionary zeal, transcendentalism). To my mind this dichotomy maps onto two representations of library history. The first sees library history as the development of concrete, technical, instrumental work—requiring no explicit ideology as such, and in fact *resistant* to the idea of theorizing beyond the necessary practical level. This reproduces ideological and material structures of domination through the work itself, as can be seen most clearly in the case of particular values encoded in subject headings[8] and search algorithms.[9] The second representation of library history posits an influencing, enlightening, in some ways a *civilizing* mission for libraries. The transcendental discourse of librarianship informs both of these historical models; it gives a basic orientation to practical, technical library work, and it provides a more fleshed out, progressive ideology to underpin the philosophy of librarianship and "library science." We can call this a distinction between materialism and idealism, in all senses of those terms. In his own discussion of librarianship as a profession, Archibald MacLeish sees the book as a metaphor for these two strains of librarianship, since the book combines both materiality and textuality. Librarians, for MacLeish, can either see themselves as the keepers of the physical book ("the small, clothbound object of 110 pages of text and vi of front matter") or of the immaterial "intellectual book":

> It makes a difference whether the book is the cloth and paper of the intellectual image. If it is the physical book of which the librarian is keeper, then the character of his profession is obvious enough. He is a custodian as all keepers of physical objects are custodians, and his obligations are a custodian's obligations... But if it is not the physical book but the intellectual book of which the

---

8   Sanford Berman, "Libraries to the People," in *Revolting Librarians*, edited by Celeste West (San Francisco: Booklegger Press, 1972), 56.

9   Matthew Reidsma, "Algorithmic Bias in Discovery Systems," *Matthew Reidsma* (blog), March 11, 2016. https://matthew.reidsrow.com/articles/173.

> librarian is the keeper, then his profession is of a very dif-
> ferent kind.[10]

In MacLeish's view, it seems that these two strains of library work are incommensurable, the occupations of two completely distinct types of worker. And indeed, we have seen how this distinction is, almost from the beginning, a gendered one: women are custodians, men are keepers of the intellectual book, influencing and directing society. For MacLeish, who was a poet as well as Librarian of Congress, the intellectual book is sacred ("the intellectual book is the Word"), and this very sacredness calls for partisanship and advocacy. At the time MacLeish was writing—1940—civilization itself seemed to be under attack by the combined forces of Fascism and Nazism and, as he writes in another article from the same year, "no one can ask with earnestness and intelligence how our own democracy can be preserved without asking at the very outset how his own work, his own activity, can be shaped to that end."[11] It is easy to understand how a poet—a "keeper of the word"[12]—faced with what Churchill memorably described as "the gathering storm" could hold transcendental views such as these, and in the current conjuncture it is tempting to subscribe to them oneself. Certainly, it is refreshing to read a librarian advocating something other than neutrality, even if the cause was a crisis of capitalism's own making:

> Keepers of books, keepers of print and paper on the
> shelves, librarians are keepers also of the records of
> the human spirit—the records of men's watch upon
> the world and on themselves. In such a time as ours,
> when wars are made against the spirit and its works, the

---

10   Archibald MacLeish, "Of the Librarians' Profession," in *Landmarks of Library Literature, 1876–1976*, ed. Dianne J. Ellsworth and Norman D. Stevens (Metuchen, NJ: Scarecrow Press, 1976), 15–16.

11   MacLeish, "The Librarian and the Democratic Process," 385.

12   Tomas Venclova and Alexandra Heidi Karriker, "Czesław Miłosz: Despair and Grace," *World Literature Today* 73, no. 4 (1999): 679.

keeping of these records is itself a kind of warfare. The
keepers, whether they wish so or not, cannot be neutral.[13]

This perspective in and of itself is connected to a whole history of
class, technology, and power. In "The Paradox of the Book," James
W. Carey draws the same distinction between the physical and the
immaterial book, connecting textuality and literacy to a complex
social history:

> The Book refers less to a manufactured object than to
> a canon: a selective tradition of the best that has been
> thought and written in the Western tradition. But it
> condenses, as well, certain skills and values: hieratic lit-
> eracy, the ability to write, comment upon and interpret
> these texts in some depth; *homo literratus,* a certain type
> or figure of unquestioned rectitude and honor; and a
> certain way of life in which the intercourse with books
> connects to wider habits of feeling and conduct—hab-
> its which we will call, in the honored sense, bourgeois...
> The equation linking the book and literacy with wisdom
> and progress is seen as part of a complex ideology that
> justified the technology of printing as it served the inter-
> ests of those who controlled it.[14]

What I want to underscore here is that the tension around "neutrality," in MacLeish's framing, is inextricably connected with the
contradiction between pragmatic and vocational librarianship, between competence and enthusiasm. MacLeish is wrong to see the
"custodians" and the "keepers of the human spirit" as two distinct kinds of profession; librarianship includes both, and just as
those who would like to "remain neutral" and occupy themselves
purely with the work of "running information agencies" must be

---

13   MacLeish, "Of the Librarians' Profession," 20.

14   JW W. Carey, "The Paradox of the Book." *Library Trends* 33, no. 2 (1984): 106–7.

awakened, so too must those who see the library as an unmixed pro-
ponent of civilization and the human spirit be made to see the complicity of library work—in both its aspects—in the inequality and
oppression of capitalist society.

Perhaps it is the case that all of the cultural problems with
librarianship spring from the productive dialectic between these
two poles. Indeed, Pierce Butler argues that the theoretical, not to
say transcendental, aspect of librarianship arose out of the long history of concrete practice itself, in a clear example, I would argue,
of historical materialism in action. Butler writes that while libraries
have a long history, they generally supported pragmatic or concrete
library work. Butler sees the modern library as developing "spontaneously and almost inadvertently" "without anyone planning or
foreseeing very far ahead."[15] Institutionally speaking, this may not
quite be the case (tax-funded public libraries in Britain and the US
required acts of legislation which—one hopes—implies a certain
level of deliberation and foresight). Butler sees this evolution as the
normal way of cultural phenomena, and along with the modern library, the "intellectual content" of librarianship arose only gradually. Butler writes that

> Theory followed practice instead of leading it. As the li-
> brary system was forming itself, librarians were becom-
> ing ever more aware of the larger significance of their of-
> fice. Librarianship, figuratively speaking, was becoming
> self-conscious.[16]

However, the self-consciousness of librarianship has always been
subject to the dynamics and pressures of ideology, to the extent that
what is generally accepted as library history might more properly be
described as a library myth.

---

15   Butler, "Librarianship as a Profession," 25.

16   Butler, 25.

Capitalist Hegemony and the Library Myth

In 1940, Archibald MacLeish wrote that "the principal difficulty" of the attempt to "put librarianship on a professional basis" was that "it has proved impossible to arrive at a common agreement as to the social end which librarianship exists to serve."[17] Such a view of the importance of consensus or social solidarity—both in terms of the need for librarianship to have a social end *and* a need for a common agreement upon it—prefigured the discursive or ideological basis of the welfare state after 1945. The problem, in MacLeish's view, was made acute by the "crisis of democracy" inaugurated by the rise of Fascism and made manifest by the Second World War. In order to be adequate to the crisis, to side with and support "democracy" in the struggle then taking place, it was not enough for librarians to restrict themselves to the practical, technical duties they were engaged in.

> If librarians accept a responsibility for the survival of democracy insofar as they can assure that survival, if librarians accept a measure of responsibility to make available to the people the precedents (in the form of documents) upon which the people's decision and action must be based in order to govern, then librarians cannot satisfy that responsibility merely by delivering books from the stacks as they are requested. Nor can they satisfy that responsibility in reference libraries merely by supplying scholars with the materials of scholarship. They must do far more.[18]

Once again, the primacy of the transcendental term in the dialectic of librarianship is expressed and reinforced. However, MacLeish is also expressing what Pierce Butler sees as a "third phase" in the

---

17   MacLeish, "The Librarian and the Democratic Process," 385.

18   MacLeish, 388.

development of librarianship as a "socially-minded" profession.[19] The 1939 Library Bill of Rights was the culmination of this initial outflow of social-mindedness, a reconstructed social solidarity for the new, mass democratic society that was coming into being out of the "Age of Empire."[20] At the same time, the socially-minded profession did not expunge the technical, pragmatic view of librarianship. Instead it inaugurated what might be thought of as a second, parallel stream, one that posed reading and hermeneutics against an instrumental view of texts and information,[21] social responsibility against "intellectual freedom,"[22] humanism against technocracy and, indeed, lifeworld against system.[23] This parallel track within the profession is still with us today, as can be seen in the debates over the ALA's Bill of Rights interpretation in 2018, and the continued significance of "critical" versus "mainstream" librarianship. The discipline of LIS occupies an uneasy, ambivalent relationship with both of these tendencies.

In his call for social solidarity and a defense of democracy, however, MacLeish relies on a fictitious library history, one in which the library, in the words of more recent scholars,

> had championed the cause of community by promoting social class mixing, a democratic ethos and a mild doctrine of outreach/extension into society. This interest in community can be traced back to the idealist vocabulary of social fellowship uttered by early supporters and promoters, but has resurfaced in the post-war, welfarist

---

19   Butler, "Librarianship as a Profession," 25.

20   Eric Hobsbawm, *Age of Empire: 1875–1914* (London Abacus, 1987).

21   Day, *Indexing it All*, 15.

22   Samek, *Intellectual and Social Responsibility*, 77.

23   Jürgen Habermas, *The Theory of Communicative Action, Volume 2: Lifeworld and System: A Critique of Functionalist Reason* (Boston: Beacon Press, 1987), 340.

era in a more virile form, backed by both community 'as state' and 'as service.'[24]

Such a view, as work by Black on the social and intellectual context of the early British public library, as well as the "revisionist" history done by Michael Harris in the 1970s has shown, is completely fictitious, an ideological justification for libraries instrumental in the maintenance of capitalist hegemony and the reproduction of capitalist subjectivities. Not only, then, did librarians like MacLeish have a desire to support the post-war consensus but they saw in the fictitious narrative a historical justification and professional responsibility to do so. Librarianship, post-war reconstruction, and revival of the capitalist economy went hand in hand with the shift of global hegemony from Europe to the United States.

Alistair Black's *New History of the English Public Library* begins by interrogating this fictitious history. "For the vast majority," Black writes, "the public library is today viewed superficially" in that both librarians and the broader public subscribe to a library myth.

> Its social neutrality and impartiality are almost mythical, reflecting, as it were… characteristics of moderation, gradualism, reserve, tolerance, fair play, reflective investigation, seriousness, respectability, quaintness, rational leisure, mild eccentricity, and respect for tradition… Yet the true story of the public library, certainly in its early years, does not read so simply. Fictitious narrative, which constitutes the essence of myth, is the defining factor in popular attitudes—generally revolving around an innocuous dissemination of 'sweetness and light'— towards the public library's past development and, indeed, present purpose.[25]

---

24 Alistair Black and David Muddiman, *Understanding Community Librarianship: The Public Library in Post-Modern Britain* (London: Ashgate, 1997), 6.

25 Black, *New History*, 2.

From his perspective, MacLeish's call for librarians to "step up" in the name of democracy was simply the reaction of the liberal, Arnoldian belief in 'sweetness and light' to the challenge of Fascist barbarity.

Much of the glorifying of library history—despite Harris' work to revise it, which we will look at next—relies on this kind of uncritical view of libraries as institutions essential for the flourishing of democracy, liberalism, and the bourgeoisie, as maintainers of a culture "open to all," as neutral, objective, and impartial. Even those who criticize the current state of libraries—Ed D'Angelo and John Buschman, for example—see them as having fallen from a prior period of uncorrupted sweetness and light, desecrated and corrupted under the pressure of postmodernism, consumerism,[26] or the "new public philosophy."[27] Such a view not only relies on an erroneous belief in the sanctity of libraries, but also in periods of "good capitalism" during which the library as a democratic institution could pursue its proper mission. Still, in 2018, Buschman attempts to hold on to a vision of a democratic American society supported by the library. The nature of American democracy may have changed, Buschman argues, but new theoretical approaches—such as he finds in the work of Jane Jacobs and Amartya Sen—"helps us locate the individual's actions within social results healthy to society and democracy—and what library places do for them."[28] Buschman does not argue with the traditional view (the fictitious narrative) that the role of libraries is to "foster informed discourse and exchange" in order to produce the informed citizenry necessary for a democratic society:

> This of course is a cornerstone of the field and, given political history and its relationship to control/manipulation

---

26 D'Angelo, *Barbarians,* 1.

27 Buschman, *Dismantling the Public Sphere,* 170.

28 John Buschman, "Everyday Life, Everyday Democracy in Libraries: Toward Articulating the Relationship", *The Political Librarian* 4, no. 1 (2018): 24.

of information, it would be perverse to argue with these approaches and the principles behind them.[29]

At most, Buschman finds such approaches "too one-sided... often essentializing it down to an information literacy problem." "What we need," Buschman argues, "is a theory of how democracy works on the ground socially... and what role libraries play in those social processes."[30] Buschman's presumption is still of a democratic American republic supported and made possible by libraries and librarians.

1939: The Library Bill of Rights

While public libraries retreated behind a newly formulated "neutral" and technocratic (practical) mission, academic libraries were being incorporated by the developing military-industrial complex. "Campus scholars (especially from the sciences) fought for a share of the research and development money being allocated by government and industry to the public sector and in many cases formed partnerships with corporate and industrial America to conduct that research"[31] which increased the demand on academic libraries while also providing opportunities for expansion and diversification. Despite a push from some library directors to recenter books and reading within the network of library services, librarianship embraced military-industrial work:

> In the early 1950s, [Jesse] Shera [then dean of Western Reserve's School of Library Science] wanted librarianship to form links with a group of scientists that traced its roots to World War II, when the federal government established an Office of Scientific Research and

29   Buschman, "Everyday Life," 18.

30   Buschman, 18.

31   Wiegand, "Tunnel Vision," 14.

Development to accelerate the war effort. In it director Vannevar Bush supervised 6,000 scientists, many of whom worried about controlling the rapidly expanding body of scientific and technical information with which they had been dealing.[32]

Libraries thus aligned with the requirements and aims of the military-industrial complex. However, material inequalities continued despite the postwar consensus, leading in the late 1960s to the existence of an alternative press, indeed an entire counterculture, that represented the lives of many constituencies that did not conform to the dominant culture and thus fell outside the concerns of military and industrial librarianship. These constituencies included political radicals, feminists, queer activists, rebellious teenagers, and minorities, and many of the most outspoken members were, significantly, students. Writing about changes in the media during this period, cultural theorist Stuart Hall argued that

> Whereas the value of the political consensus is the adherence to 'legitimate means for the pursuance of interests without resort to open conflict' [i.e. liberal pluralism], the highly heterogeneous groups I have mentioned are characterized either by political militancy, leading through extra-parliamentary politics to the varying types of 'confrontation', or by social disaffiliation, leading through collective and expressive acts of rebellion to the various types of civil disturbance. Civil righters, students, Black Power militants, political hijackers and kidnappers, shop stewards, fall into the political militancy category. Skinheads, hippies, squatters, soccer hooligans, psychedelic freak-outs, fall into the social disaffiliation category.[33]

---

32 Wiegand, 14.

33 Hall, *Selected Political Writings,* 113.

Such widespread social disaffiliation in the face of a responsibility to support the liberal/pluralist postwar consensus was bound to cause problems for librarianship. For Hall, there was a "hidden consensus" within the media to treat each side in a conflict much differently. Hall recalls

> numerous instances when Ulster civil rights militants were confronted with the consequences of violence. But I cannot recall a single instance when an Ulster magistrate or politician was confronted with the equally tenable view, succinctly expressed by Conor Cruise O'Brien, that since Ulster society has for so long been based on the dominance of a minority over a majority, no fundamental change in that structure can be expected without its accompanying release of the 'frozen violence' inherent in the situation.[34]

The hidden consensus that determined *how* things were reported, however, "must be located outside the broadcasting media proper, at the heart of the political culture itself."[35] The (liberal, pluralist) postwar consensus contained within it

> a view of politics based on the relative absence of violence… the relative degree of integration between the powerful corporate interest groups within the state. This negotiated consensus is both a historical fact and a source of ideological comfort.[36]

The 1939 Library Bill of Rights enshrined this consensus in a document that has provided ideological comfort to the profession ever since. By the late 1960s, however, as Hall mentions, cracks in the

---

34   Hall, 111.

35   Hall, 112.

36   Hall, 112.

consensus were beginning to appear. The debate over objectivity that emerged in the 1960s, and similar in many ways to the debates in the media which Hall analyzes, "introduced a professional identity crisis"[37] that mirrored the crisis of the entire postwar consensus in the industrialized West. It is no surprise that 1967—the Summer of Love—was a watershed year for both American Librarianship and Vietnam War protest: the two tendencies came together when a group of librarians protested a pro-War speech during the ALA conference in San Francisco.[38]

Social Justice and Social Responsibility

Between 1967 and 1973, a debate emerged over the continued applicability or desirability of the "balanced" viewpoint enshrined in the Library Bill of Rights. David Berninghausen's 1972 article, "Antithesis in Librarianship" framed the antagonism as between intellectual freedom and social responsibility. The intellectual freedom argument was essentially as follows: librarians ostensibly follow technical, value-free, and neutral processes when developing a collection, thus creating a collection that is not biased to one side or another, allowing users to fully employ their intellectual freedom in using the collection. The social responsibility side argued that library collections are *never* neutral: besides the fact that a given library can never purchase *everything*, librarians *always* use their judgement in selecting materials for acquisition. As we are painfully aware today, even when we seem to take human judgement out of the equation, our automated processes simply encode and reinforce the values of the humans who create them in the first place. As Safiya Noble puts it in relation to library search systems, "the digital interface is a material reality structuring a discourse, embedded with historical relations, working often under the auspices of ludic

---

37   Samek, *Intellectual and Social Responsibility*, 2.

38   Samek, 3.

capitalism."[39] Berninghausen essentially argued for what today we would think of as an ostensible objectivity of algorithms. Intellectual freedom, in his view, required a neutral or objective collection policy, and any deviation from this objectivity—to collect materials by or about under-represented groups, for example—was tantamount to censorship.

In a collection of responses to Berninghausen's article, various authors took issue with this dichotomy, both for arguing that intellectual freedom was the only ethical concern for librarians, and for misunderstanding (or misrepresenting) the social responsibility movement. In this context, then, Toni Samek's work uncovers the emergence of a political challenge to mainstream librarianship (which in North America tends to mean hegemony of the ALA). This challenge was not restricted to librarianship but was part of a growing tension within information professions—like the media in Hall's article—and in Western society at large. Such changes within librarianship can be mapped to the transition from mass, industrial, postwar society to the neoliberal society that arose out of the dismantling of the welfare state in the 1970s and 1980s. Such a mapping can, I think, allow us to connect the social responsibility debate in librarianship to the 1968 revolutionary moment, as well as the transition from Fordist/Keynesian welfare-state capitalism to the neoliberal conjuncture.

In his history of neoliberalism, David Harvey argues that "values of individual freedom and social justice are not… necessarily compatible," and it was this conflict that gave space to neoliberalism to repurpose the explosive energy of the 1968 movement into its project of economic and political restructuring. Harvey identifies a tension between the demand for individual freedoms, such as that espoused by the alternative press in California, students in Paris, and factory workers in Turin, and the solidarity required for social justice. The root of the tension lay precisely in this solidarity, which can and was used to justify both the power of the welfare state *and* the critique of the state itself. In Harvey's view, Left movements in

---

39   Noble, *Algorithms of Oppression*, 148.

1968 failed to recognize or confront, let alone transcend, the inherent tension between individual freedoms and social justice.

It was precisely this contradiction that also lay at the heart of the Berninghausen debate and other debates around social justice in librarianship in the early neoliberal period. Thus Berninghausen sees "social peace" through neutrality and "intellectual freedom" as of more importance than mitigating the dominance of the American state and bourgeois culture, both abroad (as in the Vietnam War) and at home (in the promotion of white, heterosexual, middle-class values, and the erasure of alternative perspectives, lifestyles, etc.). Berninghausen, following Weber, recognized the importance of social, economic, and political issues, and believed that librarians were free to engage with these issues privately, but he saw professional practice as by necessity separate from them, and professional engagement with them as detrimental to the work. What Berninghausen was unconsciously proposing was a Weberian model of professionalism in which practice serves to maintain hegemony under the guise of value-free neutrality. In welfare-state capitalism, balance and neutrality served to maintain social peace and stability. Under neoliberalism, the push for representation by alternative or marginalized populations served to support the dismantling of the social safety net. The point is that both sides of the social responsibility debate were used to maintain capitalist hegemony: before 1973, balance and neutrality supported the welfare state, while after 1968, social responsibility—perversely enough—was recruited to support the neoliberal project.

Seen from this perspective, the role of the ALA after 1945 was to maintain a balance of competing interests in order to keep the lid on social antagonisms that threatened to boil over and challenge the hegemony of positivism, liberalism, and the postwar way of life. In a perspective that resonates again at the current conjuncture, Berninghausen argued that "all sides" of controversial topics should be represented in library collections, supporting a position of class collaboration and social solidarity. On the other hand, the social responsibility movement promoted the selection and dissemination of specific materials in the furtherance of social justice, supporting a narrative of consumer and lifestyle choice easily coopted by neoliberal ideology. This malleability or polymorphism is one of the main mechanisms by which the liberal view—classical, embedded, or neo—unconsciously supports capitalist domination. If some form of liberalism always underpins librarianship as its "political unconscious", then librarianship can only resist capitalism if it gives up on liberalism. For both MacLeish and Berninghausen, library values needed to be firmly "centrist", opting for the "lesser evil" compared first to Fascism, then to left-wing social revolution on the 1968 model. But if capitalism is always to be supported as the "lesser evil," then what chance do progressives have for real social change?

Social Responsibility and Freedom Today

Today, bourgeois democracy—such as it is—faces a crisis similar to, though perhaps more insidious than the one it faced in 1939: the rise of far-right movements and related populist demagogues, combined with the tracking and surveillance made possible by the technological revolution of the 1990s, itself part of a broader process of capitalist restructuring under neoliberalism. Both the far-right movements and the technical capacity for surveillance benefit corporations and the state. And yet in the face of this new crisis, it seems that librarianship has not really changed very much. "No one can think of librarianship," MacLeish wrote in 1940, "without concluding that the notions of librarianship sometimes held are less than adequate." Eighty years after the Library Bill of Rights—inadequate to its purpose as soon as it was issued—and fifty years after the founding of the ALA's Social Responsibility Round Table, we still cannot agree on the principles and purposes—the social end—of our profession. Just as in 1940, "no generally accepted or acceptable definition of the function of librarianship has yet been found." And now, as then, the rise (or resurgence) of Fascism, "forces us as librarians to reconsider our librarianship, not in a vacuum, and not in relation to ourselves, but in relation to a democratic society." If we want to "do more" to combat fascism or the ideological reproduction of capitalism, we must resist these uncritical platitudes, especially given the resurgence lately of critical perspectives on librarianship and information science.

Such critical perspectives are not new, of course; indeed social critique led to both the Bill of Rights and the SRRT. The continuing presence of the Progressive Librarian Guild on the library scene provides continuity with past struggles, and the loose but vibrant #critlib movement, as well as the many unaligned interventions in race, gender, disability, and social class, all attest to a polyphonous movement of social justice within the library profession. That this movement has roots going back nearly a century without seeing much concrete change in the day to day work and organizational cultures of the profession itself is a sign that this struggle is long and arduous. But there remain librarians who are attempting not only to critique the dominant discourse of librarianship— of technical mastery and hierarchical organizations that stifle justice and change more than they encourage it—as well as librarians who are attempting to formulate strategies to address structures of oppression and domination *before* the crisis becomes acute. There are librarians who are trying, each in their own way, to follow MacLeish's injunction to "do more."

But we can't be sanguine about our ability to do more. There is a contradiction at the heart of MacLeish's view of librarianship. As I have been trying to demonstrate, library history—including its progressive wing—is embedded in the socio-economic changes taking place in society at large. Capitalism is expert at coopting or recuperating protest movements, bending them to the logic of profit and exploitation, while allowing a "false consciousness" of social justice to prevail. Social protest movements in the larger society are paralleled in librarianship as library activists try to oppose domination, support equality, facilitate participatory democracy, persuade politicians to take on social issues, and mobilize the general public to become more active participants in their civil institutions. However, most of our colleagues simply want to be left alone to do the "value free" job they were trained to do, comfortable within the liberal, technocratic hegemony of bourgeois culture. Just as library activism mirrors developments in the broader social and political world, so too does this contradiction between hegemony and dissent reflect wider contradictions in other social movements.

   In today's terms, we can recognize this tension in the ambiguity and overlap between some communists/anarchists and libertarians, as well as in the pernicious false equivalence between
Fascists and Antifa. The recognition that these tensions and contradictions exist in social reality and not merely in our understanding—as positivist social science holds—requires a different kind of
theory, a critical theory whose purpose is not merely to explain phenomena, but to describe the social realities which give rise to them,
and to offer strategic proposals to change them. Such a critical theory is encapsulated in Marx's eleventh thesis on Feuerbach: "The
philosophers have only interpreted the world, in various ways: the
point is to change it." Any critical theory of librarianship cannot be
satisfied with interpretation—the attempt to overcome contradictions by correcting error—but must concern itself with change. It is
in this respect that critical theory can look at the successes and the
failures of 1968 in order to continually reposition itself in opposition to the status quo of hegemonic power, whether that be the wider power of the state and civil society, or the narrower but no less
potent hegemony of the culture of librarianship itself.

Libraries and the State

In 1991, Mark Rosenzweig, editor of *Progressive Librarian*, wrote
that while

> most American librarians today take it for granted that
> our profession stands for the unequivocal defense of in-
> tellectual freedom, freedom of speech, and a number of
> other very fine principles... this static image of librari-
> anship is... a myth.[40]

Rosenzweig was writing in the context of an attempt to get the
ALA to take a position on the First Gulf War and the consequent

---

40   Mark Rosenzweig, "Politics and Anti-Politics in Librarianship," in
     Questioning Library Neutrality: Essays from Progressive Librarian, ed. Alison
     Lewis (Duluth: Library Juice Press, 2008), 5.

censorship by the US government. For Rosenzweig, it was precisely the apparent intrusion of politics into a supposedly neutral profession that made taking such a position so contentious to the ALA.
But the "intrusion" itself was an illusion, as Rosenzweig goes on to
remind us that politics and ideology have always been a structural component of libraries. This example provides a good illustration
of the way a particular "common sense" tries to limit the context of
a phenomenon (in this case, libraries themselves), endeavouring to
prevent "irrelevant" things like politics, social theory, and history
from complicating or tarnishing a worldview or reputation. Essentially, the hegemonic discourse of librarianship—and in a broader
sense liberalism itself—is predicated on a Cartesian rationalist theory of how libraries are in the world. As the philosopher Hubert
Dreyfus has written about artificial intelligence,

> Rationalists such as Descartes and Leibniz thought of
> the mind as defined by its capacity to form representa-
> tions of all domains of activity. These representations
> were taken to be theories of the domains in question, the
> idea being that representing the fixed, context-free fea-
> tures of a domain and the principles governing their in-
> teraction explains the domain's intelligibility.[41]

Dreyfus criticizes artificial intelligence research from a Heideggerian perspective: not only are we born into a particular history,
context, and tradition, but we can only ever see, understand, and
engage in the world through the framing provided by our social experience. To deny that in favor of a view of autonomous and unconstrained institutions—as the ALA does—is not only misguided, it
is positively dangerous: it is the position of the software engineers
that believe in the objectivity of the algorithms that are taking over
the post-neoliberal world. By linking the Gulf War and the history of libraries, Rosenzweig is attempting to remind librarians of the

---

41   Herbert Dreyfus, *What Computers Still Can't Do: A Critique of Artificial
     Reason* (Cambridge: MIT Press, 1992): xvii.

unavoidable social and historical context in which we live and operate. Such a reinstatement of the context—seen as unwarranted muddying of the waters by the ALA—creates a critical perspective on the issue at hand. The continuing relevance of the Progressive Librarians Guild (PLG) as well as newer movements like #critlib and radical librarianship in the UK attest to the fact that such conflicts between "neutrality" and "politics," between a dominant bourgeois "common sense" and radical resistance to it, also remain in full force.

The history of public libraries, as we have seen, is inextricably linked with the development of capitalist society and the rise to power of the bourgeois class. As a result, from their inception, public libraries have been implicated in the power and social control wielded by a new form of the state: the liberal-capitalist governments of the mid-nineteenth century. The role of public libraries in that period was to spread bourgeois ideology and to condition people to life under industrial capitalism. After the Second World War, the postwar consensus laid the foundation for the rise of the welfare state, and more importance was given to the social and collective values of librarianship, as the capitalist state needed to find ways to deradicalize and pacify a working class that had been plunged in war and economic depression for the best part of thirty years. Currently, the role of the "neutral" library is to create subjects appropriate to algorithmic, cognitive, surveillance capitalism.

The Chicago Graduate School and Positivism

At the turn of the present century, Wayne Wiegand took stock of the profession and found that "the body of critical scholarship detailing the historical role and impact of all types of libraries in the United States" was "too small, too light, too marginalized within librarianship, and too easily ignored" to counter wild fantasies proposed, for example, by technological evangelists.[42] In many ways, of course, we are still in this situation, with many even within the profession promoting the latest "disruption" or "pivot" either to bury

---

42   Wayne Wiegand, "Tunnel Vision," 3.

the obsolescent library or to solve all its problems. Wiegand suggests a way in which librarianship can address this problem:

> Perhaps the time is right to apply broader, more interdisciplinary and theoretically rich perspectives on that past in order to focus some attention on what I see as tunnel vision and blind spots affecting plans now being crafted for librarianship's future.[43]

This should sound familiar, for the call for broadening our theoretical perspectives, of taking advantage of other disciplines and other theoretical approaches has, *contra* Wiegand, long been a part of the culture of librarianship. Perhaps it is borne out of insecurity, perhaps out of a genuine desire to create a *discipline* out of librarianship; perhaps, in the end, it stems from a dissatisfaction with the pragmatic and positivist "library and information science" that is hegemonic within the profession. Such a theoretical position maintains a supposed objectivity (if not neutrality) and adopts the mantle of evidence-based social science. It subscribes to an instrumental view of texts and information informed by Paul Otlet's field of documentation,[44] but at the cost of a more hermeneutic approach that, as a result, we are constantly feeling the lack of and therefore are always trying to "bring back" into librarianship.

    While we tend to associate "library science" with the social-science turn in the 1920s and 30s, and specifically with the beginning of library graduate education in Chicago, the scientific pretensions of librarianship go back to the end of the 19th century, a time of rapid technological and scientific change. Otlet's first published work on bibliography appeared in 1892,[45] and at the 1893

---

43   Wiegand, 3.

44   Day, *Indexing it All*, 15–25.

45   Paul Otlet, "Something about Bibliography," in *International Organisation and Dissemination of Knowledge: Selected Essays of Paul Otlet*, ed. W. Boyd Rayward (Amsterdam, New York: Elsevier, 1990), 11–24.

ALA conference, Wiegand writes, "the 'library science' Dewey and his allies constructed for the library profession" made its first appearance.[46] Despite the theoretical work being done in the fields of documentation, bibliography, classification, etc., library education continued to focus on its practical or pragmatic side until the late 1920s. As opposed to the system set up by Dewey in the late 19th century, the Chicago Graduate Library School (GLS), which opened in 1928, "was designed to concentrate on research and to admit only Ph.D students."[47] The University of Chicago was part of a trend towards "mak[ing] the social sciences more 'scientific' by using quantitative methods," and as a result the work of the GLS "extrapolated from political science, sociology, and education to concentrate its research on the scientific investigation of reading."[48] From the early 1930s, however, the focus on reading was replaced by the study of library management and administration—technical work. For Wiegand, this move towards research into management practices constituted a missed opportunity:

> On the one hand, it failed to address concerns voiced by Helen Haines, who loudly complained about 'the mechanistic non-literary attitude' she thought characterized postwar library practice... One the other hand, the GLS also ignored newer research on the act of reading.[49]

Rather than focusing on reading as an act of engagement and interpretation (hermeneutics), "librarians continued to emphasize and improve professional expertise and management," conforming to the instrumental logic of capitalism which, in Horkheimer and Adorno's words

---

46 Wiegand," Tunnel Vision," 5.

47 Wiegand, 10.

48 Wiegand, 10.

49 Wiegand, 10.

> offered Enlightenment thinkers a schema for making
> the world calculable… For the Enlightenment, anything
> which cannot be resolved into numbers, and ultimate-
> ly into one, is illusion; modern positivism consigns it
> to poetry.[50]

In this period, as Ronald Day remarks, science (including library science) became part of a political economy of research projects and grants, in which "texts are treated as documents containing information, which are then usefully appropriated with other documents and information toward advancing research."[51] Libraries, then, become part of the infrastructure of this economy, with "library science" as the instrumental theory required for efficient management and operation of the library within its parent organization:

> Libraries or other information sources are viewed as part
> of this apparatus of production and reproduction. The
> needs of the scholarly user thus are often defined or re-
> fined by the system of scientific production in which
> they are located.[52]

In this context there is no room for "reading," or the hermeneutic exploration of texts—and the neat division between public and research libraries institutionalizes this division, one which goes back to the earliest days of the GLS. Research libraries—and the theory or philosophy underpinning them—are part of a "business of knowledge"[53] that is anything but independent, autonomous, or neutral. The empirical focus of much library research (i.e. evidence-based library and information research and practice) can be

---

50   Max Horkheimer and Theodor W. Adorno, *Dialectic of Enlightenment: Philosophical Fragments* (Stanford: Stanford University Press, 2002), 4–5.

51   Day, *Indexing it All*, 24.

52   Day, 24.

53   Day, 24.

explained by a cultural and historical shift towards science "under-stood as formally or informally collaborative and systemic research procedures and authorship, privately and publicly funded, which are project based and epistemically grounded in empirically gener-ated 'information,' whose current privileged form in our day is now quantifiable 'data.'"[54]

Just as early library practice and education responded to concrete pragmatic needs, especially when, at the beginning of the First World War, the state took the pressure of evaluation, judge-ment, and decision out of the hands of librarians,[55] "library sci-ence" is conditioned by the socio-economic structures in which it finds itself. The "political economy of knowledge" is a conjuncture in which both research and public libraries are deeply embedded.

After the Second World War, despite the resurgence of a "fundamentalist" view of books and reading as central to librari-anship (i.e. what we are calling the hermeneutic approach), librar-ianship extended its financial and research connection to the hard sciences underpinning the developing post-war "military-industrial complex."[56] This push—spearheaded by Vannevar Bush—required a transformation of libraries in order to partake in the increased funding available from the federal government. Not only has li-brarianship always been embedded within particular socio-eco-nomic conjunctures, but its theoretical apparatus has proved mal-leable enough to fit whatever form it is called upon to take. By the late 1950s,

> what Bush had called 'science information' was well placed to benefit from an infusion of federal funds, and because scientists generally agreed that tradition-al libraries were not meeting their needs, they began to

54   Day, 24.

55   Wiegand, "Tunnel Vision," 8.

56   Wiegand, 14–15. The term itself arose right after the Second World War and became widely known after Eisenhower used it in his 1961 Farewell Address.

> establish science information centers and initiate their
> own indexing and abstracting services to more rapidly
> retrieve the information they needed. Out of these ef-
> forts a postwar 'information science' was born.[57]

Information science, in Wiegand's view, privileged the instrumental over the hermeneutic approach to reading, information, and knowl-edge, and was designed "to serve the specific information needs of particular clienteles who enjoyed political or economic power."[58] Far from the ALA's stated goal of "making the American library a force for an ordered, enlightened, educated, and informed citi-zenry,"[59] librarianship in the Cold War became a force for the sci-entific and technological extension of American hegemony across the world.

The instrumental focus of library research continued un-abated until the early 1960s, as "the vast majority of postwar library literature and library research continued to address issues of library expertise and institutional management."[60] Very little had changed for library school graduates by then either:

> The model of library education they inherited grown
> from apprenticing in the nineteenth century into a train-
> ing program that by the 1920s was sometimes connect-
> ed to a major public library, sometimes to a universi-
> ty as an undergraduate program, and finally after 1950
> into a professional program located in a university grad-
> uate school... Once enrolled in library schools they took
> a core curriculum usually consisting of cataloging and
> classification, reference, management, book selection,
> and often a generic "Library in Society" course. The first

---

57   Wiegand, 15.

58   Wiegand, 15.

59   Wiegand, 3–4.

60   Wiegand, 18.

four addressed institution and expertise; the last was intended to socialize students to the "library spirit" and inculcate the "library faith" by celebrating the library as an institution.[61]

It was not until the 1970s, in Wiegand's view, that the "library faith" was finally challenged. Harris' 1973 article on the purpose of the public library and Harris and Spiegler's 1974 work on the "social control" thesis as it applied to the founding of the Boston Public Library were milestones in critical librarianship.[62] Wiegand argues that while Harris and Spiegler's work "struck at the heart of the library faith," this perspective was part of larger critical movement active within librarianship:

> The ALA had just weathered a revolt occasioned by hundreds of its younger members who saw in the principle of "neutrality" most often advocated by veteran librarians an excuse *not* to address inequities in library practice caused by racism, sexism, and homophobia, a rationale *not* to confront a government bent on conducting an unjust war in southeast Asia, and a mechanism to give the Library Bill of Rights a strict construction that rendered it ineffective in the fight to include alternative perspectives in library collections.[63]

For Wiegand, the history of the library in the twentieth century has been one of the privileging of an instrumental information science over a hermeneutic "personal information economy" focused on reading.

---

61 Wiegand, 19.

62 Harris, "The Purpose of the American Public Library."; Harris and Speigler, "Everett, Ticknor and the Common Man."

63 Wiegand, "Tunnel Vision, "19. Samek, *Intellectual Freedom,* 127–43.

> One gets the impression of a profession trapped in its own discursive formations, where members speak mostly to each other and where connections between power and knowledge that affect issues of race, class, age, and gender, among others, are either invisible or ignored. One also gets the impression of a profession much more interested in process and structure than in people.[64]

Wiegand also quotes from historian Leon Litwack's 1998 criticism of the University of California—Berkeley library system, a criticism which resonates even more today:

> In our eagerness to implement the new information technology… there is no sense of the need for balance, little or no awareness that different academic disciplines may have different needs, not all of them fulfilled by the new technology. We find ourselves, instead, embracing that technology uncritically, without considering cost, maintenance, reliability, and value.[65]

The latest round of such uncritical technological adoption involves the race to develop digital scholarship centers, which risks subsuming disciplinary difference under a generic conception of "scholarship" with little regard to cost or consequences. As Jane Schmidt remarked in her opening keynote for the 2018 conference of the Canadian Association of Professional Academic Librarians, "we are terrible at business but we spend a lot of money."[66]

---

64 Wiegand, "Tunnel Vision," 24.

65 Wiegand, 24–25.

66 Jane Schmidt, "Innovate This! Bullshit in Academic Libraries and What We Can Do About It," *RULA Digital Repository*: 15.

Epistemology and "Library Science"

Following his work in "revisionist" library history, Harris turned his attention to the theoretical underpinnings of librarianship. Drawing on "a long litany of severe critiques" of LIS research, Harris summarizes the problems identified within the literature as a combination of six factors:

1. there is too little research
2. what there is is methodologically primitive
3. LIS research lacks appropriate paradigms
4. progress would require more money and more planning
5. LIS researchers can't reach practitioners
6. practitioners aren't paying attention to research[67]

Each of these factors, to a greater or lesser extent, remains a common refrain within librarianship. However, Harris argues that these factors "not only fail to explain the problem but actually tend to mask its real nature,"[68] and that the problems with LIS research and practice lie in its pluralism and its positivist epistemology. In Harris' view, "the widespread, and generally uncritical commitment to a 'pluralist' paradigm (or world view) combined with a narrowly 'positivist' epistemology has severely delimited our perspective when defining relevant questions and the nature of relevant answers," concluding that "we suffer not from a lack of research, but rather from too much trivial work on the wrong questions."[69] In addition to defining the pluralist paradigm and how such a paradigm came to be combined with a positivist epistemology, Harris offers his own theory of library service in the United States.

---

67   Michael Harris, "State, Class, and Cultural Reproduction: Toward a Theory of Library Service in the United States," *Advances in Librarianship* 14 (1986): 211–12.

68   Harris, "State, Class and Cultural Reproduction," 212.

69   Harris, 212.

For Harris, both pluralism and positivism came to dominate the social sciences as a whole in the 1930s. From the 1930s and 40s on, he writes,

> the library was now portrayed as an institution that could play a vital role in promoting and preserving democracy in America by assisting the successful working of pluralist self-government [i.e. liberalism]. Librarians were seen as apolitical servants of the "people" and were expected to be completely neutral on social, economic, and political questions—a passive "mirror" of societal interests and values.[70]

This hegemonic liberal-pluralist view of democratic society had an effect on the perspectives available within LIS itself:

> Since society is pluralistic, and based on democratically arrived at consensus, and since libraries simply reflect that pluralist and democratic consensus, it follows that research should focus its themes of performance, productivity, and usefulness, that is, research that has come to be called "administrative."[71]

Thus the orientation of the field depends on a presumption of the pluralist, democratic credentials of American society. Such a perspective—ostensibly "value-free" and "neutral" but in reality upholding a liberal vision of society—led to the adoption of a positivist epistemology alongside the other social sciences. Harris argues that the quest for such a scientific footing was present in the profession from the beginning. In the last quarter of the nineteenth century, with science and technology developing apace, it is understandable that librarians should have sought to participate in such

---

70   Harris, 215.

71   Harris, 216.

innovation. Whatever the reason, "by the 1920s, strong voices were calling for the creation of a new awareness of science as the key to unlocking the mysteries of library management."[72] Like the library credentialism which developed after the founding of the ALA in 1876 and the opening of the first library schools—institutionalizing the difference between men's and women's library work—the adoption of the mantle of "social science" had as much to do with the academic and social standing of librarians as it did with a "value free," "objective" search for certainty. For the early library scientists of the Chicago Graduate Library School (GLS, founded in 1928),

> The positivist epistemology was in perfect harmony with the pluralist perspective, and offered researchers an "apolitical" method for investigating what were seen to be essentially technical questions. That is, since pluralism was both dominant and desirable in American life, library researchers could devote their attentions to perfecting their science while maintaining a "good" status quo and improving the profession's status within the prevailing order.[73]

By the 1960s, however, many social scientists were beginning to see the flaws in a one-sided positivism. However some fields, like librarianship and social psychology,[74] have continued to hold onto an uncritical positivism as their default epistemological position. In 1986 Harris could write that "[LIS] researchers assumed that [their] stance was value free and totally consistent with democratic premises of the pluralist perspective lying like an all-encompassing blanket over work in the field."[75] Periodically, the positivist privileging

---

72   Harris, 217.

73   Harris, 219.

74   Tom Bartlett, "'I Want to Burn things to the Ground'," *Chronicle of Higher Education*, (September 11, 2018).

75   Harris, "State, Class, and Cultural Reproduction, 221.

of "science" will be reformulated—as with "evidence-based" LIS, which derives from medical research—but a quick glance at recent library literature and research indicates that an uncritical positivism remains dominant within the profession, although it must be said that more and more space is being opened up for critical engagement.

Harris sees such uncritical adoption of both pluralism and positivism as dangerous:

> the pluralist perspective so widely and uncritically adopted by librarians has dictated long and broad structured silences relative to the ways in which social, economic, and cultural power relations shape the nature and extent of library service in America. Further... the positivist epistemology that has gained hegemony among researchers in this field has severely limited the range of questions that can be investigate and has rigidly defined the characteristics of relevant answers.[76]

In the face of such a reliance on pluralism and positivism, Harris offers an "alternative paradigm" for LIS research. In Harris' case, the theory draws from the thought of Gramsci and the field of cultural studies in order to try to develop a theory of ideology, culture, and social practice which might be of more relevance to librarianship. From careful consideration of these various intellectual strands, Harris concludes that

> What emerges is a sense of the library as an institution embedded in a stratified ensemble of institutions functioning in the high cultural region, an ensemble of institutions dedicated to the creation, transmission, and reproduction of hegemonic ideology. Such an interpretation challenges the "apolitical" conception of the library held by library professionals, and strips the library

---

76   Harris, 221–22.

of the ethical and political innocence attributed to it by
the pluralist social theorists.[77]

Such a conclusion is a core component of the long-standing trend
of (what's now called) critical librarianship running parallel to the
value-free hegemonic paradigm. However, Harris' position that his
theory "explains the central role of libraries—*the preservation, trans-
mission, and thus reproduction of the Book, and the audience of the
Book*"[78] is itself an attempt to close off debate, argument, and collective decision-making around precisely what the "central role" of libraries should be. The central role of libraries changes with the historical conjuncture, but it is also the site of debate and dissensus,[79]
constantly being challenged and defended. Thus, while we might
agree with the core of Harris' theory, such a theory can only be the
starting point in an attempt to *change* the library. In other words,
we should read Harris' theory in light of Marx's eleventh thesis on
Feuerbach. The basis of Harris' theory reads as follows:

> Libraries are marginal institutions embedded in a hier-
> archically arranged set of institutions designed to pro-
> duce and reproduce the dominant effective culture in
> print form. Power is asymmetrically distributed among
> these institutions, with some, like publishers and review-
> ers, empowered to create and produce cultural prod-
> ucts and others, like libraries limited to the transmis-
> sion and reproduction of the dominant effective culture.
> The library's structural and functional characteristics are

---

77 Harris, 241.

78 Emphasis in the original; by "Book" Harris is referring to the Book as
intellectual object, not the physical book, see J. W. Carey, "The Paradox of
the Book," *Library Trends* 33, no. 2 (1984): 103–14.

79 "There is politics because the common is divided," Jacques Rancière, "The
Thinking of Dissensus: Politics and Aesthetics," in *Reading Rancière: Critical
Dissensus*, ed. Paul Bowman and Richard Stamp (London, New York:
Continuum, 2011): 1.

> determined by its definition as an institution contrived
> to consume, preserve, transmit, and reproduce high cul-
> ture in printed form.[80]

This is fine as far as it goes, but Harris' "culturalist" stance pre-
cludes a wider understanding of the role libraries play within capitalist society: as a force which reproduces not merely high culture,
but the rules and behaviors required by class society itself. In other words, the ideological reproduction made possible by libraries
serves a more materialist purpose: the reproduction of capitalist relationships.

Unfortunately, Harris' theory only argues for *interpretation* ("we need to think about what libraries do in the much broader context of why libraries matter") rather than *change*. In order to
change libraries, which both requires changing wider society and
can contribute to such change, we have to go further than the prof-
fering of various alternative or "corrective" theories in an attempt
to adjust the theoretical framework without committing to a project of transformation. Since Harris' article appeared, a subfield of
library literature has arisen offering new theoretical models which
will address the shortcomings of LIS research. For example, John
Budd has responded to Wiegand's challenge for a "broader perspective" with the construction of a theory of "the library, praxis, and
symbolic power" drawing on Bourdieu.[81] Budd, too, restricts library theory to an interpretative rather than a transformative role:
"To avoid some blind spots and tunnel vision, librarians should become more reflective so that we can understand more completely
the complex exercises of symbolic power and cultural production
that can be embedded in human action generally and in praxis in librarianship specifically."[82] Similarly, Gary Radford offered his own

---

80   Harris, "State, Class, and Cultural Reproduction," 242.

81   John M. Budd, "The Library, Praxis, and Symbolic Power," 19–20.

82   Budd, 31.

response to Wiegand's challenge in the form of an engagement with communication studies and the work of Foucault.[83] For Radford,

> Invoking Foucault's archaeology in the context of Wiegand's problematic provides a framework in which to understand how (a) the discursive formation of LIS is itself a problem to be analyzed beside others, (b) the nature of the discursive formation hinders potentially fruitful research in LIS, and c) understanding Wiegand in terms of Foucault can help generate a new self-reflexive and critical attitude among LIS scholars to their own discursive formation and the discursive formations of others.[84]

Like Wiegand and Budd, Radford sees the problem with LIS research as a lack of reflexivity, something which can be addressed simply via the adoption of new critical attitudes. Once more, the interpretive aspect of theory ("a new self-reflexive and critical attitude... to their own discursive formation") is privileged over the transformational aspect. Radford's theory is constructed on the notion that "at its foundation, library scholarship, like all scholarship, consists of people talking to each other."[85] But in order for library scholarship to be anything but self-referential, it must be able to engage with its object of study, which is not library scholarship, but librarianship, not *representations* of libraries, but libraries themselves.

In his stirring defense of historical materialism as a social theory appropriate to a drastically warming world, Andreas Malm challenges the view that "everything is discourse." For Malm, postmodern discursive constructionism is an "epistemic fallacy": "just because we come to *know* about global warming through

---

83 Gary P. Radford, "Trapped in Our Own Discursive Formations: Toward an Archaeology of Library and Information Science," *Library Quarterly* 73, no. 1 (2003): 1–2.

84 Radford, 4–5.

85 Radford, 5.

measurements and comparisons and concepts and deductions," does not mean that "it *is in itself made up of those things*."[86] Indeed, Malm's argument supports the claim that while it is the case that "scholarship consists of people talking to each other," we cannot therefore conclude that talking is all there is. "As humans, we cannot say what a storm is like without deploying language, but that does not mean that the storm is a linguistic entity or consists of speech acts."[87] By the same token, while LIS scholarship requires the mobilization of language and consists in nothing else, librarianship is not a linguistic entity, nor does it consist entirely in speech acts. The bodily discipline of, say, silence in the library may be announced by signage, but it is enforced by very real, very physical security forces. Radford's conclusion, that the value of Foucauldian genealogy lies in "not giving clarity but in making strange" assumes an *idealist* position rather than a materialist one: intellectual unmasking is sufficient to change the world. In his discussion of constructivist theories of nature, Malm uses an argument that can serve to critique Radford's position. According to constructionism, Malm writes,

> The ontological status of global warming is that of an *idea*. So when the villages in a valley in Pakistan are swept away by a flood, or a monarch butterfly population collapses, or cities in Colombia run out of water due to extreme drought, it is not a real biophysical process but an idea that strikes them. The way to stop climate change would then be to give up that idea. Perhaps we can exchange it for global cooling.[88]

If we recognize the embeddedness of the library in social, cultural, and political dynamics, the role of the library in ideological and

---

86 Malm, *Progress of this Storm*, 25.

87 Malm, *Progress of this Storm*, 27.

88 Malm, *Progress of this Storm*, 24–25.

social reproduction, the support the library gives to racism, sexism, etc., then simply "making strange" the dominant discourse is not enough to effect real change. Changing the minds of library workers is not enough to change the culture or oppressive structures of libraries and librarianship. It is a component, to be sure, but as we have seen, our own ideological positions are difficult to overcome, and such overcoming can only come about through material struggle, partisan commitment to a cause of fundamental social change, and a collective—not individual—commitment at that.

Such proposals for alternative theoretical perspectives not only serve to embed a contemplative rather than a transformational scholarship within LIS—one whose legitimacy depends on your opinion of the status quo and your position in its structure of privilege and power—but it also ends up reproducing the very pluralism and positivism Harris criticized, thereby remaining constrained within the narrow confines of LIS as described by Wiegand. Only collective, material practice can free us from these theoretical constraints.

Chapter Seven

Truth Machines

According to the schema developed in Chapter Five, we can provisionally characterize industrial capitalism as a society of discipline and neoliberalism as a society of control. How then can we understand the changes in information and technology from one society to the other? What is the relationship between the truth and our machines? In *Discipline and Punish*, Foucault wrote: "written, secret, subjected, in order to construct its proofs, to rigorous rules, the penal investigation was a machine that might produce the truth in absence of the accused."[1] In the "post-truth" era of truth machines, what is the political economy of command and control?

In the first place, we have to recognize that the society of discipline does not come to an end with the advent of the society of control. The physical discipline of bodies remains an integral part of the state apparatus, even while technologies of control expand their sphere of operation. In *Between the World and Me*, Ta-Nehisi Coates warns his son that

---

1 Michel Foucault, *Discipline and Punish: The Birth of the Prison* (New York: Vintage, 1995), 37.

> destruction is merely the superlative form of a dominion
> whose prerogatives include friskings, detainings, beat-
> ings, and humiliations. All of this is common to black
> people. And all of this is old for black people. No one is
> held responsible.[2]

Just because capitalism has discovered new and subtle ways to exercise control over one—predominantly white and affluent–segment
of the population does not mean that physical discipline does not
retain its oppressive power and its potent violence. "Simply because we police ourselves… does not mean that there is no longer a distinction between the citizens and the police."[3] Recognizing
this distinction, we are still justified in asking how this self-polic-
ing came about, and what is the relationship between what Deleuze
has called "the societies of control"[4] and the regime of truth proper to those societies?

Inflection Points

The socio-economic changes that we can, since Deleuze, think
about in terms of a transition from societies of discipline to societies
of control are part of a larger cluster of changes apparent in every discipline: from the Fordist assembly-line to immaterial labor,
from the Keynesian welfare state to free-market neoliberalism, from
modernism to post-modernism. Indeed, the far-reaching nature of
these changes provides a multitude of options for periodizing this
transition, for defining its various moments. The May 1968 revolts,
the end of the Bretton Woods accords in 1971, the 1973 oil crisis,
the end of the Vietnam War in 1975, the 1979 election of Marga-
ret Thatcher, or the 1980 election of Ronald Reagan; these are all

---

2   Ta-Nehisi Coates, *Between the World and Me* (New York: Spiegel and Grau, 2015), 9.

3   Moufawad-Paul, *Austerity Apparatus*, 121.

4   Gilles Deleuze, "Postscript on the Societies of Control", *October* 59 (Winter 1992), 3.

significant moments in a transition that encompassed all of the centers of capitalism to say nothing of its effects on the periphery.

What is clear from this list of inflection points is that between the late 1960s and the early 1980s we witnessed a change in the socio-economic orthodoxy, as well as the power relations, of the capitalist world. The economic blueprint for this new orthodoxy[5] was laid down in 1962 in Milton Friedman's *Capitalism and Freedom*, written in the context of the society of discipline theorized a few years later by Foucault in *Discipline and Punish* (1975). In this society, discipline and coercion, just as much as social services and full employment, were equated with the "big state" of the New Deal and the post-war consensus. For Friedman, economic and political liberty were tightly coupled, and both were violated by the constraints of the welfare state. Liberty, in Friedman's view, was defined as an absence of coercion which could only be guaranteed by the free-and-equal contractual relationships between sovereign parties:

> The possibility of co-ordination through voluntary co-operation rests on the elementary yet frequently denied proposition that both parties to an economic transaction benefit from it, provided the transaction is bi-laterally voluntary and informed... Co-operation is strictly individual and voluntary provided: (a) that enterprises are private, so that the ultimate contracting parties are individuals and (b) that individuals are effectively free to enter or not to enter into any particular exchange, so that every transaction is strictly voluntary.[6]

---

5   It was hardly new, simply given a new twist. The sanctity of contract was an integral part of classic liberalism (cf. Rousseau's *Social Contract*) but was also a major part of Proudhon's critique of liberalism, roundly criticized by Marx. See William Clare Roberts, *Marx's Inferno: The Political Theory of Capital* (Princeton and Oxford: Princeton University Press, 2017), 161.

6   Milton Friedman, *Capitalism and Freedom* (Chicago: Chicago University Press, 1982), 19–20.

In this view, both the factory discipline of early capitalism and the Fordist/Taylorist discipline of the assembly line must be replaced by "voluntary" (self-)control. It follows that the transition from the society of discipline to the society of control is, in large part, a transition from the *external* disciplining of the labor force to the internalization of labor discipline through technologies of control, in order to bring about the apparent voluntarism and illusion of non-coercion of the neoliberal order. In effect, by taking labor discipline away from the state and making it a function of machines operating according to algorithms and statistics, social control itself is automated, and workers' participation in their "specific mode of subjection"[7] appears entirely voluntary. The neoliberal order thereby fits Friedman's model of voluntary and informed transactions, that is, freedom.

This argument is not entirely new. Friedman's insistence on the liberty of contractual parties is reminiscent of the formal requirement of capitalism that workers be "free in a double sense"— free both of traditional political bonds (to a feudal lord, for example) and free to sell their labor-power. Marx understood that this double freedom—socio-political and economic—was not real, but merely formal or logical—only the appearance of freedom. In the same way, Friedman's contracting parties are only formally free, free for the sake of argument. Friedman posits a world in which individuals, acting according to their interests, are free from all responsibility towards others.[8] This is the position Marx deconstructs in his critique of the "eighteenth century Robinsonades," the positing by classical political economists of a "state of nature" in which individual human beings were entirely self-sufficient, ignoring the social qualities of human activity which is a precondition of human society itself, let alone the individual. In the "Introduction" of 1857, Marx writes that this presumed state of individuals outside of and

---

7   Foucault, *Discipline and Punish*, 24.

8   Milton Friedman, "The Social Responsibility of Business is to Increase its Profits," *The New York Times Magazine*, September 13, 1970, 3.

not responsible to society was nothing but an *anticipation* of capitalist society, its origin myth:

> In this society of free competition, the individual appears detached from the natural bonds etc. which in earlier historical periods make him the accessory of a definite but limited human conglomerate... Not as a historic result but as history's point of departure. As the Natural Individual appropriate to their notion of human nature, not arising historically, but posited by nature. This illusion has been common to each new epoch to this day.[9]

Because *under capitalism* people are alienated from society and each other, this condition is made the *origin* of capitalist society, rather than its result, in an attempt to legitimate the capitalist order of things. The concept of free, uncoerced individuals voluntarily entering into exchanges is the "noble lie"[10] on which bourgeois economics and politics are based.

The "free" laborers thrown off the land and into the factories as capitalism developed found themselves part of the process of transition from a regime of bodily punishment to behavioral discipline described in *Discipline and Punish*. The techniques of maintaining social order changed focus in this period; in Foucault's words, their purpose became "not to punish the offense, but to supervise the individual."[11] By 2019, as we shall see, these techniques have changed again, to *internalize* the function of supervision itself. This new model of labor discipline, of social control, indeed the pacification of all society, is a modulation of the techniques for maintaining order from an external supervisory discipline (the

---

9 Karl Marx, *Grundrisse: Foundations of the Critique of Political Economy (Rough Draft)* (London: Penguin, 1973), 83. Marx had previously made the same argument in *The Poverty of Philosophy* (1847).

10 Plato, *The Republic*, 181–82.

11 Foucault, *Discipline and Punish*, 18.

Panopticon, Taylorism), to an internalized (self-)control (individualized tracking, gamification, hyper-Taylorism). With each modulation, then, the formal, apparent freedom of the disciplined subject
increases, while their real freedom decreases; the technologies of coercion only become more subtle.

Cybernetic Capitalism

The transition we have been discussing—from discipline to control,
from welfare state to neoliberalism—marks a shift in the moment of
capitalism itself. In 2015's *Cyber-Proletariat*, Nick Dyer-Witheford
calls attention to the ways in which digital technologies have played
a major role in the transition from a capitalism driven by mass, assembly-line labor in the immediate post-war period, to the cybernetic or "immaterial" capitalism that has developed since the end of
the 1960s. Writing in 1989, Ursula Franklin notes that "we are living in a very difficult, very interesting time, a time in which a major
historical period is coming to an end."[12] The process which began
with the socio-political upheavals of 1968 and witnessed both the
Vietnam War and the 1973 oil crisis, led in the late 1970s to the political victory of neoliberalism, the cultural victory of postmodernism, and the technological dominance of robotics, networks, and
cybernetics. Dyer-Witheford writes that

> From the 1970s on capital's 'cybernetic offensive'… re-
> lentlessly destroyed the factory bases of the mass work-
> er, reducing their workforce by automation, relocating
> them from the north-western quadrant of the globe to
> the former periphery of the world system via contain-
> er transportation and electronic networks, and, in the
> core, shifting from industrial jobs to service and tech-
> nical work.[13]

---

12   Franklin, *The Real World of Technology*, 1.

13   Dyer-Witheford, *Cyber-Proletariat*, 38.

These material changes in the way we work have had consequences for the way we experience our lives and the way we experience the world. As David Harvey argues in his history of neoliberalism, the neoliberal worldview

> has become hegemonic as a mode of discourse. It has pervasive effects on ways of thought to the point where it has become incorporated into the common-sense way many of us interpret, live in, and understand our world.[14]

Our connections with machines running on data gleaned from surveillance and tracking have made the post-truth societies of control properly cybernetic. Even the association of Fox News with Donald Trump supporters implies an ongoing, totalizing connection between the television (and the internet) and the consuming subject who both absorbs and emits information along various cybernetic channels. That information in turn feeds back into the system as yet more statistical training data. Neoliberalism, holding that prosperity and freedom are a function of unencumbered and uncoerced market transactions, has overseen the creation of a massive cybernetic organism, one whose human parts constantly report their condition, and which uses feedback to correct and control the human parts in their turn.[15] It seeks—unevenly—to bring all human action into the domain of the cybernetic market. In Harvey's view,

> this requires technologies of information creation and capacities to accumulate, store, transfer, analyze, and use massive databases to guide decisions in the global marketplace. Hence neoliberalism's intense interest in and pursuit of information technologies (leading some to proclaim the emergence of a new kind of 'information society').[16]

---

14 Harvey, *Brief History of Neoliberalism*, 3.

15 Marx, *Grundrisse*, 692–95.

16 Harvey, *Brief History of Neoliberalism*, 3–4.

Made possible by the same improvements in computing power and precision as robots and networks, cybernetics is both a way of modeling computation systems on biological processes and of tying those systems back into the biological organisms themselves. For Norbert Wiener, the "father of cybernetics," cybernetics did not require implants, though of course these are increasingly common today; he would have recognized the FitBit, for example, as a cybernetic feedback mechanism joining human organism and controlling machine. With this coupling of the human and the machine in technologies of control, we are forced to come to terms with the different senses of the word "truth." There is truth whose opposite is the lie, and there is logical, statistical, quantifiable truth, whose opposite is falsity.

From the perspective of information technology, the transition from discipline to control is inscribed in the history of computing through the dominance of formal logic and its view of truth, which have spread from the domain of nature to the domain of human affairs. Historically, the truth of formal logic was restricted to the realm of the natural sciences, while a more dialectical view of the truth was proper to the human sphere, as witness the dialogues of Socrates. Formal logic equates truth with validity, which requires abstraction; dialectical logic maintains the importance of the truth of concrete reality.[17] The cyberneticization of capitalism has been at least in part the process of replacing social and political (dialectical) truth with abstract, formal, binary truth. The fears prevalent throughout the history of science fiction of the inhuman and dehumanizing effect of machines rests precisely on the nature of this logic. True/False, binary 1/0, is an abstraction and forces logic into the most basic and unnuanced of discrete and closed positions. True<->Lie is a continuum: multitudinous, free-form, open, and contextual.[18] Like the machines which monitor our every action, True/False

17   Richard Norman and Sean Sayers, *Hegel, Marx and Dialectic: A Debate* (Brighton: Harvester Press, 1980), 123.

18   For example, texts such as this one are neither "true" nor "false" according to the discrete/binary model of formal logic.

is unchallengeable: a behavior either conforms to the norm or it does not. There is no room here for any of the human virtues or justifications, no room for social and political contradictions. Truth/Falsity is true only insofar as it is effective, as it does what it sets out to do, like the "effective procedure" of computer science,[19] which in this case is to maintain a social order based on a notion of quantity, discreteness, either/or; like mathematics itself, this order is fair, neutral, objective. From this perspective, then, if we follow Friedman's argument, the lie of the Truth/Falsity binary is a noble one insofar as it restricts politics and economics to the constrained logic of the contract.

Feedback: Cybernetics and Truth

Truth has been a human—as opposed to a divine—prerogative since Descartes, for whom truth was both clear and distinct.[20] The obtuse interrogator in Asimov's *Foundation* argues that "the truth should be clearer… less mysterious, more open to the mind"[21]—a police view of truth. It is one of the qualities of critical theory, beginning with Marx, Nietzsche, and Freud, that truth is recognized as often not only obscure and indistinct, but unconscious and irrational. For Marx, human beings "make their own history, but they do not make it just as they please,"[22] indicating that there is a truth created by social forms independent of the truth of any individual within them. This puts truth at odds with the (neo)liberal

---

19 Alonzo Church, "An unsolvable problem of elementary number theory," *American Journal of Mathematics* 58, 1936: 345–63; A. M. Turing, "On Computable Numbers, with an Application to the Entscheidungsproblem," *Proceedings of the London Mathematical Society* 42, no. 1 (1937): 230–65.

20 Rene Descartes, *Meditations on First Philosophy* (Cambridge: Cambridge University Press, 1986), 24.

21 Isaac Asimov, *Foundation, Foundation and Empire, Second Foundation* (New York: Everyman, 2010), 25.

22 Karl Marx, *The Eighteenth Brumaire of Louis Bonaparte* (New York: International Publishers, 1963). 15.

view of society as composed of individual, fully understood, mutually beneficial transactions, where truth is only significant as it exists within a given contractual relationship. For Foucault, both the view of truth as knowledge and the amenability of social forms *to* knowledge, could only come about through a "specific mode of subjection," and I would argue that post-truth is precisely the form of knowledge of the mode of subjection of our current historical moment.

In Marxist terms, truth belongs to a particular conjuncture of a mode of production and the social relations and culture appropriate to it. The question then becomes, what are the social relations that have given rise to "post-truth" as a form of knowledge in the conjuncture we call neoliberalism? The question is one of political economy. If cyber-capitalism, the computerized global capitalism of hyper-automation, networks, and robotics, is the specific economic form of our time, and neoliberalism its specific political form, then we might understand post-truth as its specific epistemological form. In this sense, then, Foucault's "machine that might produce the truth" can be understood as the *episteme* of cybernetic capitalism, indicating not only the sociality of truth, the technology of truth production, but also its emerging non-human nature. We are perhaps witnessing the alienation of human beings from the truth, a transformation as far-reaching as the Cartesian moment.[23]

Just as truth and objects of knowledge differ according to modes of subjection and production, so too, for Deleuze, "types of machine are easily matched with each type of society."[24] What kind of machines, then, are producing the truth of post-truth society? For Deleuze, human bodies—the bodies on which penality is

---

23   Antonio Negri, *Political Descartes: Reason, Ideology and the Bourgeois Subject* (New York: Verso, 2007), 315–16.

24   Deleuze, "Postscript," 6. Marx puts this another way when he writes: "Technology reveals the active relation of man to nature, the direct process of the production of his life, and thereby also lays bare the process of the production of the social relations of his life, and the mental conceptions that flow from those relations." Marx, *Capital, Volume 1*, 493.

inscribed—are desiring machines, and the distinction between animal and machine is lost in the bravura opening of *Anti-Oedipus*:

> Everywhere it is machines—real ones, not figurative
> ones: machines driving other machines, machines being
> driven by other machines, with all the necessary coupling
> and connections. An organ-machine is plugged into an
> energy-source machine: the one produces a flow that the
> other interrupts. The breast is a machine that produces
> milk, and the mouth is a machine coupled to it.[25]

This is cybernetics, the study of "control and communication in the animal and the machine," the type of machines proper to cybernetic capitalism. For Norbert Wiener, developments in computing during the Second World War made possible solutions to engineering problems common to both machines and animal organs. Initially, the connection between the animal and the machine proceeded by analogy:

> It became clear to us that the ultra-rapid computing
> machine, depending as it does on consecutive switching devices, must represent almost an ideal model of
> the problem arising in the nervous system. The all-or-
> none character of the discharge of the neurons is precisely analogous to the single choice made in determining a digit on the binary scale, which more than one of
> us had already contemplated as the most satisfactory basis of computing-machine design.[26]

Wiener's research led him to investigate the improvement or replacement of organic functionality by a combination of the animal

---

25 Gilles Deleuze and Felix Guattari, *Anti-Oedipus: Capitalism and
Schizophrenia* (Minneapolis: University of Minnesota Press, 1983), 1.

26 Norbert Wiener, *Cybernetics or Control and Communication in the Animal
and the Machine* (New York: MIT Press and John Wiley & Sons, 1961): 14.

and the machine, predicting both functional prosthetics, but also the cyborgs and cybernetic implants—not to mention the entire discourse of "posthumanism"—of the present day. Wiener also predicted the substitution of machines for humans in the "mode of subjection" of capitalist society:

> Long before Nagasaki and the public awareness of the atomic bomb, it had occurred to me that we were here in the presence of another social potentiality of unheard-of importance for good and evil. The automatic factory and the assembly line without human agents was only so far ahead of us as is limited by the willingness to put such a degree of effort into their engineering as was spent, for example, in the development of radar in the Second World War.[27]

Between 1948, when these words were written, and 1992, when Deleuze inaugurated the "societies of control" working through "computers, whose passive danger is jamming and whose active one is piracy and the introduction of viruses," a "mutation of capitalism" took place which made Wiener's vision a reality. In Deleuze's terms,

> Capitalism is no longer involved in production, which it often relegates to the Third World, even for the complex forms of textiles, metallurgy, or oil production. It's a capitalism of higher-order production. It no longer buys raw materials or assembles parts. What it wants to sell is services and what it wants to buy is stocks. This is no longer a capitalism for production but for the market, which is to say, for being sold or marketed.[28]

---

27   Wiener, *Cybernetics*, 27.

28   Deleuze, "Postscript," 6.

This cybernetic phase of capitalism developed out of the kernel of Wiener's research.[29] In 1948, he could look on the potential of cybernetic automation as holding possibilities for both good and evil. For Deleuze, on the other hand, such automation moved us from a society of discipline to a society of control, part of the larger transition or inflection within capitalism that we have been discussing. Studies of post-war capitalism like Dyer-Witheford's support Wiener's contention that "the metaphysical dominance of machines [has become] a most immediate and non-metaphorical problem."[30] To understand the mechanisms by which such metaphysical dominance, such internalized control, might work, we must look at the concept of *feedback*.

One of the cybernetic problems Wiener and his colleagues identified was how to allow a machine to self-regulate its performance. It is possible to program a robotic arm, for example, to move to a certain position relative to an absolute frame of reference. In contrast, a human being can move an arm to a given position relative to another object. The mechanism by which this is achieved is feedback, where the difference between an expected result and an actual result is fed back into the mechanism, allowing it to continually adjust the action to minimize the difference. The feedback loop in the muscles of a human being is generally so subtle as to be unconscious, except in conditions where the neuromuscular system is operating differently. The "control of a machine on the basis of its *actual* performance rather than its expected performance" involves "tell-tales or monitors, that is... elements which indicate a performance."[31] Thus cybernetics brings together data, surveillance, tracking, gamification, and truth in the service of the self-control, self-adjustment, or self-regulation of individuals. (Post-)truth, in this sense is merely the measure of conformity

---

29   Dyer-Witheford, *Cyber-Proletariat*, 39–45.

30   Wiener, *Cybernetics*, 27.

31   Norbert Wiener, *The Human Use of Human Beings: Cybernetics and Society* (Boston: Houghton Mifflin, 1954), 24.

with expected performance, the deviation from the statistical norm mined out of zettabytes of self-reported and illegally captured data.

This new period of capitalism was heralded as "the coming of post-industrial society" or the knowledge or information society,[32] a period when the advances in cybernetic control that date from the end of the Second World War were presumed would lead to regimes of immaterial and affective labor free from scarcity or coercion, increased leisure time and standards of living. All of this would be supported by software and algorithmically-controlled robots. Instead, we are living in a long period of economic downturn,[33] often slow, but punctuated as in 1973, 1987, and 2008 with increasingly harsh crises. Like Dyer-Witheford's vortex, this process has been compared with storm formations amenable only to statistical analysis. We live in a world of civil war, religious fundamentalism, drone strikes, "dodgy dossiers," "alternative facts," and a resurgent fascist right. We also live in a world of ubiquitous surveillance, data mining, wearable technologies, hyper-Taylorism, tracking, targeted advertising, the "deeps" (deep web, deep learning, and deep state), and the ultra-rapid, statistically-based financialization of the economy—all made possible by the all-too-material hyper-exploitation of the global South, and the prison-industrial complex[34] at home. Indeed, it is vital to remember that not only is the "society of control" mainly a phenomenon of the capitalist metropoles, but it is also unevenly applied: what is self-regulation to the affluent, predominantly white, cultures of the capitalist center remains brutal, bloody, bodily "discipline" to oppressed and marginalized populations. We need only think of the crimes that gave rise to the Black

---

32 Bell, *The Coming of Post-Industrial Society,* 37.

33 Robert Brenner, *The Economics of Global Turbulence: The Advanced Capitalist Economies from Long Boom to Long Downturn, 1945–2005* (London, New York: Verso, 2006), 2–9

34 Angela Davis, "Masked Racism: Reflections from the Prison-Industrial Complex," *Indigenous Law Bulletin* 4, no. 27 (2000), 6.

Lives Matter movement[35] or the violent suppression of Indigenous protests against pipelines, not to mention the "starlight tours" and the horrific number of missing and murdered Indigenous women in Canada, to recognize that there is no neat dividing line between societies of discipline and of control. If anything, discipline and control tends to break down along class, gender, and racial lines *within* a given society.

Statistics, Data, and the Society of Control

Many of the algorithmic systems that have marked the advent of this new world rely on statistical modeling or prediction. Machine learning systems like the "deep learning" TensorFlow software library from Google or the financial algorithms whose out-of-control velocity led to the financial crisis of 2008 essentially use machinery to enable the rapid parsing of historical data ("training data") to perform statistical prediction at speeds and scales impossible for human beings. Indeed, speed is one of the most marked characteristics of the period under discussion, along with increased militarization, as Paul Virilio has shown:

> Just as speed led to the Germans' incredible domination over continental Europe in 1940, fear and its administration are now supported by the incredible spread of real-time technology, especially the new ICT or new information and communications technologies.[36]

The roots of this statistical revolution can be traced to developments of 19th century science, especially in the work of Ada Lovelace and Charles Babbage, but as Marx demonstrates, it also arises from capitalism's reliance on abstract, aggregate, statistical labor

---

35   Taylor, *From #BlackLivesMatter to Black Liberation*, 3.

36   Paul Virilio, *The Administration of Fear* (Pasadena: Semiotext(e), 2012), 16.

rather than the specific labor of individuals.[37] It has been argued that the introduction of statistics into physics formed the basis of the revolution of Newtonian into Relativistic science in the 20th century. Writing in 1950, Norbert Wiener argued that statistics allowed physicists to ignore characteristics of systems that had previously been seen as significant or defining. Instead, they argued that the only feature distinguishing two systems was the amount of energy contained in each.[38] In physics, the reciprocal of energy is entropy, a measure of the amount of potential work available within a given system. In information science, on the other hand, the entropy of a system can be used to inform predictions about future states of the system through probability. While the definition of entropy differs for physical and information systems, its usefulness in terms of statistical prediction is clear. Adami's concept of information as "that which allows you to make a correct prediction with accuracy better than chance"[39] connects the concept of information-entropy with that of feedback—the ability to achieve an end result through historical data rather than by chance. Feedback measures actual performance against expected performance and is concerned with the difference between them. Adami writes:

> We can never know the actual uncertainty that we have about any physical object, unless the statistics of the possible measurement outcomes of that physical object are for some reason known with infinite precision (which you cannot attain in a finite lifetime). It is for that reason that I suggest to the reader to give up thinking about the uncertainty of the physical object, and be only concerned with differences between uncertainties (before and after a measurement, for example). The

---

37   Marx, *Capital, Volume 1,* 135.

38   Wiener, *Human Use of Human Beings,* 10–11, 21–22.

39   Christoph Adami, "What is Information?" *Philosophical Transactions of the Royal Society* A374 20150230: 8.

> uncertainties themselves we call entropy. Differences be-
> tween entropies (for example before and after a measure-
> ment) are called information.[40]

Differences between measurements, differences between actual and expected performance, prediction, achievement: these are the mechanisms by which information regulates action and behavior.

By mid-century, Western culture had become fascinated by statistics. Asimov's *Foundation*, published in 1951, is predicated on an application of statistics to history and social movements. Echoing Lenin, we could say that contemporary capitalism is "statistics plus computerization,"[41] the fulfillment of Babbage's wish that "these calculations had been steam."[42] In statistics, whether applied to physics, information, or social prediction, probability replaces certainty. Insofar as a probabilistic model of the truth can be applied to the statistical totality of human beings, the truth can only be measured in terms of its effectiveness, that is of its power to predict or control.[43] Indeed, it is precisely this transition from certainty to probability, from power over an individual to power over a population, that has led from Foucault's society of discipline to Deleuze's society of control, from power over individual bodies to control over statistical populations. This power is felt as the power of a norm. Monitoring and gamification, from FitBit to Untapped, reinforces the internalized control of the mean by penalizing underachievement and deviation. This is especially stark in struggles around disability and accessibility. Control is enforced by norms embedded

---

40 Adami, "What is Information?", 5.

41 "Communism is Soviet power plus the electrification of the whole country", V. I. Lenin, "Our Foreign and Domestic Position and Party Tasks", in *Collected Works*, Volume 31, (Moscow: Progress Publishers, 1965), 419.

42 Harry Wilmot Buxton and Anthony Hyman, *Memoir of the Life and Labors of the Late Charles Babbage Esq, FRS* (Cambridge: MIT Press, 2003), 46.

43 "A broader principle of cybernetics... was the idea that information is not about *knowing* but *doing*." Dyer-Witheford, *Cyber-Proletariat*, 42.

in our built environment, but it is also monitored and enforced by self-tracking systems, for example in Amazon warehouses.

For Foucault, the transition to statistical truth entails a change in the status and function of truth itself. It is a question of *episteme* (scientific truth) as opposed to *doxa* (common sense truth or opinion). Foucault described *episteme* as

> the strategic apparatus which permits of separating out
> from among all the statements which are possible those
> that will be acceptable within, I won't say a scientific the-
> ory, but a field of scientificity, and which it is possible to
> say are true or false.[44]

In the post-truth era, "true" and "false" are a matter of statistical probability; what is true is what is normal, average. Hence the common critique of "post-truth" during the 2016 US presidential election was the critique of "normalization." Normalization is not, I think, the "making normal" of a given phenomenon in *reality*, but making its existence and belief in it the statistical norm, a question of mass or preponderance, of weight in a population or discourse. In the post-truth era, the ability to say whether something is true or false ("alternative facts") depends on where it falls on a statistical distribution of belief. Crudely put, if enough people believe something, it is true, which helps to explain the rise of proponents of new and previously discredited theories, from anti-vaxxers to flat-earthers, as well as the prominence of conspiracy theories in contemporary discourse.

This position clearly has enormous implications for politics. In *Hatred of Democracy*, Jacques Rancière writes that in the current conjuncture,

> our basic reality does not leave us the choice to inter-
> pret it and merely requires responses adapted to the

---

44   Michel Foucault, *Power/Knowledge: Selected Interviews and Other Writings* (New York: Vintage, 1980), 197.

circumstances, responses which are generally the same,
whatever our opinions and aspirations.[45]

The post-truth societies of control are ones in which our very understanding of truth now serves the purposes of docility and the restriction of agency. The rationality of binary logic, its mathematical purity and lack of ambiguity, driving a statistical, probabilistic
model of truth, is simply the latest legitimating principle, or noble
lie, for societies that—with the advent of postmodernism—deny all
legitimating principles. Post-truth as statistics is true insofar as it
satisfies this logic, but as with all legitimating principles, it must always be contested. Its purpose is always discipline and the maintenance of social order; the societies of control have merely automated legitimacy as they have automated everything else. My insistence
on the continuity of neoliberalism with prior phases of capitalism,
in contrast to the view of it as something entirely new, is important to show the transitional developments from early capitalism
(the society of discipline) to cyber-capitalism (the society of control). Moufawad-Paul describes this development as a purely "formal transformation that... has not altered the underlying logic of
capitalism,"[46] the logic of exploitation and profit.

Such an insistence on the basic continuity of capitalist exploitation is also in part to counter the liberal critique of neoliberalism: that it is just a mistake, an error that can be corrected simply through "the shaping of a new social contract."[47] There was no
period of "good capitalism" prior to this period of deregulation,
austerity, and the dismantling of the social safety net. Even the
post-war consensus was simply a temporary compact, an "imperial détente,"[48] between labor and capital in which a small sector of
the Western working class was bought off at the expense of people

---

45   Jacques Rancière, *Hatred of Democracy* (London, New York: Verso, 2009), 77.

46   Moufawad-Paul, *Austerity Apparatus*, 53.

47   Franklin, *Real World*, 132.

48   Moufawad-Paul, *Austerity Apparatus*, 34.

of color, gender and sexual minorities, people with disabilities, and the working class of the rest of the planet. Similarly, the transition from a society of discipline to the society of control mustn't be seen as a rupture: it is a change in emphasis, rather than a fundamental transformation. While Deleuze's "Postscript" marks a particular moment in this transition, studies of the history of labor show us that in fact the movement from discipline to control began sometime in the late 1960s. We haven't yet reached the end.

Conclusion: Excess and Emancipation

Feedback restricts and controls excess or deficiency in movement. This is as true in the cybernetic organism as it is in democratic society, where the restriction of "democratic excess" is a political requirement. Liberal democracies seek to contain the "excesses" of individualism, of identities, of the demand for rights—excesses that are engendered by the ideology of liberalism itself—by supplying a homogeneous set of values, ideas, and mores to the populace through education and mass consumer culture. They hope that this will provide a substitute, an alternative legitimacy to the "natural" order of birth and wealth of the *ancien regime*. These principles, however, risk asking for more than liberal democracies are prepared to provide, in terms of recognition, rights, agency. But in order to avoid repressing this democratic excess by discipline or force, in order for ruling oligarchies to *make use of* individualism, identity, and human rights, individuals must feel that they are acting freely, without coercion; they must control *themselves*.[49] It is not enough, anymore, for the state to discipline the "docile bodies" of its subjects, for this would destroy the illusion of freedom, equality, consumer choice, and self-determination which lies at the bottom of neoliberal contractual relationships. In the societies of control each individual, each cog in the massive cyborg of global capitalism,

---

49   It would also go against the (neo-)liberal principle of small government to use state apparatuses to repress the population. In essence, the state automates repression, following the same logic of automation as everything else.

must rely on impersonal feedback loops to gauge the distance between their own expected and actual performance.

But it is precisely this reliance of the individual on mechanisms of feedback that open up a space to resist post-truth, to replace self-regulation with emancipation. In Rancière's view, the radical equality of one person with another is not the mathematical equivalence to which the cybernetic machine reduces us. Rather it is a

> movement that blurs the given distribution of the individual and collective, and the accepted boundary of the political and the social... the action that constantly wrests the monopoly of public life from oligarchic governments the omnipotence over lives from power of wealth.[50]

The debasement of choice to feedback, of the dialectical plurality and richness of human truths to the binary despotism, the "single choice," of digital truth, requires for its functioning the individual's awareness of their inadequacy, their inequality with respect to others, the vast gulf between their performance and what is expected of them. Our docility is made possible by our feelings of failure. We are required to feel like failures, incompetents, "less than." This is the truth of post-truth societies of control, a truth learned from advertising: in order to be controlled, one must feel like an imposter. "The austerity subject is... unsure of itself; this is both its strength and weakness."[51] In terms of information, our feeling of failure comes about through comparing ourselves with the massive aggregate of data that describes the *average* against which we judge ourselves and come up short. As much as we deviate from the norm, we are deviant, and our feedback loops are the means by which we register our deviance and by which we can approach the safety of the norm again. Our own individual intelligence becomes

---

50 Rancière, *Hatred of Democracy*, 93–96.

51 Moufawad-Paul, *Austerity Apparatus*, 86.

subordinated to the massive online database of global cybernetic intelligence, leading to what Rancière calls "stultification" (*abrutissement*), the subordination of one intelligence to another. It is only by recognizing our own fundamental adequacy, the equality of our own intelligence and identity, that we can escape the domination of control, the subjection of our human truths to "post-truth;" that we can achieve something out of fashion in today's fractured discourse: the communal emancipation of a world of equals.

Chapter Eight

Dual Power and Mathesis

Getting organized, negotiating strong collective agreements, and being prepared to strike, illegally if necessary: this might sound— to those enamored of the liberal and democratic discourse of librarianship—squalid and material, tainted, as Dewey put it, by trade-unionism. But the material nature of organizing, the kind of class consciousness that comes about through organized resistance, is paramount. Indeed, as Jana Bacevic has pointed out, demystifying critique is not enough. Speaking of the widespread critique of neoliberalism in higher education, she points out that "what makes the proliferation of critique of the transformation of universities particularly striking is the relative absence—at least until recently—of sustained modes of resistance to the changes it describes... by and large forms of resistance have much more taken the form of a book or blog post than strike, demo, or occupation."[1] Because of this, critique under neoliberalism becomes incorporated into the neoliberal ways of understanding and engaging with the world, idealistic assumptions that "the more we know about how

---

1   Jana Bacevic, "The Paradox of Resistance: Critique, Neoliberalism, and the Limits of Performativity," *Jana Bacevic* (blog), February 7, 2018, para. 2.

neoliberalism operates, the better we will be able to resist it."[2] Discursive denunciations abound, while material resistance to neoliberal structures are less forthcoming.

The dominant view of critique, that ideas precede action, therefore becomes a constraint on any notion of resistance. This view is based on the notion of effectivity of speech-acts (drawing on Austin and Searle), but Bacevic reminds us that speech only becomes effective under certain circumstances:

> In other words, it's not enough to exclaim: "Universities are not for sale! Education is not a commodity! Students are not consumers!" for this to become the case. For this begs the question: "Who is going to bring this about? What are the conditions under which this can be realized?" In other words: who has the power to act in ways that can make this claim true?[3]

There are few things here that need to be unpacked. In the first place, Weber's prioritizing of ideas before action is absent from the Marxian theory of (class) consciousness, where theory and praxis are in a dialectical relationship, and where material practice "in the last analysis" precedes ideas. This has major implications for how we think about the practice of resistance in neoliberal or neoliberalizing institutions like universities and libraries, institutions which were previously "outside" capitalist relations, but have become subject to commodification and subsumption.[4]

In addition, Bacevic's query—"what are the conditions under which this can be realized?"—is an important one. The problem with exclamations like "education is not a commodity," "libraries are the cornerstone of liberty" or "libraries are institutions

---

2   Bacevic, para. 10.

3   Bacevic, para. 11.

4   Sam Popowich, "Libraries, Labour, Capital: On Formal and Real Subsumption," *Journal of Radical Librarianship* 4 (2018): 9.

of democracy" is that by making what seem to be descriptive state-ments about the *current* state of affairs, it obscures the fact that cur-rent reality is *not like that*. The language of "ought" slips into the lan-guage of "is;" the normative is made to seem descriptive. Education is (now) a commodity; libraries are not institutions of "democracy". In making such exclamations we are mystifying the current situation by projecting a hoped-for future society onto the present. In other words, we are talking about utopia, without recognizing the fact.

Before turning to the question of utopia, however, I want to reflect briefly on one final component of Bacevic's argument: for intellectuals, the very fact that our practice engages with ideas, cri-tique, and the "practice of thinking" in the first place, means that all our intellectual activities are "inextricably bound up in practices, institutions, and—not least importantly—economies of academic knowledge production."[5] This goes a long way towards explaining why librarianship, despite a lot of research into information, society, and library practice, remains almost incapable of turning that cri-tique upon itself in any sustained way. For every article like Fobazi Ettarh's "Vocational Awe" we have a thousand thinkpieces by ALA officials, chief librarians, or vendors uncritically parroting the tran-scendental—that is, uncritical—discourse of librarianship. Bacevic ends by raising two concepts that have long lineages within Marxist theory: the totality and Utopia. The reason we can never take a per-spective (or even breathing room) outside of capitalism (or neoliber-alism, or postmodernism) is that these structures are total systems.

> This means coming to terms with the fact that neolib-eralism is the Research Excellence Framework, but neo-liberalism is also when you discuss ideas for a super-cool collaborative project. Neoliberalism is the requirement to submit all your research outputs to the faculty web-site, but neoliberalism is also the pride you feel when your most recent article is Tweeted about. Neoliberal-ism is the incessant corporate emails about 'wellbeing,'

---

5   Bacevic, "The Paradox of Resistance," 13.

> but it is also the craft beer you have with your friends
> in the pub.[6]

Coming to terms with this totality—"the fact that things can be two different things at the same time"—is one of the core projects of Marxism, may allow us to move beyond projects of demystification and explication, assuming that once all the intellectual mist has been blown away then radical, revolutionary action is bound to follow. For Bacevic, "if there is something critique can learn from neoliberalism, it is the art of speculation. If economic discourses are performative, then, by definition, critique can be performative too. This means that futures can be created."[7] We must be careful not to equate critique with social transformation, but holding space for utopias is an important element in the discursive struggle.

Materialism and Utopia

In his 2016 book *An American Utopia: Dual Power and the Universal Army* (2016), Jameson argues that utopian thinking—usually dismissed as unscientific and unrealistic—allows us to think *seriously* about alternatives in the guise of thinking *unseriously*. It is precisely its unscientific and unrealistic nature that makes utopian thinking worth deploying in the struggle to deal with the contradictions of our world and our profession.

Given that the capitalist values of efficiency, measurement, property, etc., are seen as "common sense," any idea or project which rejects these values will seem to us irrational and unrealistic on their very face. Utopian thinking looks, at first glance, like the worst kind of fantasy, something not grounded at all in the realities of our world. But Jameson argues that it is precisely this that allows utopian thinking to avoid being caught in the lure of reproducing capitalist values. Also, the "cognitive shock," the surprising

---

6   Bacevic, para 14.

7   Bacevic, para 15.

audacity of utopian thinking, can make us see our world different-ly, can allow us to imagine things differently by letting us question the very common-sense truths of the world as we see it, to ask, "why can't our world be different than it is?" Utopian thinking is limit-ed by nothing but our imaginations. However, in the real world, all imagination runs inevitably into the immoveable force that is the power of the state.

In the last forty years, state power has been used increasing-ly to push through the reforms of the neoliberal project led by Mar-garet Thatcher, Ronald Reagan, Augusto Pinochet, and their cli-ents in various other countries. Essentially, this meant dismantling the infrastructure of the welfare state in order to allow corporations to take over those services for profit. Historically, the abandonment of a society to capitalist enterprise (e.g. under classical liberalism in the later 19th century) has led to a decline in the standard of liv-ing and eventually to the rise of fascism both as a reaction to the capitalist takeover of social services, but also as the most efficient and effective way to organize society for the benefit of capital itself. Forty years into the neoliberal project, we are seeing the rise of the ultra-right across the developed world as the poor and the work-ing class see their standard of living and their social safety-net de-stroyed by decades of neoliberal policy, blaming this on anyone but capital. Jameson's theory of dual power, then, does not simply of-fer an alternative to neoliberal structures of government services but *now*, at this moment, it offers a potential way of arresting the slide into fascism that seems inevitable.

The starkest example of state power is the monopoly of vi-olence, both in the forms of the army and the police (and these days the distinction is increasingly difficult to draw). Jameson asks the utopian question, "what if we were all members of the army?", to which the answer in the US is, "well, we would all have health-care for the rest of our lives." Jameson is obviously speaking about the American context, but the idea that joining the armed forc-es entitles one to basic social services dates back at least to the GI Bill of 1944. Jameson takes this idea not to its logical, but to its utopian, conclusion, by asking what would happen if the army be-came *the mechanism* by which social services–the welfare state–were provided to citizens. In the face of an increasingly neoliberal (or, under Trump, perhaps increasingly fascist) state, how else would social services be provided to an increasingly abandoned populace?

Jameson links this idea with Lenin's formulation of dual power, where an alternative, non-state organization arises to provide social services in cases where the state has abdicated that role. In Lenin's case, such an alternative was provided by the soviets (councils) formed in Moscow and Petrograd after the liberal February Revolution of 1917,[8] but Jameson also sees dual power in the provision of "unofficial" social services by the Black Panthers in disadvantaged (i.e. Black) parts of the US, and Hamas in the occupied territories of Palestine. In reading Jameson's book, I began to wonder—given the "increased corporatization" and the influence of the state in academia, as well as the "austerity" measures and the depredations of neoliberalism outside of academia—what role might libraries play in the institution of dual power in Canada, given that the importance of the army in Canadian society is not, for the moment anyway, as pronounced as it is in the US?

Jameson doesn't talk about libraries. He considers and dismisses various institutions (the church, the post office, the mafia) before settling on the army as his preferred institution of dual power. One of his criteria is distributed reach, like that possessed by the postal service—indeed, this argument has been used with respect to the possible extension of Canadian postal services to other social services, like banking.[9] Libraries, especially if we consider both academic and public, exist in every major center, in every province and territory. Spatially, they are spread throughout the fabric of Canadian society.

But ideologically too, libraries are woven into our culture. Indeed, this is one of the things that makes libraries so useful to capitalist society: libraries are machines for the reproduction of ideology. Indeed, the structure of libraries in this country mirrors

---

8   V. I. Lenin, "The Dual Power." In *Collected Works,* Volume 24 (Moscow: Progress Publishers, 1964), 38.

9   "Postal Banking," *Canadian Union of Postal Employees.*

the structure of that other ideological apparatus, the school system. Many of us were introduced to the public library at about the age we started school, or a little before. If we go on to post-secondary education, we tend to leave the public library behind, "graduating" to the academic library for *advanced* ideological reproduction. When we return to the public library as adults, the library is used less as a place of education or research, than as one out of a vast number of entertainment content providers, again, mirroring the ideological requirements of the state.

It is the ubiquity of libraries, both spatially and culturally, that makes them such good candidates for dual power. Academic libraries are spread throughout the educational system; public libraries are part of core municipal infrastructure at least down to a certain level; and special libraries exist within their own professional networks and structures. The infrastructure and processes (e.g. interlibrary loan) are already present to move goods around the country. Many libraries already provide social services and outreach to the groups hit hardest by austerity and capitalist logic. Even our supposed neutrality and disinterestedness helps, by giving libraries a level of trustworthiness that few, if any, other institutions possess.

What Jameson (and Lenin) envisaged was a collective project to break away from the reliance on the state, a state which is subject not to the values and codes that we, as citizens, hold dear and important, a state which has only one value, the maintenance of the exploitative and oppressive system we call capitalism. This state abandons and oppresses all those who do not fit into the structure of capitalist production, holding out a promise of social welfare only if ways of life and struggle are given up. Dual power offers a collective project *in the face of* state power, it offers a chance for the recovery of at least a certain amount of agency and power by the collective. And it does this not by rebellion or uprising and not by trying to change the system from within, but by doing *something else*. The power of utopian thinking is that it allows us to imagine what that something else is—even if it's impossible, even if it's unrealistic—because it is so tempting to think that the world will never change. But not changing is impossible, the world will change whether we like it or not, the question is how we prepare to harness that change to fit our values—as librarians, as a collective, as a society—rather than have the world changed for us. Dual power, as an unrealistic, utopian idea, at least gives us a means to begin thinking about this kind of change.

What I am arguing is that libraries as a whole a) are already present in the lives of vast swathes of the population and b) are already structured to provide services to their constituents. As a result, libraries are well-placed as exactly the "already organized institution" on which Jameson contends dual power must be based.

There are two immediate objections to such an idea, however. On the one hand, the question of library neutrality itself. For libraries to provide the services required of the dual power institution, they must give up any pretence to neutrality. They must—just like Jameson's Army—recognize the socialist content of what they are doing. Rather than serving their current function, that of maintaining the population in their positions within capitalist culture, they would have to insist on their function as a socialist service layer, as effecting what Jameson calls "cultural revolution" in antagonism to capitalist culture.

In order to do this, however, we require new ways of talking about libraries and our parent organizations, new commitments to principles that recognizes the gap between values on paper and values in practice. And I think we have to be very clear about our commitments and values in order to let people know what services we provide. First and foremost, this means standing up to our parent organizations when they insist on policies and procedures that run counter to our commitments. This flies in face of much of our professional discourse, which centers around demonstrating and proving our value to those who fund us. However, we can't have it both ways: we can either maintain a spurious neutrality *or* be valuable to society, but not both.

At the time of writing, we have witnessed the 2016 US election of Donald Trump, the 2018 election of Doug Ford to the premiership of Ontario, and the rise of right-wing and neo-fascist activity across the developed world. While still insisting upon the importance of utopian thinking and exposing the contradictions of capitalism ("heightening" them, as Lenin put it), we therefore now have a more imminent problem. Given the explicit rise of the far right, libraries and library workers will have to decide what side they are on. As the state moves rightward in order to pander to far-right voters, lobbying, and intimidation, libraries will only become more and more complicit in far-right government policies. There is no such thing as neutrality. We have to be prepared to start fighting far-right tendencies wherever we see them: in our plans, in our policies, and in our procedures, but especially within the policies and procedures of our parent organizations. This is hard to ask: we are so afraid of being seen as obsolete or difficult, afraid that our funding will be cut and that we will cease to exist. I have only this response: under fascist governments libraries as we know them will cease to exist anyway, and the best way to prove our relevance to the communities we serve is to fight for their interests, the interests of a collective and just society. In many ways, this perspective is at the heart of Paolo Freire's emancipatory pedagogy.

Freire: Dialogism and Anti-dialogism

It is difficult to fully appreciate Freire's liberatory project without placing it in the broader idea of the Marxist philosophy of praxis. In *Pedagogy of the Oppressed*, he refers to Lukács' formulation of the dialectical combination of theory and practice. Indeed, Freire's pedagogy is based on the intimate connection between the two:

> In dialectical thought, world and action are intimately interdependent. But action is human only when it is not merely an occupation but also a preoccupation, that is, when it is not dichotomized from reflection. Reflection, which is essential to action, is implicit in Lukács' requirement of 'explaining to the masses their own action,' just as it is implicit in the purpose he attributes to this explanation: that of 'consciously activating the subsequent development of experience'. For us, however, the

> requirement is seen not in terms of explaining to, but
> rather dialoguing with the people about their actions.[10]

Freire sees the pedagogy of the oppressed as a pedagogy of liberation, of "the critical intervention of the people in reality through
praxis"[11] in order to free themselves from oppression. This is why the
oppressors cannot develop or practice the pedagogy of the oppressed.
"It would be a contradiction in terms if the oppressors not only defended but actually implemented a liberating education."[12] In his
book on philosophy and librarianship, André Cossette dismisses the
idea of a pedagogical mission for libraries precisely because

> In maintaining the illusion that the ultimate goal of
> the library is education, thinkers in library science per-
> petuate an ideology that is inseparable from the divi-
> sion of society into classes, which exists in the interest of
> the dominant class. This bourgeois librarianship, which
> aims to disseminate high culture, to grant access to the
> treasures of civilization, is alienating for the vast majori-
> ty of working people.[13]

Cossette recommends instead an "informational" mission which
supports the democratic, enlightening project which constitutes
the hegemonic discourse of librarianship. It should be clear, however, that we must reject the democratic perspective, and with it the
"neutral" idea of library as a mere information provider. The library
is *already* an educative, pedagogical institution, and it *does* represent the desires and requirements of the ruling class. However, rather than rejecting the pedagogical perspective, in favor of one that
appears less problematic, we need to take a partisan position with

---

10   Paolo Freire, *Pedagogy of the Oppressed*, 53.

11   Freire, *Pedagogy*, 53.

12   Freire, 54.

13   Cossette, *Humanism and Libraries*, 46.

respect to pedagogy itself, if we are to recuperate education as part of the library's role in society.

This, however, raises its own set of problems: "If the implementation of a liberating education requires political power and the oppressed have none, how then is it possible to carry out the pedagogy of the oppressed prior to the revolution?"[14]

This is, indeed, one of the fundamental problems of a critical librarianship. Freire draws the distinction between "systematic education, which can only be changed by political power, and educational projects, which should be carried out with the oppressed in the process of organizing them."[15] Any radical pedagogy, any radical librarianship, *must* abandon any and all pretensions to neutrality or level playing fields. It must be open and up-front about power, especially differential power, intersectionality, reification, alienation, and the political economy of its own conjuncture, if it hopes to engineer the kinds of educational projects required of a truly liberating pedagogy.

For Freire, such a pedagogy can only be constituted through dialogue, and only from a position of radical egalitarianism is dialogue possible. In his formulation, "dialogue cannot occur between those who want to name the world and those who do not wish this naming—between those who deny others the right to speak their word and those whose right to speak has been denied them."[16] The issue of dialogue explicitly links equality (i.e. social justice), education, and intellectual freedom. Freire counters a mainstream model of education (in his case, the banking model) with a "problem-posing model," one which sees humanization and emancipation as its goal:

> Problem-posing education, as a humanist and liberating praxis, posits as fundamental that the people subjected to domination must fight for their emancipation.

---

14 Freire, *Pedagogy of the Oppressed*, 54.

15 Freire, 54, emphasis removed.

16 Freire, 88.

To that end, it enables teachers and students to become
Subjects of the educational process by overcoming authoritarianism and an alienating intellectualism... The
world—no longer something to be described with de-
ceptive words—becomes the object of that transform-
ing action by men and women which results in their humanization.[17]

In answer to his own question as to how a pedagogy of the oppressed could work before the revolution, Freire responds that

while only a revolutionary society can carry out this education in systematic terms, the revolutionary leaders
need not take full power before they can employ this
method. In the revolutionary process, the leaders cannot
utilize the banking method as an interim measure, justified on grounds of expediency, with the intention of *later* behaving in a genuinely revolutionary fashion. They
must be revolutionary—that is to say, dialogical—from
the outset.[18]

The idea that revolutionary leaders need not take full power suggests that a partial taking of power—dual power—is perhaps sufficient. However, the crucial point is that dialogue without subjection is the key to an emancipatory pedagogy. Such a dialogue

is the encounter in which the united reflection and action of the dialoguers are addressed to the world which is
to be transformed and humanized, this dialogue cannot
be reduced to the act of one person's "depositing" ideas
in another, nor can it become a simple exchange of ideas
to be "consumed" by the discussants. Dialogue... is an

---

17   Freire, 86.

18   Freire, 86.

> act of creation; it must not serve as a crafty instrument
> for the domination of one person by another.[19]

We will see below how the purest site of this encounter is between the student and the book, which can then provide us with a liberating mission of libraries while allowing for the self-education of students. We might then leave teaching to the teachers and professors and let libraries be sites of "mathesis," of learning instead of teaching, abandoning the inherent inequality of teacher and student, and gaining instead a commitment to an education through radical equality, and therefore a commitment to humanization and emancipation.

Rancière: Mathesis and the Ignorant Librarian

Rancière's "ignorant schoolmaster" could perhaps be part of the solution to Freire's point about the oppressed needing to liberate themselves. In this sense, while the library has a pedagogical mission, this does not mean that librarians should be *teachers*; indeed, this might be the crux of the difference between a library and a school. I think the combination of pedagogical library and non-teaching librarians might be a productive one which, in fact, connects with the feeling that, despite the transcendental discourse, libraries are without a solid, concrete, well-understood purpose. All our discussions around what to call our users/patrons/customers suggest it; the silos that exist in any library of a certain size, to my mind, prove it. And the idea is given weight by the constant rehashing of the same tired intellectual freedom/social responsibility arguments. It appears unlikely that librarians or staff working in cataloging, collections, acquisitions, systems, public services, information literacy, or scholarly communication, have a shared set of goals that apply to all those areas. Part of this is due to the privileging of technical knowledge in librarianship, though this is strong in some units (like metadata and cataloging) and very weak in others (like public services), and

---

19   Freire, 88–89.

in still others is rigorous but, if done properly, not library-specific (like library systems units). The values and mission statements of libraries, which are primarily brand- and optics-related, only make the problem worse: the lack of actual values and sense of mission is obscured by the fact that we have value and mission statements on our websites; the long history of missionary posturing in the profession renders these statements functionally meaningless.

Many of the possible missions for libraries are, unfortunately, predicated on a liberal ideology that may be in the process of collapse after a hegemony of two or three centuries. Individualism, pluralism, and self-reliance/self-improvement tend to be the values underpinning our mission statements, as well as the presumption of a democratic and free society. That these values remain implicit and often unconscious only testifies to their hegemony. These unspoken values lie at the heart of librarianship's perennial argument over "neutrality." Would it be possible to come up with a mission (if only provisionally) that was not based on these spoken and unquestioned values?

Jacques Rancière, in a way, asks similar questions of liberalism in another area, that of education. *The Ignorant Schoolmaster: Five Lessons in Intellectual Emancipation,* is a meditation on the radical educational strategies of Jacques Jacotot, a teacher and politician who, after the restoration of the French monarchy in 1815, went to Belgium and established a school. Jacotot spoke no Flemish and his students no French, but he was able to develop a pedagogy by which *a pupil could be taught something the teacher does not know.* Rancière argues that Jacotot's method departs from the traditional view of education, which is *explication*: a teacher explains things to a student with an aim to bringing their level of knowledge up to the teacher's own (compare this with Freire's "banking model"). For Rancière, this model of teaching requires that the intelligence of the student be subjected to the will of the teacher; it is a model of intellectual submission. A condition in which the intelligence of one is dominated by the will of another is a condition of subjection, and in the intellectual field, Jacotot and Rancière refer to the result as "stultification" (*abrutissement*, "making into a brute," compare Freire's "dehumanization"). On the other hand, what Jacotot's educational method aims at is not instruction, but emancipation: the condition of "an intelligence in the service of a will" that nonetheless evades subjection. Traditional pedagogy is predicated on an inequality of intelligence (teachers know more than students, the middle classes know more than peasants, etc.), while Jacotot's method is based on a fundamental commitment to the "equality of intelligence."

Rancière's description of the world of the "Old [School] Master" is that of a system of explication and instruction that results in stultification and self-contempt based on the belief instilled into students that they are stupid. Freire writes that

> in the banking concept of education, knowledge is a gift bestowed by those who consider themselves knowledgeable upon those whom they consider to know nothing. Projecting an absolute ignorance onto others, a characteristic of the ideology of oppression, negates education and knowledge as processes of inquiry.[20]

He also argues that education must begin by reconciling the idea that both participants in pedagogy are at the same time teachers and students. This radical pedagogy is in stark contrast to instructional pedagogy entrenched—despite those who struggle against it—within many of the academy's structures and practices. Soviet Commissar of Public Education Anatoly Lunacharsky explained the difference between instruction and education in the following terms:

> *Instruction* is the transmission of ready knowledge by the teacher to his pupil. *Education* is a creative process. The personality of the individual is being 'educated' throughout life, is being formed, grows richer in content, stronger and more perfect.[21]

---

20   Freire, 72.

21   Boris Schwarz, *Music and Musical Life in Soviet Russia, Enlarged Edition, 1917–1981* (Bloomington: Indiana University Press, 1983), 14–15.

Indeed, for Freire, the main benefit of his dialogical ped-agogy—as opposed to the banking model—is precisely that it "is constituted and organized by the student's view of the world, where their own generative themes are found… the task of the dialogical teacher in an interdisciplinary team working on the thematic uni-verse revealed by their investigation is to 're-present' that universe to the people from whom she or he first received it—and 're-pres-ent' it not as a lecture, but as a problem."[22]

To me, this would be a fine mission for libraries, to provide a space in which interdisciplinary teams could be formed and work, teams formed of students and books, made possible and facilitat-ed by the work of librarians, in which the book as equality of intel-ligence could re-present the students' worlds to them as problems. For Rancière the role of *the book* in education as opposed to instruc-tion is to create a relationship between two intelligences:

> By leaving his intelligence out of the picture, [the teach-er] had allowed their intelligence to grapple with that of the book. Thus, the two functions that link the prac-tice of the master explicator, that of the savant and that of the master, had been dissociated. The two faculties in play during the act of learning, namely intelligence and will, had therefore also been separated, liberated from each other. A pure relationship of will to will had been established between master and student: a relationship wherein the master's domination resulted in an entire-ly liberated relationship between the intelligence of the student and that of the book—the intelligence of the book that was also the thing in common, the egalitar-ian intellectual link between master and student. This device allowed the jumbled categories of the pedagogi-cal act to be sorted out, and explicative stultification to be precisely defined. There is stultification whenever one intelligence is subordinated to another. A person—and

---

22   Freire, *Pedagogy of the Oppressed*, 109.

a child in particular—may need a master when his own
will is not strong enough to set him on track and keep
him there. But that subjection is purely one of will over
will. It becomes stultification when it links an intelligence to another intelligence. In the act of teaching and
learning there are two wills and two intelligences. We
will call their coincidence stultification. In the experi-
mental situation Jacotot created, the student was linked
to a will, Jacotot's, and to an intelligence, the book's—
the two entirely distinct. We will call the known and
maintained difference of the two relations—the act of
an intelligence obeying only itself even while the will
obeys another will—emancipation.[23]

Here is a concept of intellectual freedom distinct from the partial
perspectives of hegemonic bourgeois thought. So the question becomes: what if the library recognized and took ownership of its etymological history as *a place of books*? What if it began to take seriously a mission not of "access to information" or "access to resources,"
but of emancipation, and more specifically emancipation through
the *intelligence of books*. Such emancipation might fulfill Freire's requirement that the oppressed emancipate themselves, by the same
logic Rancière uses—that the relationship of the intelligence of the
student to the intelligence of the book is not a relationship of subjection. Instead, then, of the varied and multiple (and sometimes
contradictory) goals of cataloging, systems, or public services, what
if we engaged seriously with a mission of emancipation. This would
put us at odds with the mission of the (explicatory) university, but
perhaps we could position ourselves as complementary to it, or rather *antagonistic to it*, according to the model of dual power. In an academic context, we could provide a counterweight to the traditional model of pedagogy dominant within the academy; in the public
context, we could provide freedom from the cultural dominance of

---

23   Jacques Rancière, *The Ignorant Schoolmaster: Five Lessons in Intellectual
     Emancipation* (Stanford: Stanford University Press, 1991): 13.

neoliberal capitalism and its requirements for consumption. This would require a commitment, a partisanship on the part of an *ethics of emancipation*. In this view, the value of libraries that we would do well to take seriously, can be located in the way Rancière sums up the place of the book in a project of radical emancipatory investigation: "The book *is* the equality of intelligence."[24]

The Mathetic Library

Rancière's concept of radical equality could have a serious impact on the quest for a real mission for libraries, a mission that does not merely reproduce neoliberal goals and requirements. Currently, despite the best intentions of library workers, libraries are adrift in a current of competing interests, as capitalism attempts both to recover from the previous economic crisis and prepare for the next one (through its tried-and-true strategies of subsumption and technological innovation). In keeping with the idea of education as the broader context of intellectual freedom, at least as it relates to libraries, I want to contrast Rancière's concept of *mathesis* with the idea of pedagogy itself.

In their contribution to a recent volume on Critical Library Instruction, Cathy Eisenhower and Dolsy Smith write that "we use the word *pedagogy*, and to a lesser extent, *critical pedagogy*, to rally ourselves and our library colleagues around approaches to teaching research that go beyond the bounds of typical library instruction." Moreover, the term pedagogy is used "as a wedge to open space… for a more intellectually sustaining and reflective way of thinking about what we do, a more fruitful praxis."[25] Eisenhower and Smith rightly criticize a view of critical pedagogy that "works to create a democratic public sphere in which citizens debate critical issues and

---

24 Rancière, *Ignorant Schoolmaster*, 38.

25 Cathy Eisenhower and Dolsy Smith, "The Library as 'Stuck Place': Critical Pedagogy in the Corporate University," in *Critical Library Instruction: Theories and Methods*, ed. Maria T. Accardi, Emily Drabinski, and Alana Kumbler (Duluth: Library Juice Press, 2009), 305.

transform civil society into a more socially just network"[26] (i.e. the transcendental discourse of libraries). Given, "the absence of serious reflection on how teachers are necessarily implicated in the oppressive formations to which they draw attention,"

> We do not exactly teach what we preach, [and the] very possibility of a critical pedagogy of library instruction would seem to hinge on a prior critique of the aims and conditions of library instruction, a critique that we have not made explicit to ourselves.[27]

In one sense, then, critical library instruction is lacking a critique of ideology—a lack which Eisenhower and Smith seek to redress— but on the other hand, the intellectual and affective affordances of library instruction in the post-Fordist capitalist university, under a regime of immaterial labor, are recouped by the organization itself. Drawing on the work of Autonomous Marxists like Maurizio Lazzarato, Eisenhower and Smith do not see the situation as completely hopeless. Autonomous Marxism, unlike, say, the critical theory of the Frankfurt School, sees the antagonistic capacity of the working class as able to forge its own room to maneuver, despite all attempts by capital and domination and overdetermination. Nonetheless, Eisenhower and Smith write,

> our position remains profoundly ambivalent. As librarians, our engagement (with pedagogy) is not given but must be wrested from situations that would reduce such engagement to the motives of efficiency, even if the place of that efficiency, in the overall 'business' of teaching at the university, seems to verge on the negligible.[28]

---

26 Eisenhower and Smith, "Library as 'Stuck Place,'" 305.

27 Eisenhower and Smith, 306.

28 Eisenhower and Smith, 316.

This ambivalence only exists, however, in the context of a deontological or consequentialist ethics that looks to either "the rules of the game" (rigged by capital) or outcomes (easily recuperated by capital) as the method of assessment. A partisan pedagogy, like a partisan librarianship, one which engages with a virtue ethics, might help to solve the ambiguity.

In "Information Literacy and Social Power," Jonathan Cope's contribution to the same volume, he contrasts a mainstream, pluralist, pedagogical tradition—where "social institutions in Western liberal democracies are neutral terrain in which different groups interests, and blocs vie for power through conflict and dialogue"[29] with a second genealogy drawing on Gramsci and Foucault. Cope concludes that this second stream can provide LIS with "concepts that can facilitate the development of a critical theory of [information literacy],"[30] by placing the instructor—and, indeed, the library worker—within the same social and cultural context as the students. Cope concludes that

> The second stream of social power research problematizes social subjects' relationships to social and educational institutions; the mainstream tradition does not. The mainstream/pluralist tradition places a greater emphasis on the importance of consensus building and the importance of subjects choosing from available options. The second stream is interested in opening new avenues for critique and analysis.[31]

All of these critical perspectives and approaches are, of course, valuable. The more we can figure out theoretical and practical ways to

---

29   Jonathan Cope, "Information Literacy and Social Power," in *Critical Library Instruction: Theories and Methods*, ed. Maria T. Accardi, Emily Drabinski, and Alana Kumbler (Duluth: Library Juice Press, 2009): 16.

30   Cope, "Information Literacy," 21.

31   Cope, 21.

effectively instill critique and resistance, the better. However, as Eisenhower and Smith have noted, even the most critical of instruction practices are easily recuperable within the neoliberal university, and I would add that the library's *cultural and ideological* effects—reproducing capitalist social and economic relationships and regimes of power—in the long run undermine what is possible even within critical library instruction.

What if we were to go a step further? Rather than focusing on library instruction as a particular area of library work—and this would require undoing decades of fragmentation and siloization within the libraries themselves—what if we thought of the library's mission as itself educational. This would require, I think, also moving beyond the concept of *pedagogy* which, like "education", refers to the leading out of a subordinate (from the Greek, παιδός [child] + ἄγω [I lead]). "Pedagogy", even when it does not perpetuate the banking model of education, still tends to involve what Rancière calls the "subjection" of one intellect to another. There is an implicit inequality in the teacher-student relationship—even if the teacher adopts a critical praxis—between the one who leads and the one who is led.

Such a fundamental inequality is, obviously, the basis of the modern university itself. It seems to have been less prominent in older European universities where students were expected to "teach themselves," but those societies were built on a much firmer foundation of class inequality, which made up for a lack of "solid pedagogical principles." One could argue that the student/teacher inequality conforms to the more sublimated hierarchical requirements of late capitalism. Our mainstream pedagogical principles support what Deleuze calls the "society of control" just as physical order (school timetables and desks in rows) supported Foucault's "society of discipline," conditioning schoolchildren to accept the exigencies of factory discipline for which school was merely a preparation. The academic library, meanwhile, in a mistaken bid to be taken seriously by the academy, now attempts to play the pedagogical game by the academy's rules, including the metrics, analytics, and outcomes that reinforce the student/teacher inequality itself. This view of pedagogy might seem needlessly pessimistic, but this indeed was the lesson of Rancière's investigation: "For the teacher, the only thing is to say goodbye to any hope not only in the institution, but in the practice of teaching itself."[32]

What if, rather than conforming to such an inequality, academic and public libraries went the opposite route, to become places where this inequality does not hold, a place—perhaps the only place in the entire system of public education—where learning happens precisely *in the absence of a teacher*, where students are expected to teach themselves with the aid, naturally, of books. Such a radical equality is at the heart of Rancière's view of education, a view which connects "individual emancipation" with "collective hope."[33] This view, however, requires "going beyond the conclusion that it is impossible for a teacher to be also a citizen or a militant"[34]:

> The fight for equality, for the participation of everyone in the exercise of thought, and therefore of the government of the city, is made possible by the gaps between the cogs of the institution, in the meeting of individuals and intelligences, in the practices, in the real experiments in which what we can do is weave in the present egalitarian relationships. Equality is an autonomous dynamic, not the means to another end.[35]

Here, then, is a mission for libraries: emancipation, equality. If libraries adopted a radical egalitarianism as a principle, and emancipation as a value, then many of the ambiguities and contradictions of our work could potentially be resolved *even without the restructuring provided by the revolution*, at least provisionally. But in order to do this, library workers will have to recognize that, as Devin

---

32 Grégory Chambat, *Pédagogie et Révolution: Questions de classe et (re)lectures pédagogique.* (Paris: Libertalia, 2015): 190.

33 Chambat, *Pédagogie*, 192.

34 Chambat, 192.

35 Chambat, 192–93.

Zane Shaw reminds us, "emancipation is not an end point of a historical continuum. Instead, emancipation is only possible through the efforts of those who combat inequality and oppression through practices of reciprocity and solidarity."[36] And this, in turn, requires not merely a critical perspective on the part of library workers, but a real partisan commitment to emancipation and social justice.

Dual power and mathesis: two possible—if utopian—strategies which might provide an emancipating mission for libraries. On the one hand, dual power as the not only the antagonism with the structures, dynamics, and logics of capitalism, but erecting an alternative to them, in which social services abdicated by the state are taken over. We do much of this work already, but it is reactive, forced on us by circumstances, rather than sought out and taken up as a means to support the education (in the fullest sense) of citizens. Which leads us to mathesis, of the priority of *learning* over *teaching*, of education as the encounter between two equal intelligences, that of the student and that of the book, with the work of the library falling into place around this encounter, supporting it and making it possible. Utopian, perhaps, but as Freire argues in *Pedagogy of Hope*, the very vocation of education—a humanizing vocation—requires precisely the "adoption of a utopia." "Utopia," he writes, "would not be possible if it lacked the taste for freedom that permeates the vocation to humanization. Or if it lacked hope, without which we do not struggle."[37]

---

36 Devin Zane Shaw, *Egalitarian Moments: From Descartes to Rancière* (London: Bloomsbury, 2016), 46.

37 Paolo Freire, *Pedagogy of Hope: Reliving Pedagogy of the Oppressed* (New York: Continuum, 1994), 99.

Conclusion: Lives and Time

In *Philosophy and Real Politics*, Raymond Geuss writes that "Politics... is not and cannot be a strictly value-free enterprise, and so is in the very general sense an 'ethical' activity. Politics is a matter of human, and not merely mechanical, interaction between individuals, institutions, or groups."[1] Librarianship, then, must not rely on *presumptions* of enlightenment, virtue, good intentions, abstract values, or vague social commitments. Rather, it has to critically interrogate the material genealogies of those commitments in order to construct the kind of theory that will inform practice along the lines of Marx's 11th thesis on Feuerbach. As Geuss goes on to write, "every theory is partisan,"[2] which means on the one hand that no theory can be neutral, uncommitted, or universal, while on the other hand requiring theory to commit to concrete moments of practical struggle.

The kind of commitment or partisanship I have been calling for here raises, for those who still cling uncritically to the hegemonic liberalism of bourgeois society, questions of the "slippery slope." If we reject the abstract values of "equality" and "liberty" in favor of more concrete politics, if we abjure "neutrality" and the solemn sovereignty of individualism, if we challenge private property

---

1   Geuss, *Philosophy and Real Politics*, 8.

2   Geuss, 29.

and intervene explicitly in the intellectual and cultural lives of our fellow citizens (defined as broadly as possible) then, the liberal believes, we have started down the road to authoritarianism. At a talk given in January 2019 at the Ontario Library Association, Safiya Noble called for more government regulation of online spaces, social media, and search. One of the audience members asked the slippery slope question: once we begin to intervene in the unsullied laissez-faire freedom of the internet, don't we then risk becoming as bad as China? Noble argued that the problem is with the presumption of an uninfluenced, unmanaged internet. The internet may appear to be self-defining, a realm of pure, amoral algorithms and arithmetic, against which any public intervention would appear to be a corruption. But Noble's entire research project in *Algorithms of Oppression* denies this presumed autonomy. The internet—social media, search—are *already* realms of manipulation and intervention for very particular private aims. The choice is not between the liberal illusions of pure, individual freedom against tyranny, the choice is between both corporate and state tyranny on the one hand and a collective commitment to concrete social justice on the other.

In his 2008 collection of essays, *On Russian Music*, the musicologist Richard Taruskin discusses the effect of quoting of the opening motif of Beethoven's Fifth Symphony in Charles Ives' dissonant *Concord Sonata*. Taruskin argues that

> Having heard the Beethoven, we hear Ives differently, and having heard the Ives, we hear Beethoven differently. We carry the discourse around in our heads. We can no more ignore it—can no more listen 'innocently'—than we can follow the ancient recipe for turning lead into gold... But why should we ever want to ignore the discourse? The force and richness of our response to music (and not only music) depends on it. That is what is meant by participating in a culture.[3]

---

3   Richard Taruskin, *On Russian Music* (Berkeley: University of California Press, 2008): 341.

The point here is that we are born into a culture, we acquire our culture, our language, our social relations, our positions in networks and structures of power unconsciously and not by our own choice. There is no such thing as a state of nature populated by self-sufficient rugged individualists, as liberal political theory holds, and which we as a culture instil in children and students. There is no such thing as pure unconstrained freedom, intellectual or otherwise; we are all members of the culture of our parents and teachers, growing up faced with their values, perspectives, biases, and prejudices. There is no transcendental point outside the culture from which we can judge and decide whether or not to intervene. Our own lives are a process which we cannot pause while we decide (rationally!) what to do next. The very fact that we do not *choose* to learn our first language is a good indication of the already existing culture that "limits" our individual freedom.

Everything we do—whether we consider it neutral (or rational or "evidence based") or not—is a committed intervention in our culture. The question is whether that commitment is explicit, just as Safiya Noble calls for the regulation of search and other online spaces to be made explicit (and public) rather than be left to private interests. Because the opposite of explicit commitment is not disinterested neutrality, but unconscious commitment, ideology in the worst sense.

What is significant here is not only that the slippery slope question is itself "innocent," coming from a naïve belief in autonomy, individualism, self-reliance, etc., all the bromides which a hegemonic liberalism drums into us from the time we are born, through parents who believe the same things, schools which teach them, the "common sense" of bourgeois society, and a marketing industry that capitalizes on the effects of these beliefs. But the slippery slope question is also innocent in another way: it presumes the innocence of society. *Our* society—a society of freedom, individualism, and the social contract—is innocent, unregulated, living off manna from heaven. Any *mistakes* are simply that, unfortunate accidents or, at worst, the results of the actions of a few bad apples. Our society, in general, follows the path of progress. A rising tide raises all boats.

Other societies, on the other hand—and the current bogeyman is China—are coercive, authoritarian, denying individualism, property rights, and freedom itself. Or they are backward, uncivilized, unenlightened, and hoping for the chance to become like us. It is not hard to see in this the roots of colonialism, xenophobia, and racism.

Marx challenges the idea of a society derived from the state of nature, from rational individuals choosing to come together for their own mutual benefit. This was a mainstay not only of bourgeois economists like Adam Smith, but even of critics like the anarchist Pierre-Joseph Proudhon. Marx argued that we are never—indeed can never be—outside of society, outside the system of social and cultural relationships that pre-exist us and into which we are born and grow up: "production by an isolated individual outside society... is as much of an absurdity as the development of language without individuals living *together* and talking to each other."[4]

Economists like Proudhon got their social ideas from political theorists of the 17th century—specifically Hobbes, Locke, and Rousseau—who inaugurated the idea of an original state of nature in which self-sufficient individuals go about their business and exercise their property rights. Marx dismisses these ideas as "Robinsonades" (after Defoe's *Robinson Crusoe* of 1719). Such legendary origins are still with us, informing intellectual freedom, copyright law, labor policy, and diversity initiatives within the profession. The problem with such Robinsonades—and this, too, is part of the slippery slope question—is that it prevents us from explicitly and publicly taking control in our own society. Free societies (like free search and intellectual freedom) are, by definition, unrestricted, and any regulation or attempt to control them must then lead to Chinese-style tyranny. But the truth is that such freedom does not exist: "that is what is meant by participating in a culture." By arguing from an innocent position, we do not guarantee some purported freedom of the public sphere, or the internet, or librarianship; rather we abandon the field to the private interests who

---

4   Marx, *Grundrisse*, 84.

already control and manipulate those spaces for their own profit, avarice, and lust for power.

This innocence is a core component of many issues within librarianship, from an "intellectual freedom" that relies on a veneer of sophistication and worldliness but is still founded on an innocent liberalism, to the shocked reaction of white librarians to suggestions of structural racism within the profession. Librarianship cannot be structurally racist, sexist, or ableist, because libraries are arsenals of a democratic culture and the cornerstones of liberty! This is the fiction of innocence that is closely intertwined with the democratic discourse of librarianship. This is the fiction of innocence that allows the far-right to co-opt library trustworthiness to give themselves a coating of intellectual respectability, and it is the fiction of innocence that allows racism, sexism, ableism, and all the other structures of oppression to thrive in our profession and our professional organizations.

To return to the question raised in the introduction, the fiction of innocence also determines how we think about lives and time. It is innocence that prevents us from connecting racist incidents within the profession with the mass incarceration of Black and Indigenous People in North America; it is innocence that insists on seeing Pride parades as monuments of inclusivity rather than as memorials of radical action on the part of queer communities (and hence it is innocence that prevents us from understanding why cops are not welcome); it is innocent individualism that makes everything a matter of personal choice, responsibility, and reaction, rather than the overdetermining effects of structures of oppression. The fact that people are dying—that Black and trans and Indigenous lives are being taken—is so offensive to the innocence of hegemonic liberalism that it simply doesn't register, not until radical action is taken. But bourgeois ideology has a way of dealing with that too, condemning radicals for being violent, uncivilized, dangerous, zealot SJWs. So the innocence of liberalism would prefer to think that people are not dying, or if they are, then it is the result of bad apples (among the cops, for example) or racist belief in inherent violence (as in 'Black on Black crime'). And if no one is dying, then we can keep pretending that all's right with the world and nothing needs to change. From this perspective any call to commitment looks like a "slippery slope" on the road to tyranny. It ignores the fact that for Black people, Indigenous People, queer people, and many others, tyranny is already here.

It's the same with the lack of time. Between the melting ice, the sixth "great extinction" heralded by the collapse of insect species, over-population of the planet, and the constant need for what capitalism euphemistically refers to as "growth," we are destroying the viability of the planet for all but the simplest, hardiest, and most resilient of life-forms. Perhaps this is as it should be; perhaps our unwavering commitment to the ravages of capitalist greed require that the planet swat us away like a horse swats an annoying fly. Jameson is often quoted as saying that "it is easier to imagine the end of the world than the end of capitalism." But who in all conscience can knowingly condemn humanity to a painful, horrific, and implacable death simply because we are tired of struggling against the alienation and suffering caused by capital? And what of all the non-human species we would also be condemning? We do not have the right to choose for them, although this has never stopped us in the past.

Lives and time: the fact that lives are being taken and time is running out raises difficult political questions, not least for democratic theory. From a Marxist perspective, the Leninist and Maoist insistence on the party-form, dictatorship, and people's war may prove to be the only way to halt the advance of rapacious capitalism and save the planet. The source of this solution will almost certainly not come from the centers of advanced capitalism, but from the periphery, where Maoist insurrection and organization has a long history. But even leaving insurrection aside, the question of what to do with the people who insist that nothing is wrong, that some people are less than human, that property-rights and capitalist expansion are sacrosanct, poses serious problems for democracy. We may have to force such people to *stop*, to fall in line, or at the very least we may have to prevent them from continuing to make things worse. Such a situation will require serious rethinking of democracy and political theory. And the kiss of death for such a re-evaluation is innocence.

Ending capitalism will not solve all our problems. Patriarchy and white supremacy, to name only two insidious structures, have too long a history, are too embedded in our society, to be so easily resolved. But ending capitalism may at least buy ourselves some time and may slow the loss of life due to economic factors. However, if we want to fix these things, we must in some sense come to terms, not necessarily with *guilt*, but with responsibility, commitment, the fact that, while we do indeed develop in a particular society and culture, we are not completely determined by it. Constituent power can and must struggle against constituted power, can and must make hard choices, but those choices have to arise from concrete, collective experience, and a joyful taking on of responsibility. They cannot arise from a fatal innocence.

Bibliography

Adami, Christoph. "What is Information?" *Philosophical Transactions of the Royal Society* A374 20150230. https://doi.org/10.1098/rsta.2015.0230.

Agamben, Giorgio. *Homo Sacer: Sovereign Power and Bare Life.* Stanford: Stanford University Press, 1998.

———. *State of Exception.* Chicago: University of Chicago Press, 2005.

Althusser, Louis. *On the Reproduction of Capitalism: Ideology and Ideological State Apparatuses.* New York: Verso, 2014.

American Library Association. "Core Values of Librarianship." http://www.ala.org/advocacy/intfreedom/corevalues.

———. "Libraries: The Cornerstones of Democracy." http://www.ala.org/aboutala/libraries-cornerstone-democracy.

Amin, Samir. *Eurocentrism: Modernity, Religion, and Democracy: A Critique of Eurocentrism and Culturalism*, Second Edition. New York: Monthly Review, 2009.

Anderson, Robert. "University Fees in Historical Perspective." *History & Policy*, February 8, 2016. http://www.historyandpolicy.org/policy-papers/papers/university-fees-in-historical-perspective.

Aristotle. *The Politics.* London: Penguin Books, 1951.

Arendt, Hannah. *The Human Condition,* Second Edition. Chicago: University of Chicago Press, 1958.

Arnold, Matthew. *Culture and Anarchy: An Essay in Political and Social Criticism.* London: Smith, Elder, 1889.

Asimov, Isaac. *Foundation, Foundation and Empire, Second Foundation.* New York: Everyman, 2010.

Bacevic, Jana. "The paradox of resistance: critique, neoliberalism, and the limits of performativity." *Jana Bacevic* (blog), February 7, 2018. https://janabacevic.net/2018/02/07/paradox-of-resistance-critique-neoliberalism-and-the-limits-of-performativity/.

Bales, Stephen. *The Dialectic of Academic Librarianship: A Critical Approach.* Sacramento: Library Juice Press, 2015.

Bartlett, Tom "'I Want to Burn things to the Ground'," *Chronicle of Higher* Education, (September 11, 2018). https://www.chronicle.com/article/I-Want-to-Burn-Things-to/244488

Bastani, Aaron. *Fully Automated Luxury Communism.* New York: Verso, 2019.

Beasley, Myron M. "Performing Refuge/Restoration: The Role of Libraries in the African American Community—Ferguson, Baltimore and Dorchester." *Performance Research* 22, no 1, 2017: 75–81. https://doi.org/10.1080/135 28165.2017.1285568.

Bell, Daniel. *The Coming of Post-Industrial Society: A Venture in Social Forecasting.* New York: Basic Books, 1976.

Berlin, Isaiah. *Liberty.* Oxford: Oxford University Press, 2002.

Berman, Sanford. *Prejudices and Antipathies: A Tract on LC Subject Heads Concerning People.* Metuchen, NJ: Scarecrow Press, 1971.

———. "Libraries to the People." In *Revolting Librarians,* edited by Celeste West, 51–57. San Francisco: Booklegger Press, 1972.

Besner, Linda. "Risotto, robotics, and virtual reality: how Canada created the world's best libraries." *The Guardian* (June 15, 2018). https://www.theguardian.com/cities/2018/jun/15/risotto-robotics-and-virtual-reality-how-canada-created-the-worlds-best-libraries

Bhaskar, Roy. *A Realist Theory of Science.* Leeds: Leeds Books, 1975.

Bivens-Tatum, Wayne. *Libraries and the Enlightenment.* Los Angeles: Library Juice Press, 2012.

Black, Alistair. *A New History of the English Public Library.* Leicester: Leicester University Press, 1998.

———. The Library as Clinic: A Foucauldian Interpretation of British Public Library Attitudes to Social and Physical Disease, ca 1850–1950," *Libraries & Culture* 40, no. 3 (2005): 416–34.

Black, Alistair and David Muddiman. *Understanding Community Librarianship: The Public Library in Post-Modern Britain.* London: Ashgate, 1997.

Blackledge, Paul. *Marxism and Ethics: Freedom, Desire, and Revolution.* New York: SUNY Press, 2013.

"Boston Public Library." In *Encyclopedia of Library History,* edited by F. William Summers, Wayne Wiegand, Donald Davis, 85–86. New York, London: Garland Publishing, 1994.

Bowles, Vickery. "Update on Last Evening's Event at Richview Library," *Toronto Public Library* (July 13, 2017). https://torontopubliclibrary.typepad.com/ programming/2017/07/update-on-last-evenings-event-at-richview- library.html

Braudel, Fernand. "Histoire et Sciences Sociales: La Longue Durée." *Annales* 13, no. 4 (1958): 725–53. https://doi.org/10.3406/ahess.1958.2781.

Brean, Joseph. "Far-right Extremists Converge at Memorial for Toronto Lawyer." *National Post* (July 12, 2017). http://nationalpost.com/news/canada/ canadas-far-right-extremists-to-converge-at-memorial-for-lawyer- unless-venue-relents-to-pressure.

Brenner, Robert. *The Economics of Global Turbulence: The Advanced Capitalist Economies from Long Boom to Long Downturn, 1945–2005.* London, New York: Verso, 2006.

Brint, Michael, William G. Weaver, and Meredith Garmon. "What Difference does Anti-Foundationalism Make to Political Theory?" *New Literary History* 26 (1995): 225–37.

Budd, John M. "The Library, Praxis, and Symbolic Power." *Library Quarterly* 73, no. 1 (2003): 19–32.

Buschman, John. *Dismantling the Public Sphere: Situating and Sustaining Librarianship in the Age of the New Public Philosophy.* Westport, CT: Libraries Unlimited, 2003.

———. "November 8, 2016: Core Values, Bad Faith, and Democracy." *The Library Quarterly* 87, no. 3 (2017): 277–86. https://doi.org/10.1086/692305.

———. "On Democracy and Libraries." *The Library Quarterly* 88, no. 1 (2018): 23–40. https://doi.org/10.1086/694871.

———. "Everyday Life, Everyday Democracy in Libraries: Toward Articulating the Relationship." *The Political Librarian* 4, no. 1 (2018): 18–28.

Butler, Peirce. "Librarianship as a Profession." In *Landmarks of Library Literature, 1876–1976,* edited by Dianne J. Ellsworth and Norman D. Stevens. Metuchen, NJ, 24–43. Scarecrow Press, 1976.

Buxton, Harry Wilmot and Anthony Hyman. *Memoir of the Life and Labours of the Late Charles Babbage Esq, FRS.* Cambridge: MIT Press, 2003.

Byrn, David T. The Victory of the Proletariat is Inevitable: The Millenarian Nature of Marxism." *Kritike* 5, no. 2 (2011): 59–67.

Byrne, Alex. "Democracy and Libraries: Symbol or Symbiosis?" *Library Management* 39, no. 5 (2018): 284–94. https://doi.org/10.1108/LM-09-2017-0088.

Callinicos, Alex. "Critical Realism and Beyond: Roy Bhaskar's *Dialectic*." In *Critical Companion to Contemporary Marxism,* edited by Jacques Bidet and Stathis Kouvelakis, 567–86. Chicago: Haymarket, 2009.

Carey, J. W. "The Paradox of the Book." *Library Trends* 33, no. 2 (1984): 103–14.

Carravetta, Peter. "What is 'Weak Thought'? The Original Theses and Context of *il pensiero debole*." In *Weak* Thought, edited by Gianni Vattimo and Pier Aldo Rovatti, 1–37. New York: SUNY Press, 2012.

Caswell, Michelle. "'The Archive' is not an Archives: On Acknowledging the Intellectual Contributions of Archival Studies." *Reconstruction: Studies in Contemporary Culture* 16, no. 1 (2016). http://reconstruction.eserver.org/Issues/161/Caswell.shtml,

Chambat, Grégory. *Pédagogie et Révolution: Questions de classe et (re)lectures pédagogique.* Paris: Libertalia, 2015.

Chiesa, Lorenzo. and Alberto Toscano, "Introduction." In *The Italian Difference: Between Nihilism and Biopolitics,* edited by Lorenzo Chiesa and Alberto Toscano, 1–10. Melbourne: Re.press, 2009.

Church, Alonzo. "An unsolvable problem of elementary number theory." *American Journal of Mathematics* 58 (1936): 345–63.

Coates, Ta-Nehisi. *Between the World and Me.* New York: Spiegel and Grau, 2015.

Collins, Patricia Hill. "Gender, Black Feminism, and Black Political Economy." *The Annals of the American Academy of Political and Social Science* 568 (2000): 41–53.

"Community and Event Space Rental Policy—Revisions." *Toronto Public Library* (December 11, 2017). https://www.torontopubliclibrary.ca/content/about-the-library/pdfs/board/meetings/2017/dec11/04–community-and-event-space-rental-policy-revisions-combined.pdf.

Cope, Jonathan. "Information Literacy and Social Power." In *Critical Library Instruction: Theories and Methods*, edired by Maria T. Accardi, Emily Drabinski, and Alana Kumbler, 13–27. Duluth: Library Juice Press, 2009.

Cossette, André. *Humanism and Libraries: An Essay on the Philosophy of Librarianship.* Duluth: Library Juice Press, 2009.

Cox, Robert. "Gramsci, Hegemony and International Relations." In *Gramsci, Historical Materialism and International Relations*, edited by Stephen Gill, 49–66. Cambridge: Cambridge University Press, 1993.

Crenshawe, Kimberlé. "Demarginalizing the Intersection of Race and Sex: A Black Feminist Critique of Antidiscrimation Doctrine, Feminist Theory and Antiracist Politics." *University of Chicago Legal Forum*, 1989: 139–68.

D'Angelo, Ed. *Barbarians at the Gates of the Public Library: How Postmodern Consumer Capitalism Threatens Democracy, Civil Education and the Public Good.* Duluth: Library Juice Press, 2006.

Davis, Angela. "Masked Racism: Reflections from the Prison-Industrial Complex." *Indigenous Law Bulletin* 4, no. 27 (2000): 4–7.

Dawson, Michael C. *Blacks In and Out of the Left.* Cambridge: Harvard University Press, 2013.

Day, Ronald E. *Indexing it All.* Cambridge: MIT Press, 2014.

De Gaulle, Charles. "Discours prononcé à Bar-le-Duc, 28 juillet 1946." http://mjp.univ-perp.fr/textes/degaulle28071946.htm.

Deleuze, Gilles. "Postscript on the Societies of Control." *October* 59 (Winter 1992): 3–7.

———. *Nietzsche and Philosophy.* London: Bloomsbury, 2006.

Deleuze, Gilles, and Felix Guattari, *Anti-Oedipus: Capitalism and Schizophrenia.* Minneapolis: University of Minnesota Press, 1983.

Descartes, Rene. *Meditations on First Philosophy*. Cambridge: Cambridge University Press, 1986.

Dewey, Melvil. *Librarianship as a Profession for College-Bred Women, An Address Delivered before the Association of Collegiate Alumnae on March 13, 1886*. Boston: Library Bureau, 1886.

———. "The Profession." In *Landmarks of Library Literature, 1876–1976*, edited by Dianne J. Ellsworth and Norman D. Stevens, 21–23. Metuchen, NJ: Scarecrow Press, 1976.

DiAngelo, Robin. *White Fragility: Why It's So Hard for White People to Talk about Racism*. Boston: Beacon Press, 2018.

Ditzion, Sidney. *Arsenals of a Democratic Culture: A Social History of the American Public Library Movement in New England and the Middle States from 1850 to 1900*. Chicago: American Library Association, 1947.

Dowling, William C. *Jameson, Althusser, Marx: An Introduction to* The Political Unconscious. Ithaca: Cornell University Press, 1984.

Dreyfus, Herbert. *What Computers Still Can't Do: A Critique of Artificial Reason*. Cambridge: MIT Press, 1992.

Du Bois, W. E. B. "Marxism and the Negro Problem." *The Crisis*, 40, no. 5. (May 1933): 103–104. https://books.google.ca/books?id=xVcEAAAAMBAJ.

———. *Black Reconstruction in America: An Essay Toward a History of the Part Which Black Folk Played in the Attempt to Reconstruct Democracy in America, 1860–1880*. Oxford: Oxford University Press, 2014.

Dyer-Witheford, Nick. *Cyber-Proletariat: Global Labour in the Digital Vortex*. Toronto: Between the Lines, 2015.

Eagleton, Terry. *Illusions of Postmodernism*. Malden, MA: Blackwell, 1996.

———. *Literary Theory: An Introduction*. Minnesota: University of Minneapolis Press, 2008.

Eisenhower, Cathy, and Dolsy Smith, "The Library as 'Stuck Place': Critical Pedagogy in the Corporate University." In *Critical Library Instruction: Theories and Methods*, edited by Maria T. Accardi, Emily Drabinski, and Alana Kumbler, 305–18. Duluth: Library Juice Press, 2009.

Engels, Frederick. *Socialism: Utopian and Scientific*. London: Swan Sonnenschein and Co, 1892.

Ettarh, Fobazi. "Making a New Table: Intersectional Librarianship." *In the Library with the Lead Pipe* July 2, 2014. http://www.inthelibrarywiththeleadpipe. org/2014/making-a-new-table-intersectional-librarianship-3/.

———. "Vocational Awe and Librarianship: Lies we Tell Ourselves." *In the Library with the Lead Pipe* January 10, 2018. http://www. inthelibrarywiththeleadpipe.org/2018/vocational-awe/.

Federici, Silvia. *Revolution at Point Zero: Housework, Reproduction, and Feminist Struggle*. New York: PM Press, 2012.

———. *Caliban and the Witch: Women, The Body and Primitive Accumulation*. New York: Autonomedia, 2014.

Feenberg, Andrew. *The Philosophy of Praxis: Marx, Lukacs and the Frankfurt School*. New York: Verso, 2014.

Felski, Rita. "Critique and the Hermeneutics of Suspicion." *MC Journal* 15, no. 2 (2012). http://journal.media-culture.org.au/index.php/mcjournal/ article/viewArticle/431.

Feuerbach, Ludwig. *The Essence of Christianity*. New York: C. Blanchard, 1844.

Fischer, Suzanne. "Nota Bene: If You 'Discover' Something in an Archive, It's Not a Discovery." *The Atlantic* June 19, 2012. https://www.theatlantic.com/ technology/archive/2012/06/nota-bene-if-you-discover-something-in- an-archive-its-not-a-discovery/258538/.

Ford, Anne. "Bringing Harassment Out of the History Books." *American Libraries*, June 1, 2018. https://americanlibrariesmagazine.org/2018/06/01/ melvil-dewey-bringing-harassment-out-of-the-history-books/.

Foucault, Michel. *Power/Knowledge: Selected Interviews and Other Writings*. New York: Vintage, 1980.

———. *Discipline and Punish: The Birth of the Prison*. New York: Vintage, 1995.

Franklin, Ursula. *The Real World of Technology*. Toronto: House of Anansi, 1999.

Freire, Paolo. *Pedagogy of Hope: Reliving Pedagogy of the Oppressed*. New York: Continuum, 1994.

———. *Pedagogy of the Oppressed*. New York: Bloomsbury, 2012.

Friedman, Milton. "The Social Responsibility of Business is to Increase its Profits." *The New York Times Magazine*, September 13, 1970: 2–3, 122–24.

———. *Capitalism and Freedom.* Chicago: Chicago University Press, 1982.

Fukuyama, Francis. *The End of History and the Last Man*, 2nd ed. New York: Simon and Schuster, 2006.

Galvan, Angela. "Soliciting Performance, Hiding Bias: Whiteness and Librarianship." *In the Library with the Lead Pipe*, June 3, 2015. http://www. inthelibrarywiththeleadpipe.org/2015/soliciting-performance-hiding-bias-whiteness-and-librarianship/.

Garrison, Dee. "The Tender Technicians: The Feminization of Public Librarianship, 1876–1905." *Journal of Social History* 6, no. 2 (1972/3): 131–59.

———. *Apostles of Culture: The Public Librarian and American Society, 1876–1920.* Madison: University of Wisconsin Press, 2003.

Geuss, Raymond. *Philosophy and Real Politics.* Princeton: Princeton University Press, 2008.

Goulding, Anne. "Libraries and Cultural Capital." *JOLIS* 40, no. 4 (2008).

Graeber, David. *Debt: The First 5,000 Years.* New York: Melville House, 2011.

Gramsci, Antonio. *Selections from the Prison Notebooks.* New York: International Publishers, 1971.

Habermas, Jürgen. *The Theory of Communicative Action, Volume 2: Lifeworld and System: A Critique of Functionalist Reason.* Boston: Beacon Press, 1987.

———. *The Structural Transformation of the Public Sphere: An Enquiry into a Category of Bourgeois Society.* Cambridge: MIT Press, 1989.

Hall, Stuart. "The Problem of Ideology—Marxism without Guarantees." *Journal of Communication Inquiry* 10, no. 2 (1986): 28–44.

———. *Selected Political Writings: The Great Moving Right Show and Other Essays*, 158–171. Durham: Duke University Press, 2017.

Hardt, Michael, and Antonio Negri. *Empire.* Cambridge: Harvard University Press, 2000.

Harris, Michael H. "The Purpose of the American Public Library in Historical Perspective: A Revisionist Interpretation." ERIC Clearinghouse, 1972. https://eric.ed.gov/?id=ED071668.

Harris, Michael. "The Role of the Public Library in American Life: A Speculative Essay." University of Illinois Occasional Papers, 1976.

Harris, Michael. "State, Class, and Cultural Reproduction: Toward a Theory of Library Service in the United States." *Advances in Librarianship* 14 (1986): 211–52.

Harris, Michael H. *History of Libraries in the Western World*, 4th Ed. Metuchen, NJ: Scarecrow Press, 1995.

Harris, Michael H., and Gerard Spiegler. "Everett, Ticknor and the Common Man: The Fear of Societal Instability as the Motivation for the Founding of the Boston Public Library." *Libri* 24, no. 2. (1974): 249–76. https://doi.org/10.1515/libr.1974.24.4.249.

Harvey, David. *The Condition of Postmodernity: An Enquiry into the Origins of Cultural Change*. Oxford: Blackwell, 1990.

———. *The New Imperialism*. Oxford: Oxford University Press, 2003.

———. *Brief History of Neoliberalism*. Oxford: Oxford University Press, 2005.

———. *Social Justice and the City*. Athens: University of Georgia Press, 2009.

———. *The Enigma of Capital and the Crises of Capitalism*. Oxford: Oxford University Press, 2010.

———. "Why Marx's Capital Still Matters." *Jacobin* July 12, 2018. https://jacobinmag.com/2018/07/karl-marx-capital-david-harvey.

Hathcock, April. "White Librarianship in Blackface: Diversity Initiatives in LIS." *In the Library with The Lead Pipe* October 7, 2015. http://www.inthelibrarywiththeleadpipe.org/2015/lis-diversity.

Hegel, G.W.F. *The Philosophy of History*. New York: Dover, 1956.

Heinrich, Michael. *An Introduction to the Three Volumes of Karl Marx's* Capital. New York: Monthly Review, 2012.

Hicks, Marie. *Programmed Inequality: How Britain Discarded Women Technologists and Lost Its Edge in Computing*. Cambridge: MIT Press, 2017.

Hill, Christopher. *The Century of Revolution, 1603–1714*. London: Abacus, 1974.

Hobbes, Thomas. *Man and Citizen (De Homine and De Cive*. Indianapolis: Hackett, 1991.

Hobsbawm, Eric. *Age of Empire: 1875–1914*. London Abacus, 1987.

———. *Age of Extremes: The Short Twentieth Century, 1914–1991*. London: Abacus, 1995.

Horkheimer, Max. *Critique of Instrumental Reason*. New York: Verso, 2013.

Horkheimer, Max, and Theodor W. Adorno. *Dialectic of Enlightenment: Philosophical Fragments*. Stanford: Stanford University Press, 2002.

Hudson, David James. "Unpacking 'Information Inequality': Toward a Critical Discourse of Global Justice in Library and Information Science." *Canadian Journal of Information and Library Science* 36, no. 2–4 (2012): 69–87.

———. "The Whiteness of Practicality." In *Topographies of Whiteness: Mapping Whiteness in Library and Information Studies*, edited by Gina Schlesselman-Tarango, 203–34. *Topographies of Whiteness: Mapping Whiteness in Library and Information Studies*. Sacramento: Library Juice Press, 2017.

———. "On 'Diversity' as Anti-Racism in Library and Information Studies: A Critique." *Journal of Critical Library and Information Studies* 1, no. 2 (2017): 1–36. https://doi.org/10.24242/jclis.v1i1.6.

"Indigenous groups lead protest against Kinder Morgan's Trans Mountain pipeline plan." *CBC News* March 10, 2018. https://www.cbc.ca/news/canada/british-columbia/yes-and-no-protests-kinder-morgan-vancouver-march-2018-1.4571160.

Intrator, Miriam. "UNESCO, Reconstruction, and Pursuing Peace through a 'Library-Minded' World, 1945–1950." In *The History of Unesco: Global Actions and Impacts.*, edited by Poul Duedahl, 131–53. Basingstoke: Palgrave Macmillan, 2016.

Jameson, Fredric. *The Prison House of Language: A Critical Account of Structuralism and Russian Formalism*. Princeton: Princeton University Press, 1972.

———. *Marxism and Form: 20th Century Dialectic Theories of Literature*. Princeton: Princeton University Press, 1974.

———. *The Political Unconscious: Narrative as a Socially Symbolic Act*. Ithaca: Cornell University Press, 1981.

———. *Late Marxism: Adorno, or the Persistence of the Dialectic*. New York: Verso, 1990.

———. *Postmodernism, or, the Cultural Logic of Late Capitalism*. Durham, NC: Duke University Press, 1990.

———. *Signatures of the Visible*. New York: Routledge, 1992.

———. *The Cultural Turn: Selected Writings on the Postmodern, 1983–1998*. New York: Verso, 1998.

———. "The Aesthetic of Singularity." *New Left Review* II, no. 92 (2015): 101–32.

———. *American Utopia: Dual Power and the Universal Army*. New York: Verso, 2016.

Joyce, Steven. "A Few Gates: An Examination of the Social Responsibilities Debate in the Early 1970s & 1990s." In *Questioning Library Neutrality: Essays from Progressive Librarian*, edited by Alison Lewis, 33–65. Duluth: Library Juice Press, 2008.

Kaufman, Walter. *The Portable Nietzsche*. London: Penguin Books, 1977.

Kelley, Robin D. G. "Births of a Nation: Surveying Trumpland with Cedric Robinson", *Race Capitalism Justice*. Boston: Boston Review, 2017. http://bostonreview.net/race-politics/robin-d-g-kelley-births-nation.

———. "What is racial capitalism and why does it matter?" Lecture at Kane Hall, University of Washington, Seattle, November 7, 2017. https://youtu.be/—gim7W_jQQ.

Kikutani, Michiko. "The death of truth: how we gave up on facts and ended up with Trump." *The Guardian*, July 14, 2018. https://www.theguardian.com/books/2018/jul/14/the-death-of-truth-how-we-gave-up-on-facts-and-ended-up-with-trump.

Kliman, Andrew. *Reclaiming Marx's Capital: A Refutation of the Myth of Inconsistency*. Lanham, MD: Lexington Press, 2006.

Klinenberg, Eric. "To Restore Civil Society, Start with the Library." *New York Times* (September 8, 2018). https://www.nytimes.com/2018/09/08/opinion/sunday/civil-society-library.html.

Kranich, Nancy. *Libraries and Democracy: The Cornerstone of Liberty*. Chicago: American Library Association, 2001.

Krause, Paul. *The Battle for Homestead, 1880–1892: Political, Culture, and Steel*. Pittsburgh: University of Pittsburgh Press, 1992.

Lankes, David. *The Atlas of New Librarianship*. Cambridge: MIT Press, 2011.

Larue, James. "Library Meeting Rooms for All," *Intellectual Freedom Blog*, July 10, 2018. https://www.oif.ala.org/oif/?p=14997.

Lazzarato, Maurizio. "Immaterial Labour." In *Radical Thought in Italy: A Potential Politics*, edited by Paolo Virno and Michael Hardt, 133–47. Minneapolis: University of Minnesota Press, 1996.

———. *The Making of the Indebted Man: An Essay on the Neoliberal Condition*. Cambridge: MIT Press, 2012.

Lenin, V. I. "What can be done for public education?" In *Collected Works*, Volume 19. Moscow: Foreign Languages Publishing House, 1963: 277–79.

———. "Marxism and Reformism." In *Collected Works*, Volume 19. Moscow: Progress Publishers, 1963: 372–75.

———. "The Dual Power." In *Collected Works*, Volume 24. Moscow: Progress Publishers, 1964: 38–41.

———. "Our Foreign and Domestic Position and Party Tasks." In *Collected Works*, Volume 31. Moscow: Progress Publishers, 1966: 408–26.

———. *What is to be Done?* London: Penguin, 1988.

———. *The State and Revolution.* London: Penguin Books, 1992.

———. "To G. Myasnikov." In *Lenin 2017: Remembering, Repeating, and Working Through*, edited by Slavoj Zizek, 5–12. New York: Verso, 2017.

"Library Meeting Rooms for All." *Intellectual Freedom Blog*, July 13, 2018. https://www.oif.ala.org/oif/?p=14997#comment-562504, accessed July 14, 2018.

Locke, John. *Two Treatises of Government.* Cambridge: Cambridge University Press, 1960.

———. *An Essay Concerning Toleration*. Peterborough: Broadview, 2013.

Losurdo, Domenico. *Liberalism: A Counter-History.* New York: Verso, 2014.

Lukács, Georg. *History and Class Consciousness: Studies in Marxist Dialectics.* Cambridge: MIT Press, 1971.

———. *Lenin: A Study on the Unity of his Thought.* New York: Verso, 2009.

Luperini, Romano. *La fine de postmoderno.* Rome: Guida Editori, 2005.

Lyotard, Jean-Francois. *The Postmodern Condition: A Report on Knowledge.* Minneapolis: University of Minnesota Press 1979.

Macdonald, Nancy. "Canada's prisons are the 'new residential schools'." *MacLean's*, February 18, 2016. https://www.macleans.ca/news/canada/canadas-prisons-are-the-new-residential-schools/.

MacLeish, Archibald. "The Librarian and the Democratic Process." *ALA Bulletin* 34, no. 6 (1940): 385–88, 421–22.

———. "Of the Librarians' Profession." In *Landmarks of Library Literature, 1876–1976*, edited by Dianne J. Ellsworth and Norman D. Stevens, 13–20. Metuchen, NJ: Scarecrow Press, 1976.

Malcolmson, Patrick, Richard Myers, Gerald Baier, and Thomas M.J. Bateman. *The Canadian Regime: An Introduction to Parliamentary Government in Canada,* Sixth Edition. Toronto: University of Toronto Press, 2016.

Malm, Andreas. *The Progress of this Storm: Nature and Society in a Warming World.* New York: Verso, 2018.

Malone, Kelly Geraldine. "Nearly half of Canada's incarcerated youth are Indigenous, according to Statistics Canada." *CBC News* June 24, 2018. https://www.cbc.ca/news/canada/manitoba/youth-incarcerated-indigenous-half-1.4720019.

Mandel, Ernest. *Late Capitalism.* New York: Verso, 1999.

———. *The Formation of the Economic Thought of Karl Marx, 1843 to Capital.* New York: Verso, 2015.

Marx, Karl. *Economic and Philosophic Manuscripts of 1844.* Moscow: Progress Publishers, 1977.

———. *A Contribution to the Critique of Political Economy.* New York: International Publishers, 1970.

———. *The Eighteenth Brumaire of Louis Bonaparte.* New York: International Publishers, 1963.

———. *Grundrisse: Foundations of the Critique of Political Economy (Rough Draft).* London: Penguin, 1973.

———. *Capital, Volume 1: A Critique of Political Economy.* London: Penguin Books, 1976.

———. *Capital, A Critique of Political Economy, Volume 3.* London: Penguin Books, 1981.

Marx, Karl, and Friedrich Engels. *The German Ideology.* Moscow: Progress Publishers, 1976.

———. *The Communist Manifesto.* London: Penguin Books, 1985.

Mason, Paul. *Post-Capitalism: A Guide to Our Future.* London: Allen Lane, 2015.

Max, Stanley M. "Tory Reactions to the Public Libraries Bill, 1850," *The Journal of Library History* 19, no. 4 (Fall 1984): 504–24.

Mclellan, David. *Karl Marx: A Biography.* London: Macmillan, 1973.

Mendelson, Jack. "The Habermas-Gadamer Debate." *New German Critique* 18 (Autumn 1979): 44–73.

Moufawad-Paul, J. *Continuity and Rupture: Philosophy in the Maoist Terrain.* London: Zero Books, 2016.

Moufawad-Paul, J. *Austerity Apparatus.* Montreal: Kersplebedeb, 2017.

National Inquiry into Missing and Murdered Indigenous Women and Girls. http://www.mmiwg-ffada.ca/.

Native Women's Association of Canada, "NWAC Dismayed with Ongoing Issues at National Inquiry." January 11, 2018. https://www.nwac.ca/2018/01/11/nwac-dismayed-ongoing-issues-national-inquiry/.

Negri, Antonio. *Political Descartes: Reason, Ideology and the Bourgeois Subject* (New York: Verso, 2007).

Norman, Richard, and Sean Sayers. *Hegel, Marx and Dialectic: A Debate.* Brighton: Harvester Press, 1980.

Nuyen, A. T. "Critique of Ideology: Hermeneutics or Critical Theory?" *Human Studies* 17, no. 4 (1994/5): 419–32.

Oliver, Mike. "Defining Impairment and Disability: Issues at Stake." In *Exploring the Divide: Illness and Disability,* edited by Colin Barnes and Geoff Mercer, 29–54. Leeds: The Disability Press, 1996.

Olson, Hope A. *The Power to Name: Locating the Limits of Subject Representations in Libraries.* Dordrecht: Kluwer, 2002.

Otlet, Paul. "Something about Bibliography." In *International Organisation and Dissemination of Knowledge: Selected Essays of Paul Otlet,* edited by W. Boyd Rayward, 11–24. Amsterdam, New York: Elsevier, 1990.

Pearce, Katie. "How Libraries and Other 'Public Palaces' can Bridge Divides, Safeguard Democracy." *Johns Hopkins University Hub* (October 24, 2018). https://hub.jhu.edu/2018/10/24/eric-klinenberg-agora-institute/

Piketty, Thomas. *Capital in the Twenty-First Century.* Cambridge: Harvard University Press, 2014.

Plato. *The Republic.* Harmondsworth: Penguin Books, 1955.

Popowich, Sam. "'Ruthless Criticism of all that Exists': Marxism, Technology, and Library Work." In *The Politics of Theory and the Practice of Critical Librarianship,* edited by Karen P Nicholson and Maura Seale, 39–66. Sacramento: Library Juice Press, 2018.

———. "Libraries, Labour, Capital: On Formal and Real Subsumption." *Journal of Radical Librarianship* 4 (2018): 6–19.

Popper, K. R. *The Open Society and Its Enemies*, Volume 1. London: George Routledge and Sons, 1945.

Posner, Miriam. "We can Teach Women to code, but that just Creates Another Problem." *Guardian* March 14, 2017. https://www.theguardian.com/technology/2017/mar/14/tech-women-code-workshops-developer-jobs.

"Postal Banking." *Canadian Union of Postal Employees.* http://www.cupw.ca/en/campaigns-and-issues/postal-banking.

Powers, Ron. *Mark Twain: A Life.* New York: Free Press, 2006.

"Programme of the Communist International, Comintern Sixth Congress." 1929. https://www.marxists.org/history/international/comintern/6th-congress/ch04.htm.

Radford, Gary P. "Trapped in Our Own Discursive Formations: Toward an Archaeology of Library and Information Science." *Library Quarterly* 73, no. 1, 2003: 1–18.

Rancière, Jacques. *The Ignorant Schoolmaster: Five Lessons in Intellectual Emancipation.* Stanford: Stanford University Press, 1991.

———. *Hatred of Democracy.* London, New York: Verso, 2009.

———. "The Thinking of Dissensus: Politics and Aesthetics." In *Reading Rancière: Critical Dissensus,* edited by Paul Bowman and Richard Stamp, 1–17. London, New York: Continuum, 2011.

Reidsma, Matthew. "Algorithmic Bias in Discovery Systems." *Matthew Reidsma* (blog), March 11, 2016. https://matthew.reidsrow.com/articles/173.

Roberts, William Clare. *Marx's Inferno: The Political Theory of* Capital. Princeton and Oxford: Princeton University Press, 2017.

Robinson, Cedric. *Black Marxism: The Making of the Black Radical Tradition.* Chapel Hill, NC: University of North Carolina Press, 2000.

Rosenzweig, Mark. "Politics and Anti-Politics in Librarianship." In *Questioning Library Neutrality: Essays from Progressive Librarian,* edited by Alison Lewis, 5–7. Duluth: Library Juice Press, 2008.

Ruggie, John Gerard. "International Regimes, Transactions, and Change: Embedded Liberalism in the Postwar Economic Order." *International Organization* 36, no. 2 (1982): 379–415.

Samek, Toni. *Intellectual Freedom and Social Responsibility in American Librarianship, 1967–1974.* Jefferson, NC: McFarland, 2001.

Sartre, Jean-Paul. *Réflexions sur la Question Juive.* Paris: Gallimard, 1954.

———. *Questions de Méthode.* Paris: Gallimard, 1986.

Schlesselman-Tarango, Gina. "The Legacy of Lady Bountiful: White Women in the Library." *Library Trends* 64, no. 4 (2016): 667–86.

Schmidt, Jane. "Innovate This! Bullshit in Academic Libraries and What We Can Do About It," *RULA Digital Repository.* https://digital.library.ryerson.ca/islandora/object/RULA%3A7113.

Schmidt Jane, and Jordan Hale. "Little Free Libraries®: Interrogating the Impact of the Branded Book Exchange." *Journal of Radical Librarianship* 3 (2017): 14–41.

Schwarz, Boris. *Music and Musical Life in Soviet Russia, Enlarged Edition, 1917–1981.* Bloomington: Indiana University Press, 1983.

Shakeri, Sima. "Toronto Public Library Allows Neo-Nazi Memorial For Barbara Kulaszka To Go Ahead." *Huffington Post* (July 13, 2017). http://www.huffingtonpost.ca/2017/07/13/toronto-library-neo-nazi-event_a_23028596/.

Shaw, Devin Zane. *Egalitarian Moments: From Descartes to Rancière.* London: Bloomsbury, 2016.

Shera, Jesse H. *Foundations of the Public Library: The Origins of the Public Library Movement in New England, 1629–1855.* Chicago: University of Chicago Press, 1949.

Sloniowski, Lisa. "Affective Labor, Resistance, and the Academic Librarian." *Library Trends* 64, no. 4 (2016): 645–66.

Slorach, Roddy. "Marxism and Disability." *International Socialism* 129 (January 4, 2011). http://isj.org.uk/marxism-and-disability/.

Smith, Adam. "Overdue Books: Library to Enforce Ordinance." *The News Courier*, August 31, 2016. http://www.enewscourier.com/news/local_news/overdue-books-library-to-enforce-ordinance/article_746ed512-6f01-11e6-a0e5-53e37f6a8e2b.html.

Smith, Jason E. "Jobs, Bullshit, and the Bureaucratization of the World." *The Brooklyn Rail*, July 11, 2018. https://brooklynrail.org/2018/07/field-notes/Jobs-Bullshit-and-the-Bureaucratization-of-the-World.

Swan, John, and Noel Peattie. *The Freedom to Lie: A Debate about Democracy.* Jefferson, NC: McFarland, 1989.

Taruskin, Richard. *On Russian Music.* Berkeley: University of California Press, 2008.

Taylor, Keeanga-Yamahtta. "Race, Class and Marxism." *Socialist Worker* January 4, 2011. https://socialistworker.org/2011/01/04/race-class-and-marxism,

———. *From #BlackLivesMatter to Black Liberation.* Chicago: Haymarket, 2016.

Thayer, Joseph Henry. *A Greek English Lexicon of the New Testament.* New York: American Book Company 1886.

Thomas, Peter. D *The Gramscian Moment: Philosophy, Hegemony and Marxism.* Chicago: Haymarket Books, 2011.

Tovoté, Christina. "Marketing and Swedish Libraries: About the Situation Today and the Importance of Visible Librarians." In *Adapting Marketing to Libraries in a Changing and World-Wide Environment*, edited by Réjean Savard, 40–44. Munich: IFLA / KG Saur, 2000.

Truth and Reconciliation Commission of Canada. *Final Report of the Truth and Reconciliation Commission of Canada: Volume 1, Summary.* Toronto: Lorimer, 2015.

Turing, A. M. "On Computable Numbers, with an Application to the Entscheidungsproblem." *Proceedings of the London Mathematical Society* 42, no. 1 (1937): 230–65.

Tuveson, Ernest L. "The Millenarian Structure of *The Communist Manifesto*." In *The Apocalypse in English Renaissance Thought and Literature: Patterns, Antecedents, and Repercussions*, edited by C.A. Patrides and Joseph Anthony Wittreich, 323–41. Manchester: Manchester University Press, 1984.

Venclova, Tomas, and Alexandra Heidi Karriker. "Czesław Miłosz: Despair and Grace." *World Literature Today* 73, no. 4 (1999): 677–80.

Vinopal, Jennifer. "The Quest for Diversity in Library Staffing: From Awareness to Action." *In the Library with the Lead Pipe*, January 13, 2016. http://www.inthelibrarywiththeleadpipe.org/2016/quest-for-diversity/.

Virilio, Paul. *The Administration of Fear.* Pasadena: Semiotext(e), 2012.

Westol, Nick. "Toronto Public Library Board Votes to Revise Room-Booking Policy after Controversial Memorial." *Global News* (December 11, 2017). https://globalnews.ca/news/3910781/toronto-public-library-room-booking-policy/.

Wiegand, Wayne. *The Politics of an Emerging Profession: The American Library Association, 1876–1917*. Westport, CT: Praeger, 1986.

———. *Irrepressible Reformer: The Life of Melvil Dewey*. Chicago: American Library Association, 1996.

———. "Tunnel Vision and Blind Spots: What the Past tells us about the Present: Reflections on the Twentieth-Century of American Librarianship." *The Library Quarterly* 69, no. 1 (1999): 1–32.

Wiener, Norbert. *The Human Use of Human Beings: Cybernetics and Society*. Boston: Houghton Mifflin, 1954.

———. *Cybernetics or Control and Communication in the Animal and the Machine*. New York: MIT Press and John Wiley & Sons, 1961.

"Wives' Wages." *New York Times*, August 10, 1876: 4. https://www.nytimes.com/1876/08/10/archives/wives-wages.html.

Wróbel, Szymon. "Foucault Reads Freud: The Dialogue with Unreason and Enlightenment." *Polish Sociological Review* 171 (2010): 271–88.

Index

#critlib movement, 168, 226, 229
2008 financial crisis, 50, 183, 187

American Library Association (ALA), 9, 19–20,
   53, 191, 209
American Revolution, 95
ancien regime, 46, 91, 94, 266
Antifa, 227
Arendt, Hannah, 101
Arnold, Matthew, 190–92
Arrighi, Giovanni, 177–86

Babbage, Charles, 261
banking model of education, 289
Bentham, Jeremy, 95
Berlin, Isaiah, 45
Berlin Wall, 89
Black Panthers, 52, 84, 85, 274
Bolshevik Revolution (1917), 141, 151
bourgeoisie, 8, 43–47, 143, 144, 151–54, 192, 218
Braudel, Fernand, 171
Bretton Woods Accords (1944), 187, 199, 248
Brown, John, 25
Bush, Vannevar, 220, 233

Camus, Albert, 89
Canadian Charter of Rights, 106, 109
Canadian Criminal Code, 109
Carnegie, Andrew, 23–4, 197
causality, 162–3
censorship, 46, 103, 196, 223, 228
Chartism, 188
citizenship, 4, 6, 11, 19, 99, 109, 125, 193

Civil War (American), 5, 6, 97
Civil War (English), 9
Coates, Ta-Nehisi, 247
Communist International (Comintern), 141, 151
consciousness, 62, 114, 135, 139–40, 146, 161
   class, 80, 143, 144, 146, 149, 151, 269, 270
   false, 132, 141–44, 150, 160, 163, 226
consequentialism, 39
constructionism, 243, 244
consumerism, 8, 186, 218
counterculture, 204, 220
critical theory, 159, 227, 255, 287, 288
cultural logic, 129–30, 133, 166, 168, 169, 180,
   187, 189
cultural revolution, 91, 276
cybernetics, 252–55, 257, 259

decolonization, 12, 74, 146
deep learning, 260, 261
Defoe, Daniel, 296
dehumanization, 83, 97, 282
deontology, 39
deportation, 6, 105
deregulation, 179, 187–8, 204, 265
Descartes, René, 87, 228, 255
Dewey, Melvil, 54–64, 191, 209, 231, 269
dialogism, 277
Du Bois, W.E.B., 6, 76, 146

economics, 7, 101, 119, 143, 187, 190, 199, 251, 255
Engels, Friedrich, 83, 84, 109, 132–35, 138–41
Enlightenment, the, 94, 98, 129, 131
   and capitalism, 91–2, 130, 232

and liberalism, 87, 90, 93, 102
and librarianship, 12, 54, 73, 149
and republicanism, 5, 25
ethics, 39, 42–3, 286, 288
existentialism, 88, 89

fascism, 34, 90, 126, 189, 198, 200, 212, 215, 225, 273
February Revolution of 1917, 274
feudalism, 27, 46, 80, 138
Fichte, Johann Gottlieb, 132
First Amendment, 20, 103
First Nations, 73
Foucault, Michel, 131, 171, 173, 243, 247, 249, 256, 264, 288
Fourier, Charles, 83
Frankfurt School, 158–9, 287
Freire, Paolo, 52, 277–80, 283, 284, 291
French Revolution, 186
Freud, Sigmund, 130–1, 161, 255
Friedman, Milton, 249, 250
Fugitive Slave Law (1850), 5, 25

Gadamer, Hans Georg, 158, 160–1, 166
German Social Democratic Party, 177
GI Bill, 273
globalization, 182
Glorious Revolution, 95, 98
Gramsci, Antonio, 132, 141, 151–54, 168, 240, 288
Gulf War (First), 227, 228

Habermas, Jürgen, 8, 46, 143, 158–60, 166, 192
Hamas, 85, 274
Harvey, David, 27, 61, 126–7, 133, 167, 183, 189, 198–200, 204, 223, 253
Hegel, Georg Wilhelm Friedrich, 32, 87, 89, 132, 133
hegemony, 3, 102, 109, 121, 132, 142–3, 181, 192–3, 217, 223, 240
    American, 4, 177, 184, 187, 189, 234
    bourgeois, 110, 226
    British, 186–7, 189, 198
    capitalist, 13, 177, 182, 186, 188, 215, 217, 224
    Dutch, 185–6
    liberal, 44, 282
    and the library, 168, 224, 227
    political, 95, 181
    and the State, 151–4
Heidegger, Martin, 158, 160–1
hermeneutics, 157–61, 165–6, 173, 216, 231
historical materialism, 127, 133–35, 137, 139, 145, 150, 208, 214, 243

Hobbes, Thomas, 9, 106, 107, 115, 296
humanism, 155, 216

Ideological reproduction, 33, 60, 121, 155, 225, 242, 275
Ideological State Apparatus, 154–5, 195
imperialism, 105, 181
Industrial Revolution, 6, 183
information technology, 13, 236, 254
International Monetary Fund (IMF), 199
International Panel on Climate Change (IPCC), 11
Internet of Things, 119

Jacobs, Jane, 218
Jacotot, Jacques, 282, 285
Jameson, Fredric, 34, 61, 84, 90, 125, 171, 182
    and dual power, 85, 273–76
    and the financialization of capitalism, 180, 184
    and Marxist hermeneutics, 158–68
    and Marxism, 140, 164
    and the political unconscious, 133, 157
    and postmodernism, 172–3, 178–80
    and reification, 147, 165
    and the utopian principle, 120, 147, 272–3

Kant, Immanuel, 87, 88, 90, 130, 136
Kierkegaard, Søren, 89

labor theory of value, 66
Lazzarato, Maurizio, 123, 147, 287
Leibniz, Gottfried Wilhelm, 228
Lenin, Vladimir Ilyich, 1, 45–49, 52, 93, 145, 152–4
Lèvi-Strauss, Claude, 162
Library Bill of Rights, 20, 128, 216, 219, 221–2, 225, 235
library science, 29, 63, 69, 205–11, 219, 230–3, 237, 278
Lincoln, Abraham, 6, 97, 134
Locke, John, 9, 87, 90, 96, 98–103, 107, 115–17, 136, 296
Lovelace, Ada, 261
Lukács, Georg, 32, 33, 132, 141–45, 147–51, 160, 168, 277

Machiavelli, Niccolò, 152
MacLeish, Archibald, 28, 200, 211–13, 215–17, 225
Malm, Andreas, 137–8, 243, 244
Mandel, Ernest, 71, 166, 175–9
Marshall Plan, 187, 198

Marx, Karl, 27, 62, 66, 83, 119, 130, 255, 296
 and capitalism, 92, 127, 132–3, 138, 250, 261
 and the dialectic, 32, 71, 141
 and ethics, 39, 43
 and historical materialism, 133–36, 139–42
 and the problem of finance capital, 181–83
 liberty/equality as antagonistic properties, 109
 and library workers, 77–79
 and Marxism, 87–8
 and value, 67, 125
Marxism, 82, 140, 142, 159, 177, 272, 287
 and existentialism, 87–90
 and history, 164–66
 and virtue ethics, 42–3
 Western, 32, 132
mathesis, 269, 281, 286, 291
meritocracy, 72, 75–77
military-industrial complex, 219, 233
modernism, 130, 168, 189, 248
monarchy, 8, 9, 26, 95, 282
Moufawad-Paul, J., 118, 166, 172, 265

Negri, Antonio, 7, 115, 198
Nietzsche, Friedrich, 130–32, 158, 161, 255
Noble, Safiya, 122, 222, 294, 295

Ontario Human Rights Code, 109
Open Access movement, 126
Owen, Michael, 83

patriarchy, 78, 83, 299
pedagogy, 277–89, 291
periodization, 172–3, 176, 187, 209
positivism, 224, 229, 232, 238–40, 245
posthumanism, 258
post-industrial society, 180, 260
postmodernism, 89, 90, 161, 166–68, 172, 176, 180, 189, 205, 218, 252, 265, 271
poststructuralism, 89, 167–8
post-truth, 131, 132, 247, 256, 264, 267–8
postwar consensus, 198, 220–22, 229
prison-industrial complex, 260
privatization, 127
Progressive Librarians Guild (PLG), 229
propaganda, 47, 83, 109, 152, 200

Proudhon, Pierre-Joseph, 296
Public Libraries Act, 101, 174, 187–8

Rancière, Jacques, 52, 264, 268, 281–86, 289
reformism, 93
reification, 132, 136, 142, 147–51, 157, 160, 165, 168, 279
republicanism, 5, 24–5
Ricardo, David, 66
Roosevelt, Franklin, 3–4, 22, 26, 85
Rousseau, Jean-Jacques, 9, 107, 296
Russell, Bertrand, 134
Russia, 6, 154, 177

Saint-Simon, Henri de, 83
Sartre, Jean-Paul, 87–89, 104
Sen, Amartya, 218
Shera, Jesse, 23, 174, 219
sixth great extinction, 298
slavery, 5, 25–27, 86, 94–98, 186
slave trade, 91, 95–6
Smith, Adam, 296
social contract, 9, 10, 92–3, 265, 295
social control thesis, 2, 210, 235
social media, 119, 294
Social Responsibility Round Table (SRRT), 225–6
socialism, 43, 83, 140–1, 143
state of nature, 9, 107, 250, 295–6
statistical modeling, 261
stultification, 268, 282–85

Thirty Years War (1618–1648), 185, 188
Ticknor, George, 175, 195
Toqueville, Alexis de, 94
toxic masculinity, 124
transcendentalism, 159, 160
Trans-Mountain pipeline, 73
Trotsky, Leon, 52
Twain, Mark, 177

United Nations, 198–9

Wages for Housework movement, 124–5
Wayland, Francis, 22–3
Weber, Max, 153, 224
welfare state, 8, 18, 118, 168, 176, 199, 204, 215, 223–4, 229, 248–9, 252, 273
 institutions of, 76, 200, 202
 period of, 17, 36

white supremacy, 73, 75, 83, 299
whiteness, 43, 68–75, 78–80, 202
Wiener, Norbert, 254, 257–59, 262
World Bank, 199
World War I, 187, 233

World War II, 27, 104, 119, 175, 183, 187, 198, 215,
   219, 229, 233, 257–60

Yiannopoulos, Milo, 104

CPSIA information can be obtained
at www.ICGtesting.com
Printed in the USA
BVHW070440140819
555741BV00002B/5/P